Coming Out Asperger

of related interest

Asperger's Syndrome
A Guide for Parents and Professionals
Tony Attwood
Foreword by Lorna Wing
ISBN 1 85302 577 1

Pretending to be Normal
Living with Asperger's Syndrome
Liane Holliday Willey
Foreword by Tony Attwood
ISBN 1 85302 749 9

Asperger Syndrome in the Family
Redefining Normal
Liane Holliday Willey
Foreword by Pamela B. Tanguay
ISBN 1 85302 873 8

Multicoloured Mayhem
Parenting the many shades of adolescents and children with autism,
Asperger Syndrome and AD/HD
Jacqui Jackson
ISBN 1 84310 171 8

Freaks, Geeks and Asperger Syndrome
A User Guide to Adolescence
Luke Jackson
Foreword by Tony Attwood
ISBN 1 84310 098 3

Understanding and Working with the Spectrum of Autism
An Insider's View
Wendy Lawson
Foreword by Margot Prior
ISBN 1 85302 971 8

Sex, Sexuality and the Autism Spectrum
Wendy Lawson
Foreword by Glenys Jones
ISBN 1 84310 284 6

Coming Out Asperger

Diagnosis, Disclosure and Self-Confidence

Edited by Dinah Murray

Jessica Kingsley Publishers
London and Philadelphia

First published in 2006
by Jessica Kingsley Publishers
116 Pentonville Road
London N1 9JB, UK
and
400 Market Street, Suite 400
Philadelphia, PA 19106, USA

www.jkp.com

Library of Congress Cataloging in Publication Data
Coming out Asperger : diagnosis, disclosure, and self-confidence / edited by Dinah Murray.
p. cm.
Includes bibliographical references and index.
ISBN-13: 978-1-84310-240-3 (pbk. : alk. paper)
ISBN-10: 1-84310-240-4 (pbk. : alk. paper) 1. Asperger's syndrome. 2. Asperger's
syndrome--Diagnosis. 3. Asperger's syndrome--Patients--Life skills guides. 4. Self-disclosure. I. Murray,
Dinah, 1946-
RC553.A88C67 2006
616.85'8832--dc22

2005024505

British Library Cataloguing in Publication Data
A CIP catalogue record for this book is available from the British Library

ISBN-13: 978 1 84310 240 3
ISBN-10: 1 84310 240 4

Printed and bound in Great Britain by
Athenaeum Press, Gateshead, Tyne and Wear

I'd like to dedicate this book to the memory of my superbly eccentric Uncle Rupert (Crawshay-Williams), from whom I learnt the joys of freshly ground coffee and undermined assumptions. How he would have loved Google!

Acknowledgements

I must thank Jessica Kingsley, first for having the excellent idea for this book and second for getting me to make the idea a reality. I'm also grateful to her for encouraging me to take my own chapter further.

The final form of that chapter also owes much to Jane Meyerding, Wendy Lawson and Michelle Dawson, for whose constructive feedback at various points I am immensely grateful – although obviously all defects are my own. Eve Grace helped clarify the introductory chapter, much appreciated by Mike Lesser and myself. Lastly, I am of course hugely grateful to all the contributors whose hard work and dedication have gone into making this book.

Contents

Introduction

Dinah Murray

Diagnosis is not a simple and straightforward process involving the transfer of some information from one box to another box. The transfer of the diagnosis does not occur in an isolated space of its own; it does not occur instantaneously; it has a history, and it has consequences. The difference goes beyond the moment of information transfer; the diagnosis makes a difference to our memories of the past and to our expectations for the future. The diagnosis imparts information which makes a vast and ramified difference.

All the other people in the world are the social context of the information transfer. For instance, diagnosis also makes a different, complex difference to those who live with the recipient. The diagnosis makes a difference to the social embedment of the recipient: the recipient's background. The diagnosis also makes a difference in another way. It makes, or will make, a difference to the self-image of the person who receives it. Finally, everybody changes. We change in the short term, as we experience different moods. And we change in the long term as our character evolves.

Diagnosis is like a movie rather than a diagram of boxes and arrows. Boxes come and go, arrows carry more or less information and change where they are pointing, the white-paper background is a full-colour three-dimensional film and so are the contents of each box.

Medical diagnosis is a special sort of recognition. Diagnosis always has an object; its object is some condition of a human being that is identified as dis-preferred, pathological. The object of diagnosis is something to be avoided, cured or aided as the case may be. For instance, if someone is diagnosed with, say, measles, then it is immediately clear they would like to get better. Measles is a well-understood illness with a well-known course and well-known attendant risks. Also, a clear programme of beneficial action is immediately apparent. Another distinctive feature of diagnosis is that it is a form of recognition that requires the stamp of authority. It is a situation in which someone in a position of recognised authority is able to use that status and its special knowledge in order to identify and to report on the specific nature of a problem. This problem will now have an authoritative designation that in principle is recognised by everyone and with luck suggests helpful things to do. The authority who makes the diagnosis is usually a doctor, who can prescribe medical treatments appropriate for the problem. The fact that the object recognised is an illness or a medically defined disorder is what qualifies recognition as diagnosis.

Autism spectrum is recognised as a psychiatric disorder that is not sus-ceptible to any medical treatment. It is diagnosable by specialised psy-chologists such as Tony Attwood, who contributes to this volume, as well as by doctors. Unlike most doctors, psychologists may be able to allocate time to apply a set of tests yielding a highly detailed profile that will reveal strengths as well as weaknesses. Tom Berney's chapter is written from the perspective of a psychiatrist unusually knowledgeable in this field who suggests that a doctor's main role is to identify the condition so that extramedical sources of support can be accessed.

What is implied by the concept of a disorder? A disorder implies some contrast with order. Where is this order? Is it within individuals? And what is it about autism that disrupts it? Do most of us have more ordered minds than our autistic acquaintances? Disorderly relationships with other people are presented as the core of the diagnosis of any autism spectrum disorder: flawed communicating and flawed socialising are diagnostic criteria. The diagnosis implies that in any communicative/sociable situation involving an autistic individual of any age, if effective communication/socialisation does not occur, then it is because of that person's autism. Therefore, it identifies the individual as not so much a person who has problems as a person who is a problem.

Because impaired communication and impaired socialisation are among the minimum diagnostic criteria that must be met, it follows that improving either of them may mean that the diagnostic criteria no longer strictly apply, and thus the autism will, technically, be cured. Equally, a broadening range of interests and developing social imagination in an individual may mean that they are no longer judged to be excessively or extremely 'limited' or 'restricted' and, technically, will count as cured. Attwood (1997) and Shore (2001), from their different perspectives, offer the useful and plausible concept of movement over time (potentially in either direction) on a continuum that runs from severe autism through Asperger syndrome to neurotypicality. Yet autism is often described as incurable or lifelong. People with a diagnosis who may eventually become exceptionally good communicators, good company, and good friends with lively imaginations tend to deny that the acquisition of some social skills means they have lost their 'autism'.

The situation with people with Asperger syndrome is even less clear than it is with Kanner autism. Because being able to speak early in life is valued socially, Asperger syndrome is less noticeable than autism. There is no clear line of demarcation between needing or not needing social support to function – everyone needs some social support. Clinicians such as Gillberg (2002) stress that only an extreme presentation should result in diagnosis. Being detected by a clinician as 'having Asperger syndrome' is likely to occur only when what one does or says is regarded as very unacceptable or inappropriate by one's family and peers. For people like these, who are always trying to 'get it right' and can be devastated by failure, such social events may be calamitous for self-confidence and truly disabling. Yet in the right circumstances, as Liane Holliday Willey, Tony Attwood, and Tom Berney's chapters from their different angles affirm, many able people of Aspie disposition can find a welcoming niche in which they flourish. In those 'right circum-stances', such people may never attract clinical attention because they do not fulfil the diagnostic criteria of social dysfunction. They may spend their lives on the right side of the official boundary because the circles in which they mix do not find them worryingly odd. Nobody sees them as dysfunctional, and they do not experience themselves as dysfunctional: a virtuous circle of success through confidence and confidence through success keeps them free from diagnosis-attracting calamities.

Sadly, the opposite pattern is also found. Depression and anxiety are dominant emotional states for a high proportion of adults with autism of any kind. The quality of life has a very significant impact on these emotional states, but innate disposition probably contributes too. Extremes are all or nothing – not balanced, not conceptualised as gradeable by the person feeling them. Gerard Manley Hopkins – an excellent candidate for a posthumous diagnosis in our view – put it this way in his poem 'No worst, there is none':

> O the mind, mind has mountains; cliffs of fall
> Frightful, sheer, no-man-fathomed. Hold them cheap
> May who ne'er hung there

If all your attention is naturally inclined to a single focus, as we suppose to be the case in autism, then alternative prospects may be even less accessible to you when depressed than they are to a more typical person. This autocatalytic runaway tendency may also occur whenever failure is encountered: recovery will be from a steep fall. It is possible that there will be very delayed access to any other view.

Several contributors to this book suggest that recognising and working with the strengths of autistic individuals of all ages is crucial, and we wholeheartedly agree with that. But there is a problem: the people to be supported in this positive fashion have been picked out by a set of entirely negative criteria – and those criteria reflect the deepest attitudes of almost everybody concerned. The message is: 'OK, so these people can't do this really important thing, and they can't do that really important thing. But hey! Even though they are so dysfunctional, they may be capable of showing a lot of intelligence and achieving success in certain limited areas.' A diagnosis of autism or Asperger syndrome may trigger a process of recognition of needs, may release resources, and may make sense of previously puzzling behaviour, but it will – on current definitions – at the same time categorise the person as being fundamentally flawed. Michelle Dawson's chapter is a pithy summary, while Philip Whitaker sensitively addresses issues raised by telling a young person they have such a diagnosis. Potential lack of sympathetic reactions in the world beyond the child's immediate family is also a theme of Jennifer Overton's chapter. Dora Georgiou's overview explores issues around disclosure to the community for adults with high abilities on the spectrum. David Andrews' chapter makes very clear how large the negative impact can be of society's response to people who just do not fit. He has generally not found that disclosure of his autism improves that situation; on the contrary, he feels the diagnosis is perceived as invalidating his genuine and hard-won qualifications.

Disclosure of an autism spectrum diagnosis means disclosure of the fundamentally flawed personhood implied by the diagnostic criteria. It is likely to precipitate a negative judgement of capacity involving permanent loss of credibility. That is why so many writers in this book discuss what Dennis Debbaudt calls 'soft disclosure', that is, disclosure of certain difficulties, rather than 'hard disclosure' of a specific diagnosis; for example, Liane Holliday Willey's, 'Would you do me a favor? I have a learning disability that makes it hard for me to understand jargon and abstract concepts. Could you please explain [whatever I need explained] in a very concrete and simple way so I will be more likely to really understand you? I'm not dense; I just have a problem with parts of language and non-verbal communication.' Soft disclosure invites allowances and adjustments for what may come across as shortcomings and might otherwise cause trouble while at the same time not making matters worse by introducing a stigmatising disability label. This is also a feature of the approach that both Heta Pukki and Penny Barratt propose for introducing a child's Asperger problems to other children. Having an authoritative diagnosis and disclosing that diagnosis have tended to be the keys to unlocking resources, and so hard disclosure is sometimes essential for practical reasons. Jane Meyerding and Wendy Lawson both articulate more principled reasons for choosing to disclose a diagnosis as widely as possible; from different angles, they both argue that wherever possible, it should be asserted boldly, just as we used to say 'Out and proud – say it loud!' about once-hidden homosexuality.

If the whole range of autism as presently defined was not inherently dysfunctional, then the 'disclosure' part of this book's subtitle could have been 'acknowledgement', just as the 'diagnosis' part might have been 'recognition'. Disclosure implies negative judgement and rejection. *Involuntary disclosure* as someone with unacceptable behaviours is the usual route to diagnosis of any autism spectrum condition; it is the invariable route for Kanner's autism. That is, the problems implied in the word 'disclosure' are not concealed: autism involves a child producing behaviours. The developing infant does not learn to adjust his or her behaviour to the wishes or expectations of others. *Voluntary disclosure* for these children is not an issue. Not only are their differences undisguisable, but also they are not trying to disguise them and they probably are not experiencing any concern about their social impact. Using and responding to speech is a huge part of social expectations. Asperger syndrome is usually diagnosed later in life because the child who attracts that diagnosis has acquired the use of speech within the usual timeframe. Such a child has also conformed to some degree to those social hopes and developed some level of awareness of other people, which can make voluntary disclosure a complicated and uncomfortable business. Adolescence raises a whole new set of problems. Lynne Moxon draws on years of experience in encouraging realistic sex education and social understanding in young people with Asperger syndrome. She offers insight into and guidance through the troubled waters of sexual relationships, their potential for mutual misunderstandings, and their unavoidable disclosures.

The need to encourage and develop tolerance and difference is another theme of this book and is mentioned in several chapters. Voluntary disclosure can be central in that process. Jane Meyerding argues persuasively that the necessary solidarity to change consciousness, as happened in the twentieth century with women's rights, requires people to disclose their autism. Michelle Dawson makes a forceful analogy with Rosa Parks and her refusal to sit at the back of the bus, which precipitated the civil rights movement in the USA. Wendy Lawson asks for acceptance for herself and all other people who are different. Professionals such as Dora Georgiou and Philip Whitaker also emphasise the need to change public consciousness in order to increase understanding and with it acceptance. Until recently, it seems that Liane Holliday Willey has been a one-woman crusade of personal disclosure. Heta Pukki suggests that children should be taught throughout their school days to recognise and appreciate that there are many different ways of learning and being.

Jennifer Overton, writing as a parent, catches the flavour of the scary exposure of one's precious and beloved child to the potentially harsh world of school beyond the family. Penny Barratt's chapter takes us in some detail through the ins and outs of disclosing the diagnosis in secondary school, a process she has observed frequently. At that stage, the involvement of the young person in decisions about disclosure becomes a central issue: 'Time and effort must be put into developing their own understanding of their difficulties and true informed consent gained before one proceeds to share any information with the peer group.' Dinah Murray's discussion of building self-confidence equally stresses the need for people to be encouraged and given opportunities to develop understanding and to get a perspective on themselves and their concerns.

The positive feelings that many individuals have about their own autism spectrum differences are also expressed by many of those who know and work with them. But people who get a diagnosis are likely to be experiencing difficulties of various sorts that are having a very unpleasant impact on their lives. This can be summed up as losing, or never having, control; getting stuck; getting lost; explosive feelings; sensory overwhelm; inarticulacy; missed crucial information; anxiety-provoking uncertainties; and confusion. All these are likely to be part of the process of involuntary disclosure that has led to the diagnosis. The answer may be to increase an individual's control over their environment, and yet in practice getting a diagnosis of an autism spectrum disorder is likely to have the opposite result – as Michelle Dawson's chapter makes fiercely clear from an autistic perspective. From his professional angle, Tony Attwood's chapter on diagnosis in adults paints a difficult but less depressing picture. It offers subtle advice and constructive techniques to help all concerned in coming to terms with the diagnosis and its implications – much of what he emphasises are positive benefits, potentially both to the individual and to society.

A diagnosis of autism is likely to mean you lose control of your life, not only to doctors but to everyone in any way involved. People of many sorts are likely to have meetings about you in offices. Some meetings you will attend, some you will not. They will be discussing every detail of how your life must be. Because speech is part of the picture in Asperger syndrome, Aspies may receive a degree of consultation in official processes rarely offered to their less articulate peers. However, that very articulacy can generate false assumptions in the people you are talking with, who will tend to assume that your processing skills are exactly the same as theirs. For instance, they will assume equivalent speed of identifying the phonology, i.e. working out which sounds are meaningful. They will also assume equal facility in identifying explicit and implicit relevant information. As a result, in practice, these supposedly consultative processes may be a sham. In an ideal world, recognition as an Asperger person would change false assumptions and correct the way other people interact. In the real world, Aspies are likely to find their lives fluctuating unpredictably between under- and over-expectations. Their less articulate peers are almost always just treated as plain stupid. As David Andrews' chapter reveals and Stephen Shore's chapter discusses more broadly, any autism spectrum diagnosis has stigma attached. Everyone diagnosed risks being treated as lacking credibility. Yet the label is often a huge relief, making some sense at last of painful difficulties and having the potential to offer signposts. The dilemma for parents is sketched poignantly by Jacqui Jackson, wishing now that she had shared the diagnosis sooner with her son Luke.

A diagnosis of Asperger syndrome often follows other less appropriate diagnoses, such as schizophrenia, which can be acutely distressing to receive. Someone with authority is making false allegations about you, which everyone else will believe. You may think you should believe them yourself. You have been looking for answers and not finding them. You have been having a very difficult time. Things keep not working out as you expected. You want to understand what's going on, and what the doctor says makes no sense to you – yet everybody else believes it. This can make you feel worse in so many ways. And it can cause long-lasting spiritual damage.

Getting recognition as someone with Asperger syndrome is likely to be highly welcome and may even initiate a process of recovery from depression. The uncomfortable process of involuntary disclosure of weirdness – despite one's best efforts – may be made much easier by recognition as an Asperger person. It is a label that at least offers the comfort that one is not an alien, that there are others out there encountering similar problems in this puzzling world. What is more, there is a growing benevolent literature on Asperger people that emphasises the likelihood that some of the greatest eccentric scientists, inventors, artists and musicians over the years would also merit an Asperger diagnosis.

A striking feature of this book is the solidarity with more classically autistic people shown by the Asperger contributors. The only author in this volume to emphasise that there is a real and significant difference between people on the spectrum who do or do not attract a diagnosis of Asperger syndrome is strictly autistic contributor Michelle Dawson. Because of the implied good language, normal-range IQs and occasional brilliance, some clinicians and other professionals tend to see people with Asperger as belonging to a different and superior class. Michelle Dawson is keen to draw attention to key similarities between autistic people identified as high- and low-functioning, as distinct from Aspies. She is concerned that otherwise, classically autistic people will be dismissed and set aside as inadequate and inferior and their distinctive intelligence not recognised. Her own tightly focused piece is an example of that intelligence applied to the diagnostic interview. The autistic vision has qualities of clarity, accuracy and penetration that we may all learn from if we can access it.

A person's location on the range from 'extreme autism' to 'extreme normality' is a consequence not only of their innate disposition but also of the effect of that disposition on other people, and the resulting feedback. Pejorative feedback may be radically disabling. People may have their confidence punctured by repeated social failure and may lose formerly motivating interests. They may lose their capacity to proceed at all. Dinah Murray's chapter shows that a loss of the ability to speak and interact, with abrupt narrowing of attentional range, may be brought about by sudden loss of confidence. Apart from the occasional disabling outburst, when growing up her own position on this spectrum was well to the normie side of the boundary. Her story suggests that the position of that boundary is influenced by local culture, and may move over time.

We suggest that the message to people of any age beyond toddling who are being given a diagnosis should be: 'You've been having a very difficult time. Working out what's going on is much harder for you than it is for most people. Getting your feelings under control is much harder for you than it is for most people. You've really been doing very well indeed, much against the odds.' What a great thing it would be if people with autism spectrum diagnoses were given space, time, communicative tools and sensitive support to help them deal with the issues they personally find problematic.

References

Attwood, T. (1997) *Asperger's Syndrome: A Guide for Parents and Professionals.* London: Jessica Kingsley Publishers.

Gillberg, C. (2002) *A Guide to Asperger Syndrome.* Cambridge: Cambridge University Press.

Shore, S. M. (2001) *Beyond the Wall: Personal Experiences with Autism and Asperger Syndrome.* Shawnee Mission, KS: Autism Asperger Publishing Co.

Further reading

Asperger, H. (1944/1991) 'Autistic Psychopathy in Childhood.' In U. Frith (ed) *Autism and Asperger Syndrome.* Cambridge: Cambridge University Press.

Attwood, T. (2003) 'Utilising and Managing Circumscribed Interests.' In M. Prior (ed) *Learning and Behaviour Problems in Asperger Syndrome.* New York: The Guilford Press.

Bashe, P.R and Kirby, B.L. (2001) *The OASIS Guide to Asperger Syndrome: Advice, Support, Insight, and Inspiration.* New York: Crown Publishing.

Clements, J. and Zarkowska, E. (2000) *Behavioural Concerns and Autistic Spectrum Disorders: Explanations and Strategies for Change.* London: Jessica Kingsley Publishers.

Lawson, W. (2000) *Understanding and Working with the Spectrum of Autism.* London: Jessica Kingsley Publishers.

Murray, D. (1992) 'Attention Tunnelling and Autism.' In *Living with Autism: The individual, the Family, and the Professional.* Durham International Conference. Autism Research Unit, School of Health, and Social Sciences. Sunderland: University of Sunderland.

Murray, D., Lesser, M. and Lawson, W. (2005) 'Attention, Monotropism, and the Diagnostic Criteria for Autism.' In *Autism* 9, 2.

1.

To tell or not to tell: that is the Aspie[1] question

Liane Holliday Willey

I was diagnosed with Asperger syndrome (AS) five years ago. As I write this, I am 44 years old. I believe that for 39 years, my life was a myriad of misdiagnoses, misunderstandings, and missed opportunities because I did not have a proper AS diagnosis. Knowing this, you will not be surprised to hear I was very happy to hear I had AS. It was the definitive that finally made sense of my life, the missing piece of me that, once found, made me whole. For the first four years after my diagnosis, I told everyone from taxi drivers to co-workers that I had AS. I became a walking billboard for the new community I was so proud to call my own. The diagnosis became a magnifying glass through which I could see the world anew, and it only made sense that I shared that view with everyone I met. I would have felt selfish if I had kept the view a secret!

A few months ago, something happened that changed my view, my perspective, maybe even my heart. I won't discuss the event in public, but I will go on record to say it involved a young Aspie whose heart was broken and then some, after a public disclosure was made to the Aspie's peers. And now I'm left to wonder: have I been making a mistake? Am I in a complete mind-blind state when I tell everyone about all things Aspie? Does everyone have to know? Is it my right, not to mention my responsibility, to tell everyone everything? Or should I take my mother's heed when she says to me, "The truth may set you free, but it doesn't necessarily set everyone else free"?

---

1   Aspie (n.): a person diagnosed with Asperger syndrome. *I am an Aspie.*

I've no clear answer to the questions above. However, I do know me well enough to know I will never be too private a person, and above all I do remain faithful to the notion that AS is neither a dirty little secret nor something to be ashamed about. If I was the only actor in my life's play, I would continue to run full speed down the full-disclosure path. Perhaps it would be wiser and more sensitive of me to slow my pace to a nice calming walk. No, I will not abandon the pride that comes when I express exactly who I am to others; rather, I will just think twice about when and how I should express that pride. After all, I cannot guess accurately how others will take the news, and others (like it or not) do have an affect on me and mine.

OK. So I'm not going to give just anybody the Aspie lecture. I will, however, keep telling the important folks what AS is, how it affects me, and where they can go for additional information on the subject. In a nutshell, I will simply give much more thought to the Aspie question – to tell or not to tell.

Who to tell? I mentioned the important folks. Who are they? That's for each of you to decide on your own terms. For me, "important" means anyone who has an impact on the quality of my life. On any given day, it might still mean the taxi driver if I'm in a position where my thinking is going haywire due to stress or fatigue and I need someone's help in getting me safely to where I need to be. Or it might mean the ticket agent at the airport if I feel that my talking to myself and fidgeting around the crowds are giving the authorities the impression I'm someone who needs to be detained for questioning. Then again, maybe it will be my veterinarian so that I'm certain she knows to tell me everything in minute detail regarding the care of my sick dog. Obviously, I define "important" in broad strokes. But I believe a chain is only as strong as its weakest link, and I don't want to be the weakest link. I think I would be the weakest link if I wasn't honest about my difficulties and, as they fit the situation, my differences. If my strength depends on the help of others, then I have to consider them important enough to receive my lecture on who I am. After all, how could anyone help me if I didn't make them at least generally aware of how my mind tends to work?

When I do need to disclose to the everyday person, I use simple words and avoid too much detail. While what I say varies, it always goes something like this: "Would you do me a favor? I have a learning disability that makes it hard for me to understand jargon and abstract concepts. Could you please explain [whatever I need explained] in a very concrete and simple way so I will be more likely to really understand you? I'm not dense; I just have a problem with parts of language and non-verbal communication." I'd be lying if I said this was always enough information, but it is a good starter and often the other person will ask me the questions he or she needs to help me. Typical questions are anything from "What's your disability called?" to "Would it help you if I wrote things down for you?" I've never been disappointed in the responses I get if I'm with a caring person, and I am always prepared for the less-than-kind person who might answer me with a loud and slow reply as if I'm deaf or with the suggestion that I find someone else to help me. No matter the response, I do think it is best to keep the explanation of AS short and simple when dealing with someone you are only going to be in touch with for a very short time. Like it or not, the word "disability" too often carries raw nerves with it, so there's no sense in making the situation go on longer than necessary.

I'm often asked whether I feel embarrassed when I admit I'm an Aspie. No, I don't. I am also asked whether it is hard to tell people about AS. Not for me. I am blessed with a great deal of self-confidence, if not a completely healthy self-esteem. That's right: it is possible to have one without the other. Self-esteem develops when one believes in their own worth and value. Self-confidence develops when one believes they can accomplish their goals, when one believes they have what it takes to do what they need or want to do. Parents of Aspies: take heed! You are the primary influence on your child's self-confidence. Lucky for me, my parents taught me early on to believe I had the intelligence and where-withal to make my plans happen. Had they not, then I wouldn't have a few university degrees, a career, or a family. I would have folded myself into a bun and stayed there until no one was around to watch me live. It took a lot of encouragement and support to get me to open up and dare the world to tell me I didn't have what it took to make my life a good place to live.

My dad used to say: "It's too bad we can't pick our relatives." To which he would often add: "And just remember when your pick you spouse: your kids will inherit their genes too." This was his not-so-subtle way of telling me that he and I were top-drawer individuals who would be wise to keep our lineage healthy and strong. I think of my dad as a Darwinian pragmatist. To him, and later to me too, people who have AS are often the best pick for many extremely important jobs and careers. Think the kinds of careers that require hours of head-on studying and practice, strong conviction of opinion, incredible attention to detail, single-minded dedication, and outstanding memories. Think engineering, chemistry, architecture, and computer programming. Think library science, law, sculpting, acting, and music. My dad is an engineer. I am a psycholinguist. We both find joy in the tiniest of details, the most specific nuances. My dad designed airplanes. I design sentences. We are both passionate about what we do. We are lucky to practice what we love. Many Aspies are not nearly as lucky as we are. Far too many with AS who are more than capable of designing airplanes and sentences and computers and fabulous pieces of music and award-worthy ideas and great works of art and who knows what else are, instead, delivering pizzas, sweeping floors, or standing in the unemployment line. While there is no shame in any job done well, there is sadness when the job done is not the one the worker studied for, not the job the worker loves. I have to wonder how much my self-confidence played in getting me to where I am. I tend to think the answer is quite a bit.

If my parents hadn't held my attributes as precious gems worthy of praise, if they hadn't championed me as a girl who could do anything she set her mind to, would I have been able to go to graduate school and earn my terminal degree? Would I have had the courage to pursue the first few dates with my then future husband? Would I have believed in myself enough to think that I, despite my differences and difficulties, could be married, have the career I aspired to, raise a family, and live a life filled with humor and optimism? I am confident the answer to those questions is a resounding "no".

Questions. Answers. To tell. Not to tell. It's not easy being Aspie. Self-esteem gets eroded by peers and society who aren't quite ready or willing to regard our unique attributes as precious gems. Opportunities come and go before we even figure out what they were. Misunderstandings about this that and virtually everything else cloud our minds with doubt and confusion. The only real deep-down way to survive a neurotypical (NT) world as an Aspie is to rely on a very solid sense of self-confidence. For me at least, it is the very thing that continues to enable me to make the best out of everything. And it is my belief in who I am that lets me step outside of my comfort zone to admit to others I am Aspie and I might need their help now and then.

A person's self-confidence begins to take shape when they are very young. Parents who accept their children in turn help the child to accept him- or herself. Messages of acceptance come in many forms, both spoken and unspoken, both obvious and subtle. Children, even Aspie children, need to discover through all kinds of messages that their parents believe and trust that the child can do many fine things worthy of praise and applause. Subtle overtures by the parents that suggest the child's incompetence will be noticed by the child on some level. Worse, not-so-subtle remarks that express unhappiness or regret about the child's aptitude or differences will go straight to the child's heart and straight to the lock that will keep self-confidence away forever. There is no doubt it is harder to raise a child with unique needs, but there is also no doubt that self-confidence needs to be fostered in all children, no matter their difficulties, strengths, or weaknesses. Children need to be taught to believe in their own abilities, Aspie or not. They can't be coddled and kept in protective cocoons all their lives. Reality has to be brought to them, even if in small doses. Sooner or later, Aspie children have to see their challenges for what they are, just as they are led to see their strengths for what they are. In fact, it seems to me this should be the case for all children and, indeed, all people. Nonetheless, there is a distinct difference in the amount of challenges Aspie kids will face when compared with NT kids, and parents with unique kids need to understand how and when to protect and how and when to let go.

I wish I had had someone to teach me how to be less protective over my children when they were little. I was so taken by wanting to keep all ill from my children that I tended to do as much for them as I could. It never dawned on me that this was telling them they were incapable. But in many ways, it was. To their minds, Mom's ever-presence was a hint that they couldn't do much without me. To my mind, I was telling them they could always count on Mom to be their guide and helper. I had good intentions but not so good teaching. What kind of help was I providing, truly? Wouldn't my kids have been far better off if they had been allowed to discover at a young age that they could do for themselves all by themselves, without Mom looking over their shoulder and leading the way? What I saw as protection was likely transmitted to them as a message that said: "Mom's not at all confident you can do this on your own. You're just not as capable as Mom."

Because self-confidence is a rather opaque concept, it might seem difficult to foster, but it really isn't. Ironically, my doctoral work had much to do with self-esteem and self-confidence, which I flat forgot to apply when my kids were little. But it's never too late to do the right thing, so here I've written down just a sampling of ideas we now use, and some we wish we had used, to help you get your creative self-confidence building juices going. Adjust them to fit your child and then use them as a guide for coming up with your own.

- Ask the child to plan the dinner menu. Set a few guidelines to keep the child within a healthy-eating parameter, but after that let the child pick the food items.

- Starting at a young age, let the child prepare some of the family's food. How young? Well, even a toddler can put peanut butter on celery sticks, for example.

- Encourage your child to take some responsibility for their stuff as soon as they understand the concept of putting away even one toy. Let them help you decide where their toys should go, keeping in mind that even the youngest Aspie likes things "just so"; then encourage your child to put the toys there after every use. Continue this lesson as the child gets older. For instance, let them pick out bedcovers, decide the order in which he or she likes the covers laid, or choose the color of their bedroom.

- As soon as it seems possible, begin to help the young Aspie learn to separate his or her caregiver's world from his or her own world, but go slow and in little ways. One thing I used to do rather successfully was to let my child play in the toddler section of our local library. Sure, I had to come in to rescue the other kids from mine when a tad too much 'Aspie-in-charge' personality came through, but for the most part my child learned she could exist in a world where Mom wasn't holding her hand. Of course, I still held her hand when danger lurked, but I was always quick to explain why I was holding her hand sometimes and why I wasn't during other times. I firmly believe that Aspies often learn well from very direct instruction, and I also believe they need to be directed to see and understand as much about this world as we can impart to them. Chances are, they will fail to see trouble brewing more often then they will see it coming. My own personal experiences with really bad things heaped on me by really bad people make me very vigilant about keeping my kids aware of the very bad out there. The library was a safe spot for my kids because I knew there was an adult on hand to keep them safe from predators. I could let them be free to explore on their own there. But in a big shopping mall, they needed me to open their eyes to places they should avoid, situations they should run from. All the while, I'd let them know that some day, they would be big enough to keep themselves safe but that for now they were too little to risk being all alone in certain areas. And as the mom of three daughters, there are times even now when I don't allow my almost 18-year-old to go all alone. In the case of personal safety, the issue of self-confidence takes second place.

- Prove to your child you appreciate their strengths and interests. Find plenty of occasions to strike up a conversation about their favorite obsession. Put their latest invention, no matter how weird and unattractive it might be, on the mantel alongside your favorite possessions. Ask them to help you with a problem if it's the kind of problem you know they'll likely be successful with. I remember finding out how capable young kids can be during a conference I was presenting at a few years back. My computer was not working right, and after three adults could not fix it I noticed a young adolescent standing just to my left. I asked him if he was an Aspie, and he nodded yes. I asked him whether he knew about computers, and he again nodded yes. "Would you fix mine?" I asked. He smiled as big as a mouth can go and walked through the adults like Moses parting the seas. Sure enough, less than five minutes later, the computer was up and running. No surprise to me. One of the best things about being Aspie is our intellect. We are usually quite good at the things we enjoy the most, and this young man proved that to a crowd of 300.

- Encourage your child to try things that their AS might not let come easily. For instance, I have very poor bilateral coordination, but my parents always encouraged me to swim, play ball, cheerlead, take dance lessons – basically whatever I wanted to try. They knew I'd likely drop out of the events sooner rather than later, but they never said a word when I quit. They didn't even get mad when my ballet teacher suggested that I – their precious little five-year-old – not return for ballet simply because I tended to smack the other kids if they got too close to me. Replied my mom when this was brought to her attention: "Well, you did tell the kids they should be an arm's length apart. It appears my child was the only child here smart enough to understand what 'arm's length apart' means." Way to go, Mom!

- Stand up for the child's logic when it is sound. Just as my mother did with the ballet teacher, it is appropriate to reward the child for being smart and reasonable. No, I wasn't rewarded for smacking other kids, and, yes, I was sent to my room for hitting, but I wasn't chastised for my rationale. Rather, I was re-taught how to act on my logic. In the ballet example, my parents taught me merely by standing next to me, one of them on each side of me, that when someone gets too close you just keep moving away. And if that doesn't work, you tell the child to stay an arm's length away. And if that doesn't work, you tell the teacher to watch and make sure your neighbors are all an arm's length away. And if that doesn't work, you ask to be placed on the end of the line so you can always move as far away as you like. Now, this kind of "thinking it through" is nothing more than linear problem-solving, but it is the kind of problem-solving that Aspies should be able to learn and, indeed, follow. One important reminder: do talk to the adults involved to let them know what your child is doing, so they can see the problem-solving for what it is rather than precociousness.

Note of caution: Aspies are great at deciding exactly not only what they should do but what others should do as well. Early on, establish boundaries that the Aspie cannot cross. For instance, you don't want your

Aspie telling you what you will eat for dinner every night; nor do you want your Aspie deciding what kind of furniture the house should have and what kind of clothing you should wear. Within their space, be it their room or just a secret nook, they can have carte blanche, but never should they be given control over the entire world they live in. Allowing that kind of control won't build self-confidence rather, it will build the notion that their way is *the* way, and that notion will not make anyone a better person.

OK. We've covered some tidbits on building self-confidence for kids, but what if the Aspie (you?) is a teen or adult? Self-confidence is far easier to groom when it begins strong as a child. For people beyond the adolescent years, self-confidence typically will be far more difficult to change. More difficult, but not impossible. Now, it is very important to remember that what might look like poor self-confidence in a neurotypical person might not be anything of the sort when noticed in an Aspie. Let me explain. Aspies often use echolalia to fit in. Echolalia is about copying other people or other things we see and/or hear. I fall into echolalia almost every time I'm out of the house. When I come home from teaching a class or doing an interview, my kids will laugh and tell me to stop acting like I'm on stage. When I talk to my British friends, my American speech becomes peppered with British phrases. To the untrained eye, it might appear that I don't have the confidence to be myself or think for myself. But that is not necessarily the case. Echolalia is fun and, in a way I can't explain, very natural. Typically, it just happens without my even realizing it. I tend to think it is the brain's way of conserving energy, because it takes less brain power to copy others than it does to analyze and quickly re-shape and re-figure our own inclinations so that we may fit in with the NT society.

Look carefully, too, at the Aspie's actions that, on the surface, might appear as fear of failure or rejection. Personally, I know my reluctance to try new things isn't based on a fear of failure or fear of rejection; rather, it is usually because I hate change and I like my routine. I take plenty of risks, but not the kind of risks the NT world tends to see as person-ality-shapers. For instance, my idea of a risk is going to a party at the home of one of my friends. That is really putting myself out on a limb. Again, it is not a matter of fear of failure or rejection such as we might see when a neurotypical person with poor self-confidence refuses to apply for a new job because they are convinced the employer will see their impressive résumé as insufficient and dull. In an Aspie's case, it is often more a fear of the unknown and the unpredictable rather than the fear of what others might think about us or how we might fare in a contest. Hence, before one looks at developing a self-confidence-building program for an Aspie, they will need to figure out the underlying root of the behaviors. Consider: Is the Aspie reacting out of fear of being liked for who they really are or the natural inclination to copycat, as was the case in the first example? Is the behavior caused from the fear of being rejected or the fear of leaving a routine and predictable environment, as was presented in the second scenario?

To further mix the pot, it could be that the older Aspie has developed low self-confidence just like a neurotypical person would. Eventually, many of us do see ourselves rejected by peer groups because we are different or turned down for employment because our résumé doesn't quite make up for our quirks. The new question becomes: What kinds of self-confidence programs work for us, then? This is one of those questions that defies an easy answer. Remember: it is first important to analyze the root issue, seeing whether it is an Aspie trait or a real reflection of poor self-confidence. If it is an Aspie-related issue, then you refer to the experts, who tell us how to help Aspies deal with such things as too much echolalia or fear of facing the unknown. But if you are certain the issues are purely stemming from a heavy dose of low self-confidence, then you might begin by encouraging the following kinds of things:

- Remind the Aspie of her successes. Show her any awards she earned. Take her to environments where she excelled and ask her to talk about the good times she had there. Request people who know her write letters that reflect the successes and good things they see in the Aspie.

- Encourage your Aspie to use visualization, wherein she pictures herself doing a good job at the things she loves most. Ask her to write down or draw the images and then have her carry those reminders with her so she can refer to them in moments of self-doubt.

- Teach the Aspie to talk herself through moments of low self-confidence by replacing negative thoughts with optimistic concepts. Practice this out loud to be sure they really understand what you're trying to explain. For example, you might say something like: "I'm starting to feel I can't go into this party. My heart is racing, my head is starting to hurt. Oh no! What if no one wants me there? What if … *stop*! I am not going to talk like that. I am not going to fall into self-doubt. I *can* go to the party. I *can* do this. I wouldn't have been invited to this party if people didn't like me. I'll be fine!"

- Teach the Aspie to apply logic to his or her self-evaluation. This will be a tough one as Aspies tend to find introspection difficult. But with time and practice, we can learn to be introspective and self-evaluating individuals. And when we combine a sense of logic with our reality, thoughts that were bad or unappreciated will not take hold as deeply.

So, the next time your Aspie says something irrational such as "I am the worst person in the world and I'll never get the job I want," offer a logical reply that debunks that notion. "Do you really think you are the worst person in the world? Isn't that going overboard? In the whole scheme of things, you are very far from being even near the worst person in the world. You may not get the job you want, but you aren't unique to that. Lots of people don't get the jobs they want. Do the best you can do by preparing well for the interview, making sure you are qualified for the position, and presenting yourself professionally. That's all anyone can do!"

Help your Aspie to see that the best way to feel comfortable in their own skin is to believe in oneself at all costs. Share biographies of famous and everyday people who have turned their lives from failure to success. Remind the Aspie that from failure come new knowledge and new growth. Bottom line: teach that failure is neither a dirty word nor a condemnation to eternal emptiness. It is a natural phase most people go through over and over again.

To be honest, all the information I've presented on self-confidence might not be enough to bring the Aspie to a fully realized goal of high self-confidence. If that appears to be the case, then I highly recommend a consultation with a qualified counselor who specializes in autism spectrum disorders (ASDs). There is only so much the lay person can do, no matter how dedicated they are to the Aspie's success. And there is no shame in asking for help. Asking for help is a sign of strength!

Now for the bad news. No amount of self-confidence can keep away all the risks intrinsic to telling others about AS. Sure, strong self-confidence will help us to not worry about what others will say when we tell them about our AS, and it might make it far easier to disclose in general, but it won't stop others from reacting in ways that might make our lives more difficult. We with AS have to realize that. While I have very little problem telling people about my AS, I am always shocked to discover it is the listener who might have a problem when they hear the information. Even if I am filled with self-confidence and the belief that I am a solidly decent person with good attributes and abilities, people who hear I'm Aspie are still wont to look at me differently, either pitying me or worrying that ultimately I'm not up for the task at hand. These days, I'm not even surprised when I find out someone has whispered behind my back that I have a disability. Sometimes, I even find people alter the way they speak to me, using slower speech or simple terms, as if my AS means I am stupid, dense, or deaf.

No matter how many good facts you tell when disclosing your AS, there will be others who fail to hear the good stuff, so unnatural is it for them to understand that neurological differences do not mean unable. Know, then, that if you choose to tell about your AS, you will run the risk of others having reservations and doubts about your abilities and maybe even your personality on the whole. That's intimidating stuff and it demands heavy consideration while you decide whether to tell. For me, the risks are worth taking, but I have a very big group of supporters who make me whole no matter how much society tries to chop me up. If I do not keep a job because I've told my peers too much about my differences – a reality I am certain I have experienced over and over again – I can still afford to feed and house my family thanks to my husband and his career. If I am taken off the who's-who of the neighborhood list because I come out with my AS disclosure too fast – yet another reality I've suffered again and again – so be it. I have a few really good and faithful friends who see me through every storm. I just gather my daughters, husband, and parents to my heart and let the others drift from my world.

I am extremely lucky these days, but that has not always been the case. I spent ten long years in virtual hell. During the days when my parents were unable to watch over me due to the long distance between us, before I had a husband, and before I had cultivated a few close friendships, I spent my days hating my life and my nights alone and sad. And those were the good times. I experienced the worst of the worst, the kinds of things I do not like to put down in print because that gives the memories the kind of permanence that could strangle me. Those ten years taught me to tell those who are largely on their own, or those who have few if any supports, to tread lightly when they think about disclosing. It is far easier for someone with a support system to come forward. That fact cannot be denied.

Given all the problems that can chase disclosure, many may wonder why bother telling in the first place? Telling might make you feel safer if the telling brings people to your support corner. Telling might help you relax if in telling you are freed to be your real self and no longer made to pretend. Sharing will also help educate others about AS, and this education will lead to the kind of awareness that might make it possible for new Aspies to be identified and counseled. Who knows? Maybe sharing your AS story will ring a bell with another soul who will only then recognize the true song in their heart ... the Aspie song.

Make no mistake about it: sometimes you really have to tell. When it comes to matters of physical or emotional health, when your environment must be changed to accommodate your sensory issues so you can do your best at work, or when you just can't bear faking it as someone else any longer, then it really might be wise to take the risks and tell. If you're trying to establish a lasting relationship, if you're taking part in an unfamiliar activity that is too confusing to handle, or if you're attempting to continue your education and finding the regular education setting too difficult to manage, then it might be wise to face the risks and tell. Knowing what the risks are will help you psych up for the disclosure, and if you've done a good job of making your self-confidence strong and certain you can do a much better job of keeping the entire issue in perspective. As my dad always says to me: "Will what you're about to do kill you? If not, then do it, and do it as best as you can."

2.

Diagnosis in adults

Tony Attwood

The diagnostic criteria were written primarily to identify the signs of Asperger syndrome in children, and we do not have any adjustments to the criteria for the diagnosis of adults. The diagnostic assessment of adults will present the clinician with some potential problems and the risk of misdiagnosis or no diagnosis when the characteristics are denied or camouflaged. The author prefers, if possible, to conduct the diagnostic assessment with a relative, partner or friend of the adult who can provide a more objective opinion regarding the person's developmental history. For example, a young man said that when he was a child, he had many friends that came to his home; but his mother commented that the children came to play with his toys, not her son, and when they were in his home he played on his own in another part of the house.

It is possible that the adult will deliberately mislead the clinician for reasons of maintaining self-esteem or to avoid a diagnosis that may be perceived as a mental illness. Some adults may choose to conceal their difficulties in social interaction skills, while others may consider that their abilities are quite normal, using the characteristics of a parent as the model of normal interaction skills. If the person had a dominant parent with the characteristics of Asperger syndrome, then this may have influenced the person's experience and perception of normality.

Some adults with Asperger syndrome have known they were different from quite an early age. The author usually asks the person: 'Have you ever felt that you were different to other people? What were those differences? And when did you first notice you were different?' The general consensus of those who recognised that they were and are different to other people is that the first signs were noticed when they started school. They had to relate to an adult other than their mother and children other than their siblings. Throughout early childhood, the person developed a sense of social rapport with family members, but age peers were confusing and did not behave in the way that they expected or were not interested in the same things.

Psychological adjustment to being different

Children with Asperger syndrome perceive and experience a very different world to that of their peers, and gradually they can recognise and become concerned that they are different to their peers. This is not only in terms of different interests, priorities and social knowledge but also in terms of frequent criticisms by peers and adults. These young people can then develop defence and compensatory mechanisms for feeling alienated, socially isolated and not understood. The author has identified four compensatory or adjustment strategies developed by children with Asperger syndrome in response to the realisation that they are different. The strategy used depends on each individual's personality, experiences and circumstances. The personality types that tend to internalise thoughts and feelings may develop signs of depression or use imagination to create an alternative world in which they are more successful. The personality types that externalise thoughts and feelings can look to others to blame or mimic. The former can develop problems with anger management and arrogance; the latter learns how to act successfully in a social situation.

Reactive depression

Social ability and friendship skills are highly valued by peers and adults, and not being successful in these areas can lead some people with Asperger syndrome to internalise their thoughts and feelings, such that they become self-critical, overly apologetic and increasingly socially withdrawn. The person has an intellectual ability to perceive his or her social isolation and lack of social skills in comparison with others but does not know intuitively what to do to improve his or her abilities. Brave attempts to improve social integration may be responded to with ridicule; due to not yet having the diagnosis, the person does not have the necessary level of guidance and, especially, encouragement. The person desperately wants to be socially accepted and to have friends but does not know what to do and may develop a reactive clinical depression as a result of insight into being different and not being able to achieve the degree of social success required. The clinical depression can also affect motivation and energy for other previously enjoyable activities, and there can be changes in sleep patterns and appetite, a negative attitude that pervades all aspects of life and, in extreme cases, talk of suicide and indeed impulsive or planned suicide attempts.

Escape into imagination

A more constructive internalisation of thoughts and feelings of social isolation can be to escape into one's imagination. The person may develop a vivid and complex imaginary world, sometimes with imaginary friends. In this fantasy world, the person is successful socially and academically. The child may develop an interest in other countries and planets at an early age, as described in the following quotation from the author's sister-in-law, who has Asperger syndrome:

> When I was about seven, I probably saw something in a book which fascinated me and still does. Because it was like nothing I had ever seen before and totally unrelated and far removed from our world and our culture. That was Scandinavia and its people. Because of its foreign-ness, it was totally alien and opposite to anyone and anything known to me. That was my escape, a dream world where nothing would remind me of daily life and all it had to throw at me. The people from this wonderful place look totally unlike any people in the 'real world'. Looking at these faces, I could not be reminded of anyone who might have humiliated, frightened or rebuked me. The bottom line is I was turning my back on real life and its ability to hurt and escaping.

The interest in other cultures and worlds can explain, for example, the development of a special interest in geography, which may satisfy a curiosity about the very different culture of a particular place; or in astronomy and science fiction, in which the fantasy might be about the discovery of a planet where the knowledge and abilities of the person with Asperger syndrome are understood and valued; or in pre-history, such as the time of the dinosaurs, when there were no humans to relate to; or in Ancient Egypt, with its much simpler lifestyle. Sometimes, the degree of imaginative thought can lead to the development of the ability to write fiction. Some children – especially girls – and some women with Asperger syndrome can develop their ability to use imaginary friends, characters and worlds to write quite remarkable fiction. This adjustment could lead to success as an author of fiction or as a travel journalist. Another expression of this adjustment strategy is to develop an interest during adolescence in complex role-playing games.

The escape into imagination can be a psychologically constructive adaptation, but there are risks of other people misinterpreting the person's intentions or state of mind. Hans Asperger (1994, p.51) wrote with regard to one of the four children, Harro, who became the basis of his thesis on autistic personality:

> He was said to be an inveterate 'liar'. He did not lie in order to get out of something that he had done – this was certainly not his problem, as he always told the truth very brazenly – but he told long, fantastic stories, his confabulations becoming ever more strange and incoherent. He liked to tell fantastic stories, in which he always appeared as the hero. He would tell his mother how he was praised by the teacher in front of the class, and other similar tales.

The contrast between the real and imaginary worlds can become quite acute during adolescence, and under extreme stress the adolescent with Asperger syndrome may create a fantasy world that becomes not simply a mental sanctuary and source of enjoyment but also a cause of concern to others, who observe that the distinction between the fantasy world and reality is becoming blurred. This retreat into imagination as a compensatory mechanism can then become interpreted as a delusional state of mind (LaSalle 2003).

Denial and arrogance

An alternative to internalising negative thoughts, feelings and the cause and solution to interpersonal problems is to externalise the cause and solution. The person can develop a form of over-compensation for his or her feelings of incompetence in social situations by denying that there are any problems and, in an arrogant manner, insisting that the 'fault' is in other people. Such children and adults go into 'God mode', seeing themselves as omnipotent people who never make mistakes and cannot be wrong. They may deny they have any difficulties making friends or reading social situations or people's thoughts and intentions. They insist that they do not need any remedial programmes and that they should not be treated differently from others. They do not want to be considered as socially inept or having a disorder that has been diagnosed by a psychologist or psychiatrist. Their response is: 'I'm not mad, bad or stupid.'

Although such people know that they have limited social competence, they are desperate to conceal their disability. The resulting denial and arrogance can be of great concern to family members and psychologists. Their lack of competence in social understanding can result in the development of behaviours to achieve dominance and control in a social context. Such behaviours may include the use of intimidation and the development of an arrogant and inflexible attitude to achieve authority and control, as others are more likely to 'give in' to avoid a confrontation. Such people can become 'intoxicated' by their power and dominance; in childhood, this may lead to conduct problems. Another strategy, sometimes used by girls with Asperger syndrome, is not dominance but avoidance of any social demands. The child may develop an ability to manipulate and avoid situations using emotional blackmail and single-minded determination to achieve control.

Unfortunately, one of the consequences in childhood and later of the compensatory mechanism of arrogance and denial and the immature theory of mind and empathy skills associated with Asperger syndrome is to seek resolution and retribution for social embarrassment by physical retaliation. When the child is confused as to the intentions of others, or about what to do in a social situation, or has made a conspicuous error, the resulting 'negative' emotion can lead to the misperception that the other person's actions were deliberately malicious. The response is to inflict equal discomfort, sometimes by physical retaliation: 'He hurt my feelings, so I will hurt him.'

The compensatory mechanism of arrogance can also affect other aspects of social interaction. The person may have difficulty admitting being wrong and be notorious for arguing. Asperger (1944, p.48) advised:

> There is a great danger of getting involved in endless arguments with these children, be it in order to prove that they are wrong or to bring them towards some insight. This is especially true for parents, who frequently find themselves trapped in endless discussion.

There can be a remarkably accurate recall of what was said or done to prove a point, being great historians of their own past. This characteristic could perhaps lead to a successful career as a defence lawyer in an adversarial court.

The arrogant attitude can further alienate the person from natural friendships, and denial and resistance towards remedial programmes can increase the gap between the person's social abilities and that of others. While we may understand why the child or adult would develop such compensatory and adjustment strategies, the long-term consequences can have a significant effect on friendships and prospects for more intimate relationships and even employment as an adult.

Imitation

An intelligent and constructive compensatory mechanism is to observe and absorb the personas of those who are socially successful. Such children initially remain on the periphery of social play, watching and noting what to do. They may then re-enact the activities that they have observed in their own solitary play using dolls, figures or imaginary friends at home. They are rehearsing, practising the script and their role, to achieve a fluency and confidence before attempting to be included in real social play situations. Some children and adults with Asperger syndrome can be remarkably astute in their observation abilities, copying gestures, tone of voice and mannerisms. They develop the ability described by Liane Holliday Willey (1999) in *Pretending to be Normal*. This could lead to a successful career as an actor and be a constructive way of making friends and achieving social inclusion.

Becoming an expert mimic can have other advantages. The child may become popular for imitating the voice and persona of a teacher or a character from television. The adolescent with Asperger syndrome may constructively use drama classes and techniques for everyday situations, determining who would be successful in this situation and adopting the persona of that individual. However, there are two possible disadvantages. The first is observing popular but notorious models, for example the school 'bad guys'. This group may accept the adolescent with Asperger syndrome who wears the group's 'uniform' and speaks their language and knows their gestures and moral code, but this may alienate the adolescent from more appropriate models. The group may also recognise that the person is a fake or 'try-hard', and the person with Asperger syndrome may not be aware that he or she is being covertly ridiculed and 'set up'. The other disadvantage is for psychologists and psychiatrists, who may consider that the person has signs of multiple personality disorder rather than recognise that this is a constructive adaptation to having Asperger syndrome.

The diagnostic assessment

Diagnosis entails knowledge of childhood, and yet it may be several decades since the adult was a child, and recollections of childhood may be affected by the accuracy, or otherwise, of long-term memory. An aid to memory and discussion can be looking at photographs of the person when he or she was a child. Family photographs taken during social occasions can provide an opportunity to notice whether the child appeared to be participating in the social interactions. Conversation during the diagnostic assessment can be about the event and the person's competence and confidence in a particular social context. School reports can be useful in indicating any problems with peer relationships at school and any concerns with regard to learning abilities and behaviour.

The author prefers, if possible, to conduct the diagnostic assessment with a relative, partner or friend of the adult who can not only provide a second opinion on recollections of childhood abilities and experiences but also give a more objective opinion.

There are some characteristics that may be more conspicuous in adults who are referred for a diagnosis of Asperger syndrome. Generally, women are aware of current dress styles and know that their choices of clothing, colour coordination and accessories will be noticed, especially, perhaps, by other women. They are also aware of what would be appropriate clothing for a diagnostic assessment. The clinician may note that a woman with Asperger syndrome chooses clothing that is comfortable and practical rather than fashionable. A man with Asperger syndrome may have an unusual dress sense, appearing untidy and quickly dishevelled.

A partner or relative may describe the person as being a perfectionist and overly critical of others. The author has noted that some adults with Asperger syndrome are notorious for becoming agitated about what others perceive as trivial matters but are admired for being calm and rational in a genuine crisis, when typical peers are overly emotional and making unwise decisions. For example, the author knows of several physicians with Asperger syndrome in accident and emergency departments who are able to work calmly during a medical emergency and several men with Asperger syndrome who have been noted for their bravery, determination and decision-making in their active military careers.

We now have screening questionnaires to identify the ability and personality characteristics of Asperger syndrome in adults, and the analysis of the responses and scores on these questionnaires can be extremely useful for the clinician. Most of the current assessment instruments have been developed by Simon Baron-Cohen and Sally Wheelwright and have been published in Baron-Cohen (2003). One of the tests is online at www.wired.com/wired/archive/9.12/aqtest.html.

The screening instruments are designed to indicate someone who might have the signs of Asperger syndrome; they are not an alternative to a diagnostic assessment with an experienced clinician. The diagnostic assessment can provide an opportunity to examine the person's responses to the questionnaire in more depth and for the clinician to determine the validity and accuracy of the person's self-rating. The adult referred for a diagnostic assessment may provide a response based on self-perception of his or her social abilities, while a good friend or family member may have a different opinion – hence the value of having a relative, partner or friend present during the diagnostic assessment. The clinician will need to determine which response is the more accurate.

It is possible that the adult will deliberately mislead the clinician in order to maintain self-esteem or to avoid a diagnosis that may be perceived as a mental illness. For example, Ben described how:

> I was always ashamed of who I was, so I never told the truth about anything that would embarrass me. If you had asked me if I have trouble understanding others, I would have said no, even though the true answer was yes. If you had asked me if I avoided social contact, I would have said no, because I wouldn't want you to think I was weird. If you had asked me if I lacked empathy, I would have been insulted, because everyone knows good people have empathy and bad people don't. I would have denied that I'm afraid of loud noises, that I have a narrow

range of interests, and that I get upset by changes in routine. The only questions I would have answered yes to would have been the ones about having unusually long-term memory for events and facts; reading books for information; and being like a walking encyclopaedia. That's because I liked those things about me. I thought they made me look smart. If I thought it was good, I would have said yes, and if I thought it was bad, I would have said no. (LaSalle 2003, pp.242–3)

As mentioned earlier, some adults may choose to conceal their difficulties in social interaction skills, while others may consider that their abilities are quite normal, based on family experience, which, especially if a parent also had some characteristics of Asperger syndrome, may have influenced their view of normality.

During the diagnostic assessment, the person may provide a reply to a question that appears to indicate considerable ability with social reasoning and empathy, but a careful examination of the response may indicate that the reply appeared to have been achieved by intellectual analysis rather than intuition, with a fractional delay in the response. The reply may have required some cognitive processing that also produces the impression of a contrived rather than natural response.

Self-perception of difference is also an indicator, and usually adults with Asperger syndrome have known they were different from an early age. Those who recognise that they were and are different to other people frequently first noticed when they started school, when they had to interact with an adult other than their mother and children other than their siblings, none of whom behaved in the way that they had grown used to within the family, or who were not interested in the same things.

The diagnostic assessment should examine not only areas of difficulties but also areas of ability that may be attributable to the characteristics of Asperger syndrome. For example, the person may have achieved prizes and certificates for his or her knowledge regarding a special interest or demonstrated academic skills such as winning a mathematics competition. The person may draw with photographic realism or invent computer games.

For an experienced clinician, the diagnostic assessment takes from one to two hours, or perhaps longer if more information is needed or further tests are conducted. Sometimes, the characteristics of Asperger syndrome are clearly evident to the clinician within the first moments of meeting the person. The remainder of the diagnostic assessment provides confirmation of the first impressions. For other adults, it may take some time to recognise the way the person is compensating for, or camouflaging, his or her characteristics of Asperger syndrome. The initial presentation does not 'broadcast' the clinical signs, but an experienced clinician knows what questions to ask and how to recognise the qualitative differences in abilities that confirm the diagnosis.

Closure of the diagnostic assessment

At the end of the diagnostic assessment, the clinician provides a summary and review of those characteristics in the person's developmental history, profile of abilities and behaviour consistent with a diagnosis of Asperger syndrome and whether the signs are sufficient for a diagnosis. The author uses a metaphor of a diagnostic jigsaw puzzle. A typical person may have perhaps up to 10 or 20 pieces (in other words, some of the features of Asperger syndrome), but when more than 80 pieces are connected, the puzzle is solved and the diagnosis is confirmed. Sometimes, a person referred for a diagnostic assessment may have more pieces than occur in the typical population but not enough characteristics, or the key or corner pieces, to complete the puzzle and achieve a diagnosis. Such individuals do not have a diagnosis of Asperger syndrome, but they may still benefit from the strategies used for those 'pieces' that they do have.

Some adults referred for a diagnostic assessment may have the number of signs but not the impairment in functioning necessary for a diagnosis according to the *Diagnostic and Statistical Manual of Mental Disorders*, (DSM-IV; American Psychiatric Association 2000). Problems with social understanding may be reduced to a sub-clinical level by a supportive partner who provides the necessary guidance, such as a social script before an important social occasion or effective repair of comments or actions that are confusing or inappropriate to other adults. Work circumstances may be successful due to understanding colleagues and line managers. In such circumstances, the clinician may have to consider whether the apparently successful functioning of the individual warrants the diagnosis of a mental disorder (Szatmari 2004). However, if the person experiences a crisis such as divorce or unemployment, the signs may become more conspicuous and then warrant a diagnosis. It is perhaps not the severity of expression that is important, but the circumstances, expectations and coping and support mechanisms.

The author has recently noticed an increasing number of referrals of adults who have read about Asperger syndrome and have become convinced that the diagnosis is an explanation of their unusual character and childhood experiences. However, after an objective evaluation and consideration of the degree of expression necessary for a diagnosis, the clinician has been unable to confirm the client's conviction that he or she has Asperger syndrome. Sometimes, the referral can be from a partner, convinced that the relationship difficulties are due to having a partner with Asperger syndrome. A diagnostic assessment has to distinguish between what some may consider as typical male behaviour in a relationship and a mental disorder.

The final decision on where you draw the line, namely whether a person has a diagnosis of Asperger syndrome, is a subjective decision made by the clinician on the basis of the results of the assessment of specific abilities such as the maturity of theory of mind skills, observations and interactions with the person, and descriptions and reports from parents, teachers and others. The qualitative impairment in social interaction or social relatedness is central and pathognomonic to the diagnosis, but there is no weighting system for the other characteristics to help decide whether, on balance, a borderline case should have the diagnosis. The ultimate decision on whether to confirm a diagnosis is based on the clinician's clinical experience, the current diagnostic criteria and the effect of the unusual profile of abilities on the person's quality of life.

The summary needs to acknowledge the positive characteristics of Asperger syndrome, the degree of expression of each of the main characteristics, and which characteristics in the profile of abilities and behaviour are not due to Asperger syndrome. The clinician may also need to comment on the signs of any secondary or dual disorders such as depression, anxiety or conduct disorder, and whether another disorder is currently the dominant factor affecting the person's quality of life and, as a matter of expediency, should be the priority for treatment. The next stage is to discuss the known causes of Asperger syndrome, recommended remedial programmes, government support services, parent or spouse support groups, relevant publications, the likely prognosis and the monitoring of progress. However, this may be achieved in subsequent appointments once the significance of the diagnosis has been understood and acknowledged.

The author makes an audiotape cassette recording of the summary, strategies and closure stage of the diagnostic assessment so that the person can subsequently listen to the explanation of the diagnosis and implications. The author has noted that recording the summary can lessen the likelihood of being misunderstood or misquoted when others are informed of the diagnosis and degree of expression.

Explanation of the diagnosis

Adults may be reluctant to attend a diagnostic assessment that will examine their developmental history, abilities and personality, especially if the diagnostic assessment is conducted by a psychologist or psychiatrist. The diagnostic assessment can be perceived as a test of sanity. If the impetus for an appointment has come from a partner or parent, then there may be a greater risk of reluctance to attend the appointment and antagonism towards the clinician. There will need to be a personal advantage in attending a diagnostic assessment, such as to seek advice regarding employment or how to cope with changes in work responsibilities, to improve a deteriorating relationship with a partner or to seek more effective treatment of a mood disorder. The approach is to consider how the diagnosis may be a positive influence in the person's life.

The Attributes Activity

The author has developed a programme called The Attributes Activity to explain the diagnosis to the person and their family. The author arranges a gathering of family members, including the person who has recently been diagnosed as having Asperger syndrome. The first activity involves using large sheets of paper attached to the wall, or a large white board and coloured pens. Each sheet is divided into two columns, one column headed 'Qualities' and the other headed 'Difficulties'. The author suggests that another family member is the first person to do the activity, which is to list his or her personal qualities and difficulties. These can include practical abilities, knowledge, personality and the expression and management of feelings. After the focus person has made his or her own suggestions, which the clinician writes on the paper or board, the family members add their suggestions. The clinician ensures that this is a positive activity, commenting on the various attributes and noting that there are more qualities than difficulties. Another member of the family is nominated or volunteers to repeat the procedure. The person who has Asperger syndrome is then able to observe and participate in the activity to learn what is expected when it is his or her turn.

Sometimes people with Asperger syndrome are reluctant to suggest, or may not consider that they have many, qualities or attributes. The family members are encouraged to make suggestions, and the clinician can nominate a few suggestions from his or her own observations. There will need to be some care when nominating difficulties so that the person does not feel he or she is being victimised. The following is a representation of the Attributes Activity for a typical person with Asperger syndrome:

Qualities

Honest
Determined
An expert on insects and the Titanic
Aware of sounds that others cannot
    hear
Kind
Forthright
A loner (and happy to be so)
A perfectionist
Advanced in the knowledge of
    mathematics
A reliable friend
Good at art/singing
Exceptional at remembering things
    that other people had forgotten
Funny in a unique way
Observant of details that others did
    not see

Difficulties

Accepting mistakes
Making friends
Taking advice
Managing anger
Handwriting
Knowing what someone is thinking
Avoiding being
    teased
Showing as much affection as
    other family members
    expect

The clinician can then comment on each quality and difficulty as a positive and constructive activity. The next stage is to explain that scientists are often looking for patterns in nature and that when they have found a consistent pattern they give it a name. Reference is then made to Dr Hans Asperger, who saw many children at his clinic in Vienna and first published the clinical description that has become known as Asperger syndrome.

The author usually says to the person, 'Congratulations, you have Asperger syndrome', and explains that this means they are not mad, bad or defective but have a different way of thinking. The discussion begins with how some of the person's talents or qualities are due to having Asperger syndrome, such as impressing people with his or her know-ledge about the Titanic, ability to draw with photographic realism and attention to detail, and being naturally talented in mathematics. This introduces the benefits of having the characteristics of Asperger syndrome.

The next stage is to discuss the difficulties and the strategies needed to improve specific abilities at home and at work. This can include the advantages of guidance and counselling in social understanding, cognitive behaviour therapy and/or medication to help with emotion management, and ideas to help with making friends and improving relationships. The clinician then provides a summary of the person's qualities and difficul-ties that are due to having Asperger syndrome and mentions successful people in the areas of science, information technology, politics and the arts who really benefited from the characteristics of Asperger syndrome in their own profile of abilities or attributes (Ledgin 2002; Paradiz 2002).

Hans Asperger (1979) wrote:

> It seems that for success in science or art, a dash of autism is essential. For success, the necessary ingredient may be an ability to turn away from the everyday world, from the simply practical, an ability to re-think a subject with originality so as to create in new untrodden ways, with all abilities canalised into the one speciality.

The Attributes Activity can also be used with adults on their own or with their partners. If the author is using the activity with a couple, where one partner has Asperger syndrome, then the other partner can be asked what is appealing about his or her partner. The author has noted that the attributes can include being physically attractive (the silent handsome stranger), loyalty, having a remarkable intellect and original ideas, being a man with a 'feminine' side, being a challenge to get to know and, during the time of dating, being very attentive. As with all relationships, over time other attributes become more noticeable and some diminish, but some of the relationship attributes can be explained as being associated with the characteristics of Asperger syndrome in an adult.

The activity closes with an explanation of some of the author's personal thoughts on Asperger syndrome. Such individuals have different priorities, perceptions of the world and ways of thinking. The brain is wired differently, not defectively. The person prioritises the pursuit of knowledge, perfection, truth and the understanding of the physical world above feelings and interpersonal experiences. This can lead to valued talents but also vulnerabilities in the social world.

Resources to explain the diagnosis

Carol Gray and the author of this chapter were concerned that when an adult with Asperger syndrome reads the diagnostic criteria, the characteristics are almost exclusively those that are qualitatively different in terms of being less able than the person's peers with a very distinct value judgement on what is acceptable and clinically significant. We noticed that people with Asperger syndrome have some qualities that can be superior to their peers. To provide a counter-argument, we wrote diagnostic criteria that describe positive and affirmative characteristics of Asperger syndrome in adults, in an article entitled 'The Discovery of "Aspie"' (Gray and Attwood 1999), available online at www.thegraycenter.org/discovery_of.htm.

Unlike 'diagnosis', the term 'discovery' refers to the identification of a person's strengths or talents. Actors are *discovered*. Artists and musicians are *discovered*. A great friend is discovered. These people are identified by an informal combination of evaluation and awe that ultimately concludes that this person – more than most others – possesses admirable qualities, abilities and talents.

In the Gray and Attwood questions, there is a list of social advantages that has its roots in the social challenges of people with Asperger syndrome. Regarding someone as socially 'new' or 'unique' has more potential than the negative counterparts of 'awkward' or 'inappropriate'. This requires social creativity. In this case, it may be helpful for typical people to regard social interaction as a trip through immigration and customs. Anyone who travels between countries knows the anxiety of approaching a customs agent, that country's appointed keeper of the rules of entry and acceptability. Here the rules are rigid, the questions straightforward and a little rude: 'Why are you here and when are you leaving?' 'Are you here for personal or business purposes?' (In other words, 'Are you here to visit Los Angeles or buy it?') The process raises social anxiety: Do I look safe and kind enough to these people (who look dispassionately authoritarian and mannerless to me) to be among them in their country? Or, do they need to rummage through my personal belongings to judge whether I can be included? For people with Asperger syndrome, there is a daily social immigration and customs process – a continual anxiety of doing it 'right', saying it 'right' and having the necessary social "passport" that typical people constantly seek in others before befriending them.

Liane Holliday Willey (2001) has Asperger syndrome and has written a self-affirmation pledge that can be incorporated in the explanation of the diagnosis to adults:

- I am not defective.
- I am different.
- I will not sacrifice my self-worth for peer acceptance.
- I am capable of getting along with society.
- I will ask for help when I need it.
- I will be patient with those who need time to understand me.
- I will accept myself for who I am.

After explaining the diagnosis to the person, it is important to discuss who else needs to know. Adults will want to know whether it is wise to tell friends, prospective employers and colleagues. The clinician will need to examine the relevant advantages and disadvantages for each person based on that person's circumstances, the advantages and disadvantages of certain people knowing and how much information to disclose.

The advantages and disadvantages of having a diagnosis

The advantage to the person of having a diagnosis is not only in preventing or reducing the effects of some aspects of potential compensatory or adjustment strategies but also to remove worries about other diagnoses such as insanity and to aid recognition that he or she has genuine difficulties coping with experiences that others find easy and enjoyable. The person who has Asperger syndrome has no physical characteristics to indicate that he or she is different, and having intellectual ability may lead others to have high expectations with regard to social knowledge. Once the diagnosis is confirmed and understood, there can be a significant positive change in other people's expectations, acceptance and support. There should be compliments rather than criticism with regard to social competence and acknowledgement of the person's confusion and exhaustion in social situations.

The advantage of acknowledging and understanding the diagnosis for parents is that, at last, they have an explanation for their son's or daughter's unusual behaviours and abilities and knowledge that the condition is not caused by faulty parenting. The family may then have access to information on Asperger syndrome from literature and the Internet, resources from government agencies and support groups, and access to remedial programmes to improve social inclusion and emotion management that will greatly benefit the whole family. There may also be greater acceptance of the person within the extended family and family friends. The parents can now provide a legitimate explanation to other people regarding their son's or daughter's unusual behaviour.

Siblings may have known for some time that their brother or sister is unusual and may have been either compassionate, tolerant and concerned for their difficulties or embarrassed, intolerant and antagonistic. Siblings will make their own accommodations and develop their own attitudes towards a person with Asperger syndrome. Parents can now explain why their brother or sister is unusual, and how the family has had to and will need to adjust and work cooperatively and constructively to implement the remedial strategies. Siblings will need to know how to explain their brother or sister to their own friends, so as not to jeopardise their social network, and how to help them at home. Parents and professionals can provide the siblings with age-appropriate explanations for their friends.

The advantages of the diagnosis for the adolescent or adult with Asperger syndrome can be in terms of support in employment or while a student at college or university (Fast 2004; Harpur *et al.* 2004; Hawkins 2004). The recognition of the diagnosis can enable the adult with Asperger syndrome to benefit from employment agencies that specialise in adults with Asperger syndrome. The person with Asperger syndrome may need to develop ways of explaining their unusual qualities to colleagues, acquaintances and neighbours so that should he or she break the anticipated social conventions, the situation can be repaired by reference to the relevant characteristics of Asperger syndrome. The diagnostic term need not be mentioned in the conversation, but explanations should be given, such as 'I am the sort of person who goes on and on about my special interest. If I am boring you, please say so and we can change the subject.' Eric, a young man with Asperger syndrome, said that he prefers a life of openness, not secrecy, with regard to his diagnosis in order to prevent any problems occurring because of the ignorance of colleagues.

Acknowledgement of the diagnosis can lead to greater self-understanding and better decision-making with regard to careers, friendships and relationships. The adult may benefit from joining an adult support group that has local meetings or an Internet support group or chat room. This can provide a sense of belonging to a distinct and valued culture and an opportunity to consult members of the culture for advice.

The family and people in the social network of the adult can now have an explanation for aspects of behaviour that previously have been perceived as abrasive or rude and a cause for annoyance or ridicule. The person's difficulties are now taken more seriously. The person will need to decide who and when to tell and how much detail to provide. Clinical experience suggests that being open and honest regarding the diagnosis can have a beneficial effect on the person's interpersonal experiences.

We also know that acceptance of the diagnosis can be an important stage in the development of successful adult relationships with a partner, and invaluable when seeking counselling and therapy from relationship counsellors (Aston 2003). The recognition of the diagnosis may also put into perspective other potential explanations of the person's unusual character, for example early childhood experiences such as emotional neglect or abuse.

The author has noted that when an adult is diagnosed with Asperger syndrome, there can be a range of emotional reactions. The usual response is a great sense of relief. One adult said: 'I've always known I was different, but I didn't know it had a name' (Jacobs 2003). Having that name, and an awareness of the qualities and difficulties associated with Asperger syndrome, can lead to greater self-understanding and better decision-making.

Most adults report that having the diagnosis has been an extremely positive experience. There can be intense relief – 'I am not going mad', joy at ending a nomadic wandering from specialist to specialist in an attempt to discover why they feel and think differently to others, and excitement as to how their lives may now change for the better. There can also be moments of anger at the delay in being diagnosed and at 'the system' for not recognising the signs for so many years. There can be feelings of despair when they realise how much easier their lives would have been had the diagnosis been confirmed decades ago. Other emotional reactions can be a sense of grief for all the suffering in trying to be as socially successful as others, and for the years of feeling misunderstood, inadequate and rejected. There can be a new sense of personal validation and optimism: they are not stupid, defective or insane. As Liane Holliday Willey said exuberantly on learning of her diagnosis: 'That's why I'm different, not a freak or mad.'

However, another response can be denial, with the belief that there is nothing wrong or different about them. Despite such people acknowledging that the clinical descriptions match their developmental history and profile of abilities, they may question the validity of the diagnosis and reject any programmes or services designed for adults with Asperger syndrome. Clinical experience suggests that rejection of the diagnosis is rare, especially when the clinician has explained the qualities of someone with Asperger syndrome and the positive aspects of the prognosis once the diagnosis is understood and acknowledged by the person.

The disadvantages of having a diagnosis can be in terms of how the person and others perceive the characteristics of Asperger syndrome. If the diagnostic news is broadcast widely, inevitably there will be some people in the person's life who misuse the news to torment or despise the person with Asperger syndrome. This is an unfortunate part of the nature of some individuals, but more compassionate people may be able to repair some of the damage to the self-esteem of someone with Asperger syndrome who has been shunned or ridiculed for being different and having a disorder.

Having a diagnosis of Asperger syndrome could limit the expectations of others, who may assume that such people will never be able to achieve as well as their peers with regard to social and academic success. The diagnosis should facilitate realistic expectations but not dictate the upper limits of ability.

One of the concerns of adults with Asperger syndrome is whether to include reference to the diagnosis on a job application. If there is considerable competition for a particular vacancy, then an applicant having a diagnosis that is unknown to the employer might lead to the application being rejected. A potential solution is for the adult to write a brief – perhaps one-page – description of Asperger syndrome and the qualities and difficulties that would be relevant to the job. This personalised brochure could also be used to explain Asperger syndrome to colleagues, juniors and line managers. A shorter version can be reduced to a business card that can be given to anyone who needs to know about the person's diagnosis.

The diagnosis can be of considerable benefit to individuals in terms of understanding who they are and how they think differently to others, and enabling wiser decision-making in their lives based on an understanding of the nature of Asperger syndrome. The remedial programmes designed after the diagnostic assessment should be directed not only at improving social understanding and success but also at improving the talents that can be associated with Asperger syndrome. As Temple Grandin said, 'If the world was left to you socialites, we would still be in caves talking to each other.' As a society, we need to recognise the value of having people with Asperger syndrome in our multi-cultural community. And perhaps we should consider this suggestion, from an adult with Asperger syndrome, who asked the author whether he thought that Asperger syndrome might be the next stage of human evolution.

References

American Psychiatric Association (2000) *Diagnostic and Statistical Manual of Mental Disorders*, 4th edn. (DSM-IV) Washington, DC: American Psychiatric Association.

Asperger, H. (1944) 'Autistic Psychopathy in Childhood.' In U. Frith (ed) *Autism and Asperger Syndrome*. Cambridge: Cambridge University Press, 1991.

Asperger, H. (1979) 'Problems of infantile autism.' *Communication*, 13, 45–52.

Aston, M. (2003) *Aspergers in Love*. London: Jessica Kingsley Publishers.

Baron-Cohen, S. (2003) *The Essential Difference: Men, Women and the Extreme Male Brain*. London: Allen Lane.

Fast, Y. (2004) *Employment for Individuals with Asperger Syndrome or Non-Verbal Learning Disability: Stories and Strategies*. London: Jessica Kingsley Publishers.

Gray, C. and Attwood, T. (1999) 'The Discovery of "Aspie": Criteria by Attwood and Gray.' *Morning News*, 11, 1–7.

Harpur, J., Lawlor, M. and Fitzgerald, M. (2004) *Succeeding in College with Asperger Syndrome: A Student Guide*. London: Jessica Kingsley Publishers.

Hawkins, G. (2004) *How to Find Work that Works for People with Asperger Syndrome*. London: Jessica Kingsley Publishers.

Jacobs, B. (2003) *Loving Mr Spock: The Story of a Different Kind of Love*. London: Michael Joseph.

LaSalle, B. (2003) *Finding Ben: A Mother's Journey Through the Maze of Asperger*. New York: Contemporary Books.

Ledgin, N. (2002) *Asperger and Self-Esteem: Insight and Hope through Famous Role Models*. Arlington, TX: Future Horizons.

Paradiz, V. (2005) *Elijah's Cup: A Family's Journey into the Community and Culture of High-functioning Autism and Asperger Syndrome*. London: Jessica Kingsley Publishers.

Szatmari, P. (2004) *A Mind Apart: Understanding Children with Autism and Asperger Syndrome*. New York: Guilford Press.

Willey, L.H. (1999) *Pretending to be Normal: Living with Asperger Syndrome*. London: Jessica Kingsley Publishers.

Willey, L.H. (2001) *Asperger Syndrome in the Family: Redefining Normal*. London: Jessica Kingsley Publishers.

3.

Confidence, self-confidence and social confidence

Dinah Murray and Mike Lesser

Confidence is defined in my dictionary as 'firm trust'. If you are confident about something, you don't worry about its outcome, you just take it for granted that it will go well. Sports commentators tend to say things like 'She's very confident, nothing seems to faze her' or 'John's playing with such confidence today every ball's going just where he wants it – sheer mastery!' Confidence is partly about skill, about knowing what to do and how to do it. We tend to forget that even standing upright is a learned skill, that once upon a time we were all unable to do that. We build up layers of confidence in moving through the world, encountering and overcoming successive challenges.

Confidence is also about motivation. Low confidence can become high confidence only when strong motivation drives repeated experience. As confidence increases in any one area of understanding, less attentional energy will be wasted in anxiety and uncertainty and lower levels of motivation will be required to drive it. On the other hand, if confidence is misplaced and a step taken leads to a crash, then the reverse process will occur and a process of re-motivation may be needed before the experience is repeated. Over-confidence is likely to trip itself up in the end and may damage self-confidence overall – so confidence is also about having good judgement.

Self-confidence I suggest arises from a sense that the skills one has acquired are valuable and not to be scorned. It is connected with the need to fit into and flourish within one's environment, which must be universal to all animals but for social animals such as humans implies acceptance within a given society. We need to feel we belong, that we are not in a wrong or dangerous place in which our efforts to do the right thing are spurned. Not only does one have to struggle to learn a skill, i.e. become confident enough to try it out, but one may also have to endure social judgement of its execution. Two layers of confidence are thus required by people who have tuned in to social issues. If what we have to offer is rejected, then motivation can take some very hard knocks – in people with uncertain self-confidence it may flatten right out, leaving no appetite for action whatsoever. But the most deeply self-confident people are so sure of the worth of what they do, that they will carry on doing it through repeated rejection, with little or no social support. Confidence is what allows us to pursue our interests with resolve.

All of those points about confidence apply to everyone. But as this chapter shows, the attention-tunnelled (monotropic) disposition of people on the autism spectrum has a distinctive impact, making many of them particularly vulnerable to lack of confidence and to social rejection, while others appear capable of pursuing their own interests with enviable indifference to the judgement of others. Some monotropic people may be unaware of negative social input until well on in life because it has not been 'loud' enough to distract them from being so satisfactorily focused on their own concerns. Others may have acquired enough social awareness soon enough to have encountered some very discouraging social experiences fairly early in life. Anyone who acquires an autism diagnosis will ipso facto be an identifiable social misfit, at whatever stage in their life that occurs. But they are likely also to have a great contribution to make in their chosen areas of interest and a need equal to anyone's to feel they belong. We need them too. We need to use all this human potential. We need the people who do not follow the herd. That means they need to have confidence in the social process as well as in themselves – and it behoves us to earn that confidence.

Monotropism – being extremely attention-tunnelled – means that objects of interest tend to be isolated and without context or scale (Lawson 2001; Murray *et al.* 2005). That makes for an alarming and unpredictable universe in which there's no guessing what's going to happen next. To make matters worse, monotropism also tends to precipitate black-and-white/all-or-nothing reaction and assessment and emotional arousal, which can be extreme, rapid and out of tune with other people. All in all, it's a baffling and confusing world in which setbacks tend to be both frequent and subjectively catastrophic, at least in the short term. Fear of failure can be all-consuming. Such people are very uncomfortable with getting things wrong and thus tend to be absolutely dedicated to 'getting it right' – however implausible that may sometimes seem to the rest of society.

This chapter discusses how to build up confidence and resilience in people with a monotropic disposition – who will tend to be in a state of almost perpetual anxiety – and thus create a beneficial loop:

1.   Reduced fear/increased confidence.

2.   Increased exploration.

3.   Increased understanding.

4.   Increased ability to make successful predictions.

5.   Increased adaptive behaviour.

6.   Reduced crashes.

7.   Reduced fear/increased confidence.

Quantity of available attention affects the quality of monotropic experience. It varies both between individuals and within individuals over time – confidence has an impact on this both at any given moment and across time. Confidence maximises available attention in two ways: it is replete with positive affect and thus intrinsically motivating, and it can excite aroused interests above the action threshold. Events that damage confidence have the effect of draining all attention into a painful focus, which exacerbates the tendency not to reach out and connect. Being unable to proceed with confidence shrinks one's horizons of possibility. Successful experiences, in particular successful ventures, build confidence. A subjectively successful event is one that has fulfilled one's hopes, however small.

Overall, there are three possible lines of approach towards increasing confidence and decreasing fear, which have an impact on each other: maximise opportunities for getting it right; minimise occasions for getting it wrong; and develop awareness of scalar concepts – of 'shades of grey', for example, very important, rather important and hardly important at all.

Maximising opportunities for 'getting it right'

Give as much control as possible to the individual. Being involved in decisions about one's own life is something most of us take for granted and is fundamental to our sense of personal autonomy and efficacy. If people control both the topics and the timing of what they do, then from their point of view it is far less likely to go wrong and far more likely to be personally rewarding. This is particularly important for the most steeply monotropic individuals, who will have deep focal interest correlated with discomfort in switching focus when a competing alternative stimulus is presented. These young people are likely to be painfully and frequently interrupted unless they are in complete control of their worlds. That is not a good way to build confidence in the social process. For these very monotropic people, life tends to veer between intensely rewarding high-quality moments and catastrophes. These are also the people who will take longest to develop connections between their fragmented experiences and who consequently may need the most help to develop their general understanding of life. Whenever possible, we should avoid diverting the attention of such firmly focused folk – and especially avoid doing that abruptly – since doing so is likely to be counterproductive, leaving them stranded and confused. Although perhaps softened in adults by age and experience, the old autism saying, 'Start where the child is', is a reliable strategy for building up confidence and understanding.

When a steeply attention-tunnelled person also tends to have a narrow rather than broad focus of interest, they may have marked difficulties with sensory integration and be unable to take in information simultaneously through more than one sensory channel. They may be particularly likely to suffer from sensory overload and also particularly likely not to make connections between areas of interest. Making connections is fundamental to increasing understanding, and increasing understanding in order to increase the scope of their confidence may be a slow and piecemeal process. But we have to build on those limited areas – their areas of particular interest – in which an individual feels competent, confident and motivated. It will waste both their time and yours to attempt to increase their understanding of areas in which they feel none of that. Even the least promising areas of interest can be built on and developed, because the sense of personal efficacy attached to pursuing those interests and the motivation to keep doing so are likely to remain high. Wendy Lawson tells a great tale of a lad whose socially unwelcome obsession was dog turds. Some years later, he has become a proto-palaeontologist with a vast knowledge of digestive processes and what you can learn about diet – including dinosaur's diets – from excreta. Most other interests have more obvious promise for building broader under-standing, and it will be less hard to adjust one's own mindset to appreciate them as required. We just need to take it one step at a time and be confident in our monotropic children and partners.

Over a lifetime, few individuals do not broaden their horizons of interest, regardless of whether we directly try to actively encourage this process. Spontaneous shifts of perspective will occur just through living a life. Monotropic individuals sometimes start off appearing to be lost to the rest of humanity in their intensive preoccupation with objects of interest that pass the rest of the world by, but later on they are certain to notice much else and may develop interests of universal scope. The robust confidence with which steeply attention-tunnelled people pursue their interests can give them a happy indifference to other people's judgement. Even though that feels like a loss to us, it may be a benefit for them. Once they've pieced the world together later, they may be equally resolute in a common cause (see www.autistics.org for some evidence regarding this). Albert Einstein, Ludwig Wittgenstein and Alan Turing all determinedly pursued the implications of detailed observation through to general con-clusions running counter to received opinions and went on to influence world views. It has been suggested widely that these people qualify as belonging somewhere on the autism spectrum. They appear to have flourished without their monotropic dispositions causing them serious problems for most of their lives. Perhaps it used to be easier to find oppor-tunities to pursue one's own interests freely and yet be poor at teamwork or multi-tasking, while generally being socially valued and even employed for doing so?

If we do choose to encourage the pursuit of broader or more socially valued interests, then it is usually best not to do so directively. That is likely to encourage either dissent or passivity in its monotropic recipients rather than stimulate genuine interest in finding out more. But everyone can move themselves on, can move without being directed to, if they feel motivated to do so. One boy watched the rest of his family using computers for more than two years before he ventured to explore them himself. We may need to repeatedly and persistently provide opportunities to observe and join in activities that involve exploring the new in a relatively safe way (the new is always risky). This may inspire new interest and motivation. That means being a good observer – not trying to lead but noting and adjusting constantly to new achievements and developing interests. This can be a most enjoyable process and will build confidence in each other for both of you. As the process will also increase understanding and mastery, it will also build self-confidence in the children or adults who are sharing it. Work on 'scaffolding' in the learning process in the tradition of Vygotsky (1962) and Bruner (1985) makes it clear how much other people functioning as sensitively adjusted external resources can facilitate learning. The active role we can most usefully play in this may be to make success easy – but not too easy – to help motivate and engineer manageable and appealing challenges.

Every challenge met successfully is a boost to self-confidence and a contribution to a life lived fully. If those challenges happen to attract genuine social approval, such as the running successes of Alex Bain in Canada (PEI Road Runners Club 2004) and Dane Waites in Australia (Waites & Swinbourne 2001), then enduring general social confidence may be an additional benefit. Learning to take physical risks and master physical challenges is a great way to improve self-confidence. Having a sense of personal achievement and the satisfaction that one has met a challenge is intrinsically rewarding and motivating. It may also win respect from a wider range of people than the less obvious achievements that a more intimate connection may be alert to. Being treated with serious respect as a responsible and capable person rather than being dismissed as socially valueless can be transforming in terms of feeling a sense of belonging and contributing.

If we ignore the individual's interests in their early years and fail to make our own friendly interest known, then awareness or understanding of social possibilities may not occur until problematically late in life. If we constantly try to impose our own agenda and dismiss the individual's, then we are guaranteeing alienation. The individual may acquire a profound sense of not belonging – the 'wrong planet' syndrome that so many Aspies have identified. Small, carefully judged inputs of positive feedback can make a huge difference to this, although the greatest care must be taken not to offer insincerity, as it will increase neither the individual's self-confidence nor their confidence in you.

Building a community of friendly people around autistic individuals is a generally reliable long-term strategy. But the friendly community we can influence tends to be limited, and some degree of social rejection remains inevitable, given the expectations that have singled out people on the autism spectrum as dysfunctional. So we need to find further ways of helping people withstand the social disrespect that is certain to be encountered. Being a member of a proudly eccentric family that treats negative social judgements as insignificant may be of real value – so dredge up those weird cousins and ancestors to give some solid ground to the sense of belonging. However, the 'black or white' tendency of monotropic thinking may swing a person to the other extreme, and they may see themselves and family as fundamentally superior: a false belief that carries its own load of trouble. So play this hand with caution. It is a good idea also to emphasise the fact that people in general are hugely variable, and that this variety is essential to human development and inspiration. Then, being different may not seem to be a reason to lose confidence, even if hostile voices are raised and critical attitudes revealed.

A general drawback of relying on a supportive self-contained circle of friends and family is that it is but one tiny fragment of society. We want those we love to be part of a wider world. But we know how harsh that world can be. There's a limit to how much all our love and support can do, and everyone needs the wherewithal to stand up for themselves. Yet even within the small supportive circle of our love, the hopes we have and the messages of disappointment we give – in which we echo and represent the views of society at large – may be so blatant that they do not increase confidence at all. Or our expressed enthusiasm may not ring true and a significant lesson learned by the child will be how false and how unreliable speech – and people – can be. And sometimes we forget that, however infuriating and off the wall somebody is being, that they are not putting on a performance for our benefit. We need our monotropic children and partners at least to be confident in us and in their ability to interact successfully with us. Sometimes we find it hard to give people enough time even to switch attention. Steeply focused people find it really difficult to switch, and we risk closing them down if we hammer on at them instead of giving them some grace.

Monotropism is also often associated with very rapid rates of emotional arousal, which can get people into a lot of trouble, both inside and outside their own homes. Sometimes, when very extreme feelings have taken hold and led to extreme behaviours, we parade our expectations in front of the person who was upset first, who is already completely discombobulated by their overwhelming bad feelings, which they are unable to express in an acceptable form. These additional unmeetable expectations – 'Talk to me!' 'Explain yourself!' 'Pull yourself together!' – just make matters even worse. This is where we may need to back right off for as long as it takes not to make assumptions and still less express assumptions to any effect but that the person who is upset has been and is doing their best to be an OK person. The recovery of equilibrium that the distressed person needs may take many hours to occur. However long it takes, try not to butt in – and above all, avoid talking (in whispers or not) about the distressed person and their behaviour in front of them.

Not behaving in any of the counterproductive ways just described may be more than most typical people can manage when they so want a person to behave in ways that will let them fit in. But if we want to build up social confidence, then this is not the moment to compound the sense of failure. It is not the moment to rush in with blame and recrimination – much better to keep quiet and try to understand how we may have contributed to the meltdown. We somehow have to make ourselves accept the 'unacceptable' (unless it is seriously injurious behaviour), stop seeing it as unacceptable and see it as an acceptable coping strategy however superficially bizarre or maladaptive it may be, unless and until we can encourage an alternative equally effective coping strategy without negative social consequences. Over time, there may be ways of developing such alternatives and replacing behaviours that cause social distress with behaviours that are less disturbing to the general equilibrium.

Other important issues for self-confidence are related to those moments of high emotional arousal. The person having the intense and distressing experience needs to know that the feelings experienced are not disqualifications for full human-ness, but the opposite. Everybody in the world needs to have their feelings seen as making sense. Most people's feelings are typical reactions to events of certain sorts, and as such are readily affirmed by other typical people's shared feeling states or expressions of same. We may have to use our imaginations and work a bit harder than usual to tune in to the emotional states of atypical people – but it is meant to be the typical folk who are good at this work after all. So when those explosions happen and there is a bit of loss of control, the best thing you can do is tune in to *why* and sympathetically (and quietly) express some fellow feeling. Expressing fellow feeling about matters of joy or fear as well as frustration is essentially the same excellent way to build up social confidence. It is part of the validation we all require in order to feel we belong.

Another important issue, which arises from the rapid, extreme emotional arousal that is frequently associated with monotropism and has an impact on confidence, is control. One of the reasons why it feels so bad to get upset is almost certainly the loss of control itself. People with high levels of uncertainty and anxiety really like to be in control. A person in an acute distressed state is at their most autistic in the sense of being unable to function at all in the social realm and is also at their least able to move on. It is depressing and discouraging to be unable to control your own feelings or even behaviours, and it is likely to diminish social confidence even when the fierce feelings are validated. So, one possible way to overcome the threat to self-confidence posed by extreme emotions getting out of hand would be to develop ways to recognise them in time to deal with them in a way that causes minimum distress. That is likely to be only partially successful so long as the feelings continue to occur with such force. An even better way to deal with them in the long run will be to reduce the frequency and the intensity of those experiences by increasing understanding of context and scale (Lawson 2001).

Problems with identifying context or scale are corollaries of having monotropic attention and thus tending to have a lack of spontaneous access to simultaneous disparate cognitive templates. However, that need not be an all-or-nothing matter; the more understanding grows and the more connections are made, the more possible it will become to identify what is relevant more broadly. As connections multiply, one acquires a less idiosyncratic perspective and with it a means to assess context and scale and possibly see one's own concerns in more manageable propor- tions. Unfortunately, we live in such a complex age that there hardly ever is such a thing as 'the' context, and being adept at shifting with its ever-changing form and constantly adjusting to it are not skills that any monotropic individual is likely to acquire. But there are a whole lot of ways in which we can help people who tend to see things in black and white learn about the between bits – emphasise variability, gradation and imperfection at every opportunity. Retrospective reflection and discussion about events that have occurred can be useful additional ways of increasing understanding and improving perspective (Jordan & Powell 1995). Discussing emotions in the context of videos, which can be replayed and revisited as often as wished, can also be a valuable way to develop social and emotional understanding (Lawson 2001). Carol Gray's Social Stories™ may also help to resolve social issues including emotional understandings, by making meanings clearer and making people's feelings explicit (www.thegraycenter.org/). Some people might just sit in a café or mall and people-watch as a good way to learn.

All of the above ways of learning about the social context are likely to improve understanding and help get personal views into perspective so that, for example, omissions in other people's behaviour may be understood as accidental rather than being seen as targeted 'at me'. Thus, occasions for social catastrophe may be reduced steeply. But even with a really high level of social understanding, discombobulating surprises can and will still happen. This is where we reach the limits of what family and friends can do. Getting these volatile emotions under control so as not to have the sort of temperamental crisis we have been discussing is one significant way of improving social function and potentially escaping some of the crises that might otherwise undermine or destroy one's social confidence. But as I have hinted, this is not easy to achieve. How can a steeply attention-tunnelled person who might have difficulty even in recognising a full bladder pressing for attention pick up the information about their abruptly changing state of mind in time to interrupt an extremely rapid chain of events? We can reduce the occasions when such crises occur through improving understanding, as we have been discussing. But without this emotional mastery, occasional crises are certain to recur and may cause enough problems to threaten not just an individual's self-confidence but even their liberty. Cognitive therapies may be effective in promoting emotional recognition and control in more articulate individuals who are strongly motivated to achieve those goals (Attwood 2004). More generally, learning to identify certain physical signs such as increased heart rate or sweaty palms or grinding teeth may be helpful but will need careful and persistent observation and is unlikely to happen without support. A possible if inaccurate tool for encouraging such self-awareness is a 'mood ring' – an inexpensive finger ring that changes colour when certain mood changes occur. Some people may find that wearing one of these rings raises their awareness of their own moods in a potentially useful way.

Achieving some mastery over one's emotions will go a long way towards reducing catastrophic social events in society at large. If we can avoid those, then we have a much better chance of maintaining confidence in the long term. For most people on the autism spectrum, the forgiving group of friends and family that we may all hope to have is much smaller than it is for other people and may consist solely of family members. Functioning effectively in a wider society than that group involves more than just having some clues about how to stay out of trouble. It means being able to make contributions that are welcomed, recognised and appreciated. The people on the autism spectrum who have learned to speak and who have eventually been drawn to socially approved areas of interest are much the best placed to achieve an established social position and with it the 'confidence scaffolding' it can supply. They are also the beneficiaries and the victims of people's expectations that anyone who speaks normally will have equally normal intentions, perceptions and understandings. That can keep the confidence well boosted, so long as the discourse doesn't go wrong and misunderstandings surface. But even when it goes right 100 times, the one time it goes wrong can be devastating, at least in the short term. Once again, getting a general perspective on oneself and one's feelings, and knowing that one has other concerns that matter more, can be the best way to speed recovery from such a collapse. Sometimes it might be a good idea to have a recovery list of what matters most to help remind one of these relative values.

The specialised interests of monotropic people are often unrelated in any obvious way to current concerns within the social environments they physically inhabit. There are two complementary approaches to that. One discussed earlier is to connect the basic enthusiasm gradually to more and more culturally useful information, as in the case of the dog poo to palaeontology trajectory. A person's interests will tend to become both more socially acceptable and more socially rewarding the more they address issues of common concern. However, current concerns in one's local community may be petty and vain, and not sharing those may not be a disadvantage or matter for regret. People on the spectrum who do not share those concerns may have more serious and worthwhile interests to pursue.

Another useful way to approach building self-confidence and social confidence for a monotropic person is to connect the enthusiast with fellow enthusiasts; that is what clubs and societies traditionally have been for. Few things can be more encouraging and more suitable as a basis for friendship than discovering another person who shares your passion. Society at large may not appreciate the object of the enthusiasm, but it includes multiple smaller interest groups dedicated to every conceivable interest. There may be no such people in the school yard, there may be no such people in your village – but there are bound to be such people on the Internet. This is not just a matter of finding people to communicate with, it is a matter of finding people who respect and appreciate what you have to offer. In addition, they will do so without any sense that it is because they're being 'nice' – respect will be given when respect is due.

Just being able to access information freely is a great bonus of the Internet. It can be highly rewarding for people who are inclined to have more confidence in information than in people, who like to pursue matters for themselves, and who like to go fully armed with relevant information in their dealings with life. 'At first, I didn't know how to use computers, so I did microfilm in libraries. Then I learned databases. Then finally (less than two years ago) I started slowly to use the Internet' (Dawson 2005). Exchanging and discovering information of common interest can be a joyful experience, whatever the topic. Connecting with members of one's interest group over the Internet adds to the general benefits of belonging to a club. Over the internet odd manners, flat intonation or problems keeping up with the pace of social discourse will all be irrelevant.

There may be no call to disclose a diagnosis and no occasions of involuntary disclosure of difference in Web-based discourse. Such a diagnosis may seem of no consequence in that context. However, in reality, the diagnosis and what led to it is of consequence, and it could be that finding a context in which that is recognised and accepted will be of value to many people. There is a limit to how adequately people who are not monotropic and not experiencing the sort of difficulties that most people on the autism spectrum are dealing with on a daily basis can understand how it feels. So, the loving support group, however extensive or caring, is unlikely to be well placed to validate those particular feelings any more than they can confirm a wider acceptance of the individual beyond their protective reach. Both those aspects of belonging may be found in autistic-run support groups such as Autism Network International (ANI) and sites linked from there, many created and run by people on the spectrum who have rounded up a mass of useful information and are often communicating busily with each other in a generally constructive and mutually supportive way.

As Martijn Dekker puts it (Dekker n.d.):

> I also run an Internet-based support group for people like myself, namely those on the autistic spectrum, and it makes me extremely happy to realise that the group helps people and enables people who help themselves. It is also the best self-help I could have wished for; the contact and friendship I have with my autistic peers is immensely valuable to me.

It is immensely valuable to thousands of other people too. As well as giving them a sense of belonging, an important part of the value of the Internet-based autistic community to other people with autism spectrum diagnoses is the opportunities it offers to understand oneself better and in a positive light.

Self-understanding is the last part of the self-confidence equation: understanding the ways in which one is different from other people, understanding one is processing and accessing the world differently from most people, recognising how much harder one is having to work to make sense of the shared world than other people. These insights can lift a burden of felt inadequacy and can provide ways of explaining one's difficulties that do not imply that one is stupid or defective and won't automatically result in other people reacting with suspicion or disrespect.

Everybody, especially people who are unusual or different, needs to know that being who they are does not mean being sick, stupid or crazy, and they need to know that other people know that too.

References

Attwood, T. (2004) *Exploring Feelings: Cognitive Behaviour Therapy to Manage Anxiety.* Arlington, TX: Future Horizons.

Bruner, J. (1985) 'Vygotsky: A Historical and Conceptual Perspective.' In J.V. Wertsch (ed) *Culture, Communication, and Cognition: Vygotskian Perspectives.* Cambridge: Cambridge University Press.

Dawson, M. (2005) 'The Misbehaviour of Behaviourists'. www.quicktopic.com/27/H/ vJvhV4fDnBgw7

Dekker, M. (n.d.) 'On Your Own Terms: Emerging autistic culture'. www.aspiesforfreedom.com/wiki/ index.php/emerging_autistic_culture

Jordan, R.R. and Powell, S. (1995) *Understanding and Teaching Children With Autism.* New York: John Wiley & Sons.

Lawson, W. (2001) *Understanding and Working with the Spectrum of Autism: An Insider's View.* London: Jessica Kingsley Publishers.

Murray, D., Lesser, M. and Lawson, W. (2005) 'Attention, Monotropism, and the Diagnostic Criteria for Autism.' In *Autism*, 9, 139–56.

PEI Road Runners Club (2004) 'Alex Bain: 2004 Patterson Palmer Law Rookie of the Year.' www.peiroadrunners.ca/awards2004/rrroty2004.html

Vygotsky, L.S. (1962) *Thought and Language.* Cambridge, MA: MIT Press. (Original work published 1934)

Waites, J. and Swinbourne, H. (2001) *Smiling at Shadows: A Mother's Journey Through Heartache and Joy.* Pymble, NSW: HarperCollins.

4.

Psychiatry and Asperger syndrome

Tom Berney

Diagnosis and assessment

What is Asperger syndrome?

Any concept has to have a name, a label. The development of the concept of the autism spectrum disorders (in the USA, the pervasive developmental disorders) is marked by the various names that have been used to identify different disorders and the relationship between them, the confusion being reflected in an interchangeable use of terms. A disorder is defined by *criteria*, of which the most authoritative are the World Health Organization's (WHO) International Classification of Diseases 10th revision (ICD-10) and the American Psychiatric Association's *Diagnostic and Statistical Manual of Mental Disorders*, 4th edition (DSM-IV). These represent committee consensus and, although tested widely before publication, are revised steadily over time, affecting the consistency of research that depends on differing versions. This formalised construct is matched against an individual's symptoms and signs, gathered using *instruments*, i.e. the process of *diagnosis*. Often crude, the process does hold clinicians to a consistent threshold and can be refined by an algorithm, although such mechanical simplicity can be misleading, particularly when there is a comorbid overlay. Diagnosis imposes a categorical view on a dimensional disorder and is only one component of a multidisciplinary *assessment* that gives a more individual description.

Asperger coined the term 'autistic psychopathy' in 1944 in order to distinguish its innate social distance from the social distance that developed later as a symptom of schizophrenia. His concept was elaborated by van Krevelen (1962), Wing (1981) and Gillberg (1998), all of whom sought to identify a disorder similar to, yet different from, autism. Gillberg, pointing out that it was questionable whether many of the cases described by Asperger would have met ICD/DSM criteria, devised an alternative set of criteria based on the original clinical descriptions (Leekam *et al.* 2000). The resultant model includes both Asperger syndrome and autism within the group of autistic spectrum disorders (ASD). While there is reasonable agreement about the criteria defining autism, Asperger syndrome has been, and still is, identified in a variety of ways. Like autism, everyone's criteria for Asperger syndrome include impaired reciprocal social interaction and restricted, repetitive or stereotyped patterns of behaviour, interests and activities. It is the presence of normal syntactical speech that distinguishes Asperger syndrome. However, while both Wing and Gillberg emphasise current presentation, ICD-10 and DSM-IV, wishing to identify a disorder that would be an alternative to autism rather than just a variant or subtype, require normal language development from early life. At issue are the people who have had early language delay but have caught up, greatly outnumbering those whose language has been normal from the start; they would be defined as having Asperger syndrome by all definitions except those of ICD-10 and DSM-IV.

Other symptoms have been proposed as distinctive, including self-awareness (Tantam 2003), the interest in (and awareness of) others, and poor coordination of movement (clumsiness). Research has been hindered not only by the syndrome's varied definitions but also by the unnoticed circularity of the methodology used, many studies finding differences that simply reflected their own selection criteria. The predominant view at present is that, once allowance has been made for ability, there appears to be little real difference between the two disorders, except in terms of severity (Gilchrist *et al.* 2001; Howlin 2003; Kugler 1998).

What is not Asperger syndrome?

Several psychiatric disorders are likely to be mistaken for Asperger syndrome, including schizophrenia, obsessive-compulsive disorder, dissocial personality disorder, attention-deficit/hyperactivity disorder (ADHD), epilepsy and developmental disabilities.

SCHIZOPHRENIA

Until the 1970s, autism and schizophrenia were considered to be different faces of the same unitary psychosis, the age at which it emerged modulating its symptoms. Although the two disorders are now clearly distinct, their varied clinical presentations have led to a debate as to whether autism predisposes an individual to schizophrenia. Outcome studies suggest that it does not (Howlin *et al.* 2004; Volkmar and Cohen 1991), but then neither does it protect, so that at times the two disorders will coexist coincidentally as comorbid conditions.

Schizophrenia is characterised by changes in thinking (with a sense of loss of control and coherence and the development of delusions), perception (hallucinations are common but not invariable) and emotional tone (with feelings being blunted or inappropriate). There may also be changes in volition (the ability to translate thought into action), with inertia, negativism, mutism and odd posturing. Schizophrenia may come as an episode, single or recurrent, or as a long-standing continuous disorder that fluctuates in severity. It comes in so many forms that it is difficult to generalise, but when its more negative symptoms (apathy, social withdrawal, reduction in the amount of speech, blunting of emotional response) dominate the picture, it may be indistinguishable from autism, unless the clinician takes a lifelong view of the way the disorder has developed (Konstantareas and Hewitt 2001). Broadly, autism is most pronounced in early childhood and schizophrenia in late adolescence and early adulthood. Autism tends to improve with age; schizophrenia may slowly worsen with age, ending in residual schizo-phrenia, with the disappearance of positive symptoms (e.g. delusions, hallucinations) to leave the negative symptoms resulting in the person being in a slow, passive, 'burned-out' state that is easily mistaken for Asperger syndrome. The distinction is not clear-cut with indeterminate disorders such as simple schizophrenia (where there are no positive symptoms but the gradual development of a withdrawn, self-absorbed, aimless and inactive individual) and catatonic schizophrenia (which is dominated by abnormal movement). Conversely, the symptoms in Asperger syndrome may appear misleadingly psychotic at times:

- Someone who has difficulty in describing internal symptoms, like thoughts, may describe them like hallucinations.

- Incomplete answers can, at face value, sound like psychotic symptomatology. Thus, a bald agreement, omitting the circumstances, can make everyday teasing or victimisation (of somebody who is obviously different) sound like persecutory delusions.

- At times, the person may have difficulty in distinguishing what they have done from what they have observed. Video material can be particularly pervasive, leaving listeners with the sense that the individual is living in a video world that is detectable and comprehensible only when they have also seen the video.

- High arousal in a developmental disorder can produce an acute and transient psychotic state (F23) with hallucinations and thought disorder.

- A pragmatic difficulty, making it difficult to appreciate the extent or limitations of someone else's knowledge of a topic, coupled with a tendency to obsessionality, can result in over-inclusive, irrelevant speech similar to that of schizophrenic thought disorder.

- Impassivity, insensitivity to, and lack of awareness of the emotional climate can mimic inappropriate or blunted affect. However, it isn't that the person's emotional expression is reduced, but that they do not pick up on how others are feeling.

- Catatonic symptomatology, including odd mannerisms and postures, freezing or difficulty in initiating movement, occurs in ASD as it does in many other neurological conditions and schizophrenia (Wing and Shah 2000).

- A slow and unmotivated response to being asked to perform a task that has no meaning for the person may look like a loss of motivation.

- Some symptoms of both disorders can improve with neuroleptics (Campbell et al. 1996).

Some of the conceptual confusion arises from the early studies in Edinburgh that used the criteria for schizoid personality to identify a group of children who subsequently were equated with Asperger syndrome. A substantial proportion later developed schizophrenia, but it is likely that the group was a mixed one that swept in both children with preschizophrenic schizoid personality (i.e. were on the schizophrenia spectrum) and children with ASD (Wolff 1995).

OBSESSIVE-COMPULSIVE DISORDER

A natural reaction to the disorganised messiness that is everyday life is to establish order. The more success there is in achieving a set, predictable world, the greater the distress when faced with novelty and change. In somebody with Asperger syndrome, this may attain a pathological height, for example where the commonplace collection of objects and information comes to dominate his[1] life as well as the lives of those he lives with. Some people lose all sense of proportion, and the obsession leads to offending.

Clinical management includes the use of standard devices to cope with obsessions and routines – diversion, environmental changes, pictorial or written preparation for changes, and the introduction of alternative rules, routines and limits. While serotoninergic drugs can reduce the level of obsessionality, it may take a number of trials to find the right drug for a particular person and, once found, its effect may be only partial and temporary. Even so, medication can help the individual to change enough of his life and behaviour to reduce the likelihood of recurrence.

However, obsessional traits are rife, running through much of biological psychiatry as well as being an overlapping familial trait in autistic disorders (Hollander *et al.* 2003). In the absence of internal resistance and anxiety, it has been questioned whether it is truly obsessive-compulsive disorder (Baron-Cohen 1989), the more so as the content of their thoughts and the form of compulsive behaviour may or may not differ from those of the neurotypical person (McDougle, Kresch *et al.* 1995; Russell *et al.* 2005). All the same, any distinction may be academic, as the management is similar.

---

[1]   The term 'his' is used for convenience, reflecting the male preponderance.

DISSOCIAL PERSONALITY DISORDER

The lack of empathy and the focused unconcern for consequences, which comes partly from difficulty in foreseeing potential outcomes, can make somebody with Asperger syndrome appear egocentric and callously indifferent both to the needs of others and to societal rules. Added to this may be an apparent lack of motivation, poor executive function and/or other priorities to those expected of him. Although very different to the underlying psychopathology of the dissocial personality disorder, the superficial effect can be so similar as to make it difficult to say where Asperger autistic psychopathy ends and personality disorder starts. The distinction becomes even less distinct as psychiatry moves towards a more biological, developmental perception of many conditions and, in the end, it becomes difficult to define why personality disorders should be categorised and treated so differently from the pervasive developmental disorders. The distinction is an important one, as it affects professional concern, expectations, funding and resources.

ATTENTION-DEFICIT/HYPERACTIVITY DISORDER (ADHD)

There appears to be an association between ASD and ADHD, and this may go further than coincident comorbidity, as it is possible that untreated ADHD may simulate, or at any rate amplify, Asperger syndrome. Consequently, the latter is best assessed after symptomatic treatment of the former.

EPILEPSY

Epilepsy can amplify ASD, and there is an active debate about the extent to which it may mimic ASD or, at any rate, put an Asperger spin on what would otherwise present as a sociable developmental disability. Here it is not only the effects of seizures themselves but also the effects of the antiepileptic medication that can produce peculiar personality change.

DEVELOPMENTAL DISABILITIES

Social and communication impairment is frequent, and the difficulty is to define the point at which they are sufficiently pronounced to merit being categorised as Asperger syndrome. Gillberg (1992) has suggested it to be only one of a range of 'empathy disorders', while others have split off syndromes such as pathological demand avoidance (Newson *et al.* 2003), semantic pragmatic disorder (Bishop and Norbury 2002) and multiplex developmental disorder (Towbin, *et al.* 1993). Complicated by synonyms such as right hemisphere disorder and non-verbal learning disorder (Fitzgerald 1999), the result is a firmament of specific developmental disabilities on which we impose recognisable constellations of clinical disorder (Willemsen-Swinkels and Buitelaar 2002). Unfortunately, limited knowledge brings the temptation to sweep everyone into the Procrustean categories of ASD or pervasive developmental disorder (not otherwise specified).

The process of diagnosis and assessment

Diagnosis on its own is of limited value, but it is the gateway to a great deal of information, specialist groups and resources, including financial benefits. It is often not recognised that a diagnosis is simply a working hypothesis, a clinical judgement that has to strike a balance between being too broad and too narrow, and a process that can evolve with time and changing circumstances. It is essential, therefore, that it is categorical and that everyone involved appreciates its purpose, because the cut-off points will differ depending on whether it is:

- for research – excluding any doubtful cases
- clinical – a best guess to guide further treatment
- administrative – giving access to services or resources.

Diagnosis of a disorder implies that the person reaches some threshold of discomfort, either to themselves or to those around him. Asperger syndrome implies that the person has a characteristic response to his environment. If that environment is sufficiently sympathetic, e.g. he is complemented by a supportive partner and in a suitable job, then his life may run a reasonably normal course – normality is a very broad notion but implies that the person and those around them are reasonably comfortable. In these circumstances, it is questionable as to whether any diagnosis is warranted. Asperger syndrome may become evident only when circumstances change, e.g. the person finds himself struggling to cope with an unpredictable, crowded, complex job dealing with difficult and anxious people. Consequently, any diagnostic exercise has to take into account not only the characteristics of the individual but also how he functions in different environments. The diagnosis implies discomfort or limitation of what the person might take on. The problem is then that everyone is limited to some degree and the individual has to reach some agreement with the clinician that their degree of impairment is sufficient to reach that diagnostic threshold.

It is difficult for most people to be objective about how they function in relationships; this is particularly so for someone with Asperger syndrome. The comprehensive picture that is necessary for diagnosis must, therefore, draw on the accounts of others, such as parents, friends, teachers and employers (Green et al. 2000). Once the syndrome is suspected, diagnosis needs a clinician who is reasonably familiar with the syndrome as well as with potential alternatives, whether they mimic or merely amplify ASD, to make a clinical judgement. This should combine the lifelong perspective of a developmental history with a clinical examination of the person's present state that is designed to elicit the features of Asperger syndrome.

Although a number of instruments have been developed to identify autism, the few that have been designed specifically for Asperger syndrome are mostly screening questionnaires. These vary in the extent to which they are structured, ranging from the very specific self-rating Australian Questionnaire (Attwood 1999) through to the Asperger Syndrome Diagnostic Interview (ASDI), a simple framework that has good inter-rater reliability (Gillberg et al. 2001).

The more formal structured interviews, such as the Autism Diagnostic Interview (ADI), were initially developed as research instruments to identify children with clear-cut autism but broader instruments have evolved, such as the Diagnostic Schedule for Speech and Communication Disorders (DISCO). The Autism Diagnostic Observation Schedule (ADOS), a subject interview designed to elicit the signs of autism, has a module for able and fluent adolescents and adults. The International Molecular Genetic Research Consortium has developed a family history interview (FHI) in order to identify autistic symptomatology at the edge of the spectrum, the broader phenotype. This instrument uses a set of schedules that includes matching subject and informant interviews as well as a scale to record observed behaviour. Whatever instrument is used, it is essential that the clinician takes account of childhood as well as current symptomatology, so that it is clear how symptoms developed, a point worth repetition as it is so often neglected.

Many people will have diagnosed themselves from descriptions, symptom lists and self-rating scales and simply seek formal confirmation. Any diagnostic exercise must be clear as to its purpose. A screening assessment, focusing only on the current symptomatology, may be relatively brief, particularly if it complements a psychiatric interview. A more definitive, diagnostic interview can last several hours and is not something to undertake without good reason. A full assessment is best done in conjunction with the agencies that will help to provide the individually tailored plan. Results are best fed back in writing, in order to avert the misunderstandings that arise with aural communication, with sufficient examples and description to explain the conclusions. Numerical scores, which are more relevant to research than to everyday clinical practice, are not helpful and, like employment references, reports need to speak to a specific audience for a specific purpose.

Assessment follows diagnosis and should be broad and multi-disciplinary, taking account of:

- the cognitive level of ability – identifying discrepancies between receptive and expressive, verbal and non-verbal communication

- functional ability – acknowledging the extent to which subtle psychological disabilities, e.g. in executive function or theory of mind, can handicap someone who is otherwise very able

- other, comorbid developmental disabilities, notably attention-deficit disorder, tics and dyspraxia

- areas that are specific to the individual's immediate difficulties. These do not apply to everyone with Asperger syndrome and may only occur in some individuals for some part of their life. Examples of these specific assessments are the capacity to make a decision, the risk of committing a certain offence and a person's reliability as a witness.

CAPACITY TO MAKE DECISIONS

This must be judged in relation to a specific decision and start from the presumption that the person has the capacity to make that decision. From there, it will depend on the person's ability to understand and to use relevant information. As long as the person is able to take into account the implications of a decision, then it does not matter that it seems sensible or even in his best interests – we are all free to smoke, drink or commit suicide provided we appreciate the consequences much as might the 'ordinary man'. Some people with Asperger syndrome have difficulty in understanding the implications of marriage, employment, hire purchase and other everyday agreements as well as in appreciating the consequences of their decisions. Questioning the person's ability to enter into these contracts must be approached cautiously, as it can have far-reaching effects, e.g. using diminished capacity to escape from credit-card debt may exclude the person permanently from obtaining any form of credit. In addition, the assessment of capacity can be very unreliable and, for example, it is often only trial and error that reveal whether a couple is able to make a successful marriage.

THE RISK OF OFFENDING

A number of factors combine to predispose a person with Asperger syndrome to offending, often inadvertently, although it is possible that they are offset by a greater tendency to comply with rules. However, any association is likely to be masked by a reluctance to link any syndrome with criminality, the tolerance for disturbance in anybody with disability, and an unwillingness to prosecute where conviction is uncertain. Although people with Asperger syndrome are characterised by their law-abiding adherence to rules, when they do become enshrined in the law, it is important that the syndrome's contribution is recognised (Barry-Walsh and Mullen 2004).

- An innate lack of concern for the outcome can result in, for example, an assault that is disproportionately intense and damaging. Not infrequently, the individual, unable to understand what he has done wrong, will deny responsibility and ascribe blame to others – all symptoms of his inability to see his inappropriate behaviour as others see it.

- An innate lack of awareness of the outcome leads the individual to embark on actions with unforeseen consequences, e.g. fire-setting may result in a building's destruction and assault in death.

- Impulsivity, sometimes violent, may reflect a state of anxiety turning into panic or may be part of comorbid ADHD.

- The misinterpretation of relationships and social naivety can leave the individual misreading friendship or a superficial attraction for love. This also leaves them open to exploitation as a stooge.

- The misinterpretation of rules, particularly social regulations, and social signals can lead the unwitting individual into offences such as date rape.

- Difficulty in judging the age of others can land the person in illegal relationships, e.g. making sexual advances to somebody under age.

- Overriding obsessions can lead to offences such as stalking or compulsive theft. Here, admonition can increase anxiety, leading onto a ruminative thinking-the-unthinkable, which increases the likelihood of action.

- Misjudging relationships in formal interviews and the consequences can permit an incautious frankness and the disclosure of private fantasies, which, even though no more lurid than any adolescent's, can be interpreted as dangerous.

- A lack of motivation to change may leave the individual stuck in a risky pattern of behaviour.

These factors need to be taken into account when assessing the level of risk that an individual presents.

RELIABILITY AS A WITNESS

The report of an event will depend on what the observer actually saw, on their interpretation of the scene and on their memory. With Asperger syndrome comes:

- the risk of misinterpretation of what the person has seen or heard

- difficulty with the dimension of time. Although the person may recall the sequence of events correctly, his perception of the relative periods of intervening time may be so uncertain that it is unclear whether he is recounting something that happened the previous day, week or year. His temporal confusion may emerge only if his account includes sufficient corroborative material, such as details of the scene, e.g. the clothing worn and the colour and pattern of the wallpaper, as well as sequential detail of the events preceding and following the episode.

- difficulty in distinguishing their own actions from those of others so that it becomes unclear who actually did what and may extend to the point where the individual confuses reality with observed fiction.

- difficulty with the normal structure of official interviews, whether in a police station or a witness box. The interview can be distorted by the misinterpretation of rules and relationships, with undue compliance complicated by the rigid tendency to adhere to (and believe in) a story once it is in his head. Because of his ability in other areas and, in particular, a good academic awareness of right from wrong, there is the risk that he may not be recognised as a vulnerable adult. How he presents himself becomes of particular importance in the absence of a right to silence, to the extent that he may be unfit to plead (Gray *et al.* 2001). Allowance must be made for communication problems; examples are the use of words without understanding their significance; the characteristic, very literal comprehension; and the inability to take in non-verbal components. Communication may be helped by the use of visual aids, such as a computer.

Psychiatric disorders (comorbidity)

Affective disorders: anxiety, depression, bipolar affective disorder

These disorders occur more frequently in people with Asperger syndrome than in the neurotypical population, but they may not be immediately recognisable because of the characteristic difficulty in identifying, let alone labelling, internal feelings. Consequently, these feelings may be expressed in confusing and even bizarre ways.

Chronic dysphoria may merge with more clear-cut depression, anxiety with phobic states, and overarousal with panic. All can respond to serotoninergic medication, which includes not only many of the antidepressants but also drugs such as risperidone and lorazepam, raising the issue of how readily and how early it should be tried and, if successful, how long it should be continued. This debate has been sharpened by recent reservations about the use of the serotoninergics (Nutt 2003). Although one confirmatory randomised controlled trial (RCT) is available (McDougle, Naylor *et al.* 1995), most of the evidence of the effectiveness of these drugs in ASD comes from open uncontrolled trials and is limited to the longer-acting drugs such as fluoxetine. However, experience suggests that, as indicated by the variety of preparations on the market, if it is thought to be worth trying one serotoninergic, then it is worth trying a succession.

Obsessive-compulsive disorder (OCD)

Obsessive-copulsive disorder has been discussed above as one of the conditions that may be confused with Asperger syndrome (see p.71). It may coexist and, if the individual has the motivation to change, be susceptible to the standard treatments, including cognitive behavioural therapy (CBT).

Other developmental disorders

Asperger syndrome has been linked with ADHD, tic disorders (including Tourette syndrome) and various other specific developmental disabilities, notably disorders of executive function and motivation, making it difficult for the individual to take effective action.

Alcoholism

Alcohol is an effective tranquilliser, particularly in people who find social groups uncomfortable. As well as social anxiety, Asperger syndrome can bring a compulsive quality and encourage isolated drinking ungoverned by normal societal conventions. As for many of these links, the evidence is more anecdotal than quantified by systematic research. It is not known whether there is any particular association, but these factors must be addressed in treatment.

Aggression

Expressed through word, gesture or physical assault, aimed at property or people, either towards others or the person himself, there is, somehow, some assumption of a uniform underlying mechanism that allows the management of aggression to be discussed in general terms. It is the catch-all term for the final common behavioural pathway of a wealth of factors. Clinical accounts, blurring detail, lump together the different functions that it may serve with the varied contributory factors.

Everyday feelings of aggression can be made more dangerous by deficient emotional taboos or guilt, together with a failure to appreciate consequences and an inability to comprehend the feelings and perception of the victim (Baron-Cohen 1988). Another example is an adolescent girl with Asperger syndrome who, not understanding the lethality (or the permanence) of stabbing, used this to discourage a boyfriend's intimacy. Another adolescent set fire to his home to reinforce his point that his mother should not restrict his use of a fax machine.

It is usually obvious when a compulsive drive is thwarted. Other emotions can underlie the episode and, whether it is anger, fear, anxiety or depression, it is *context-dependent* and is as catching as a cold: its presence breeds an ever-widening climate that promotes aggression and an aggressive response. Consequently, the attitudes and response of those around are all important. Uncertainty about authority and control can also encourage behaviour that tests the system to find out how the land lies. Whatever its basis, violent aggression is relatively frequent (Tantam 2003), and the response needs to be informed and tailored to the individual, be it containment, anger management, medication or prosecution.

Psychiatric treatment

The treatment of comorbid disorders is the same as in other areas of psychiatry but it can be coloured by a number of elements specific to Asperger syndrome:

- An appreciation that Asperger syndrome is familial, so that other members may have subtle communication difficulties.

- The context in which the person is living – it is not unusual for the individual to be with family and friends who, if they do not have Asperger syndrome itself, have a number of its traits and assume that the therapist understands the culture.

- The network of specialist agencies. Even if none of these is involved currently, it is helpful to understand the setting from whence the person came, e.g. a special school, where disturbance might have been averted by a better-adapted environment. There is also the potential for the future involvement of specialist resources, which range from an Asperger internet network through to a specialist residential further education college.

- The background difficulties that go with growing up with Asperger syndrome.

- The altered symptomatology, particularly difficulties in communication – the question 'How do you feel?' may be very hard for the person to answer, and progress might be better gauged from their behaviour.

- A knowledge of the therapeutic culture – the diets, supplements and orthodox drugs that have been suggested as helpful.

Psychological therapies

Psychodynamic psychotherapy became discredited by Bruno Bettelheim's lack of success and, in the UK, the emphasis has been on psychoeducational work, counselling and the development of relational capacities. People with Asperger syndrome are often excluded from exploratory and cognitive therapies by an initial assessment that focuses on areas that include the capacity for verbalisation and symbolisation, the ability to access thoughts and emotions, and the ability to establish a relationship with the therapist which will be characterised by their mutual consideration of the experiences of the patient. However, Frances Tustin wrote extensively about her work at the Tavistock Clinic and there is a resurgence of interest, although knowledge and experience of this work is limited and patchy.

There are isolated reports of the successful use of cognitive behavioural therapy for social anxiety and for depression and, as in other areas of psychiatry, this seems likely to become more widespread as therapists gain experience and confidence in its use.

Drugs

In psychiatry, drugs tend to be used to treat symptoms rather than disorders. Reports about autism spectrum disorders rather than Asperger syndrome have targeted the following:

- Core symptoms of autism – the neuroleptics, of which the most thoroughly investigated has been haloperidol, have been shown to improve both core and associated symptoms (Campbell *et al.* 1990). This does not explain the mechanism and it may simply be the result of a reduction in anxiety or activity, making the child more accessible. Unfortunately, the neuroleptics are also likely to produce dyskinesia (Campbell *et al.* 1997). The neuroleptics were overused in the past, often in excessive dosage, as a reflex panacea for any form of disturbance. Thioridazine (Melleril®) was particularly popular (Rimland 1988) because it was reputed to be less likely to induce dyskinesia, but there was little research to substantiate its reputation and, because it may cause cardiac arrest, its use is now restricted to intractable schizophrenia. Its place has been taken by the newer atypical antipsychotics, of which risperidone has the most substantial publication base, although, with wider use, there is a growing recognition of its adverse effects.

- Symptoms associated with autism – aggression, ADHD, obsessive-compulsive symptoms, catatonia and habit disorders, e.g. with sleep, feeding and elimination.

- Other disorders that may amplify, or even mimic, the symptomatology of autism. Although epilepsy and depression have been cited, in fact any disorder that causes malaise, whether toothache, hayfever or an intercurrent infection, will make autism symptoms worse.

Reports of drug effectiveness are not easy to interpret, being confounded by the following:

- Non-specific clinical targets – there is often a lack of clarity about the target, and drugs alter different symptoms in different people.
- The lack of a straightforward dose–response curve, psychopharmacology being characterised by:
  - the therapeutic window – drugs may only work in a particular range of dosage, which is often lower or higher than expected in a person with autism
  - the paradoxical effect – drugs, e.g. alcohol, reverse their effects at a higher dose
  - inconsistency in response, with more frequent idiosyncratic responses, so that every new drug is a therapeutic trial with the motto 'start low, go slow'
  - the group of subjects not being homogeneous, usually covering a range of ages and abilities.
- Difficulties in measuring outcome, for example:
  - most of the ASD rating instruments that are used to describe a person's response have been designed for diagnosis rather than measuring symptom change. The exception is the Behavioural Summarised Evaluation Scale (Barthelemy *et al.* 1997)
  - most studies do not make allowance for change that results from other factors. These include *a change in environment* – the startling effectiveness of the placebo effect was demonstrated in the secretin trials; *natural development* – particularly the developmental spurts that occur at the ends of early childhood and adolescence; or the temporary blips that represent *spontaneous fluctuation*; as controlling for these effects usually requires the use of a double-blind randomised controlled trial, which is difficult to mount.

In the end, drugs are only one component of the total treatment armamentarium, and it is impossible to give a drug in isolation. Prescription will alter the expectations and attitudes of those around the individual and these, in turn, will affect the response. Drugs work best for people who believe in them, and a good therapist will enlist the placebo effect to enhance the action of the drug. The treatment should improve the relationship of the person with their environment (often simply by reducing anxiety) to enable teaching and training to take place thereby allowing a more permanent change in the relationship with the environment, once accomplished, will alter the need for further medication and allow its withdrawal. At any rate, that is the aspiration. Very often, however, some medication is always necessary, albeit at a reduced dosage.

This is an area where the debate as to whether fluoxetine, or any other serotoninergic, is indicated for a subtle dysthymia. The debate is sharpened by the uncertainty as to whether a deeper disorder is being masked by poor communication and whether there is a case for the more routine prescription of serotoninergics.

If a drug works, the result will be:

- inconsistent, with the drug working with some symptoms in some people

- transient, tolerance eventually developing as the nervous system adapts to the drug (although the hope is that this may take years rather than days)

- at a very specific dosage

- messy, the desired effect being only one of a number and, with luck, the dominant one; unwanted effects being so minor as to be tolerable. However, no drug is totally free of adverse effects.

Psychiatric services

Increasing recognition has led to increasing demand for services, both for diagnosis and for management. While there is debate about the prevalence of Asperger syndrome and the frequency of comorbid disorder, there is some agreement about meeting the need in childhood, formalised in the National Autism Plan for Children (NAPC) (NIASA 2003). There is no such convention for older adolescents and adults, a state of indecision that leaves adults with Asperger syndrome in limbo between various psychiatric specialities. Age and ability may bar access to the specialities of child and adolescent psychiatry and learning disability psychiatry. As there is less emphasis on the syndrome in general psychiatry, there is a wide variation in the level of expertise. Given the extent of the demands on adult psychiatry, it may be that the best that can be achieved is an increased awareness of the implications of autism and the ready availability of specialist advice. Similarly, while the establishment of a network of specialist inpatient units is impracticable, existing psychiatric facilities can become more autism-friendly, both through environmental adaptation and through staff training.

The development of specialist residential care in an area can mean the arrival of a group of individuals whose degree of disturbance has earned them their funding and out-of-area export. These people require specialist support from the health services which, in the absence of planning and funding, become overstretched and unable or unwilling to respond. The development of such services needs some formal machinery in order to ensure coordination between the private sector and the health service.

Psychiatric services are only one cog in the jigsaw of care that is multi-agency and multi-disciplinary, involving families and carers and people from a variety of cultures and with a variety of beliefs. Services need to bridge both home and out-of-home placements. A cost-effective service, therefore, will need to involve all parties in planning and commissioning different components of services of multiagency services. While there is active planning across the whole of the UK, there are many areas of shortfall (Powell 2002), earlier reports have been ignored (Holland et al. 2000), and more recent guidance has left matters undecided (Department of Health 2001) (Public Health Institute of Scotland 2001). This is an area that is being actively discussed and it seems probable that the interest in it will last long enough to produce real change within the next few years.

References

Attwood, A. (1999) *Asperger's Syndrome: A Guide for Parents and Professionals.* London: Jessica Kingsley Publishers.

Baron-Cohen, S. (1988) 'An Assessment of Violence in a Young Man with Asperger Syndrome.' *Journal of Child Psychology and Psychiatry and Allied Disciplines,* 29, 351–60.

Baron-Cohen, S. (1989) 'Do Autistic Children have Obsessions and Compulsions?' *British Journal of Clinical Psychology,* 28, 193–200.

Barry-Walsh, J.B. and Mullen, P.E. (2004) 'Forensic Aspects of Asperger's Syndrome.' *Journal of Psychiatry and Psychology,* 15, 1, 96–107.

Barthelemy, C., Roux, S., Adrien, J.L. *et al.* (1997) 'Validation of the Revised Behavior Summarized Evaluation Scale.' *Journal of Autism and Developmental Disorders,* 27, 139–53.

Bishop, D.V.M. and Norbury, C.F. (2002) 'Exploring the Borderlands of Autistic Disorder and Specific Language Impairment: A Study Using Standardised Diagnostic Instruments.' *Journal of Child Psychology and Psychiatry and Allied Disciplines*, 43, 917–29.

Campbell, M., Anderson, L.T. and Small, A.M. (1990) 'Pharmacotherapy in Autism: A Summary of Research at Bellevue/New York University.' *Brain Dysfunction*, 3, 299–307.

Campbell, M., Armenteros, J.L., Malone, R.P. *et al.* (1997) 'Neuroleptic-related Dyskinesias in Autistic Children: A Prospective, Longitudinal Study.' *Journal of the American Academy of Child and Adolescent Psychiatry*, 36, 835–43.

Campbell, M., Schopler, E., Cueva, J. *et al.* (1996) 'Treatment of Autistic Disorder.' *Journal of the American Academy of Child and Adolescent Psychiatry*, 35, 134–43.

Department of Health (2001) *Valuing People: A New Strategy for Learning Disability for the 21st Century: Implementation Guidance.* London: Department of Health.

Fitzgerald, M. (1999) 'Differential Diagnosis of Adolescent and Adult Pervasive Developmental Disorders/Autism Spectrum Disorders (PDD/ASD): A Not Uncommon Diagnostic Dilemma.' *Irish Journal of Psychological Medicine*, 16, 145–8.

Gilchrist, A., Green, J., Cox, A., *et al.* (2001) 'Development and Current Functioning in Adolescents with Asperger Syndrome: A Comparative Study.' *Journal of Child Psychology and Psychiatry and Allied Disciplines*, 42, 227–40.

Gillberg, C.L. (1992) 'The Emanuel Miller Memorial Lecture 1991: Autism and Autistic-like Conditions: Subclasses among Disorders of Empathy.' *Journal of Child Psychology and Psychiatry and Allied Disciplines*, 33, 813–42.

Gillberg, C. (1998) 'Asperger Syndrome and High-functioning Autism.' *British Journal of Psychiatry*, 172, 200–9.

Gillberg, C., Gillberg, C., Rastam, M., *et al.* (2001) 'The Asperger Syndrome (and High-functioning Autism) Diagnostic Interview (ASDI): A Preliminary Study of a New Structured Clinical Interview.' *Autism*, 5, 57–66.

Gray, N.S., O'Connor, C., Williams, T., *et al.* (2001) 'Fitness to Plead: Implications from Case-law Arising from the Criminal Justice and Public Order Act 1994.' *Journal of Forensic Psychiatry*, 12, 52–62.

Green, J., Gilchrist, A., Burton, D., *et al.* (2000) 'Social and Psychiatric Functioning in Adolescents with Asperger Syndrome Compared with Conduct Disorder.' *Journal of Autism and Developmental Disorders*, 30, 279–93.

Holland, T., Clare, I., Baron-Cohen, S., *et al.* (2000) *Current Issues Surrounding the Diagnosis, Management and Treatment of Children and Adults with Asperger Syndrome.* London: Department of Health.

Hollander, E., King, A., Delaney, K., *et al.* (2003) 'Obsessive-compulsive Behaviors in Parents of Multiplex Autism Families.' *Psychiatry Research*, 117, 11–16.

Howlin, P. (2003) 'Outcome in High-functioning Adults with Autism with and without Early Language Delays: Implications for the Differentiation between Autism and Asperger Syndrome.' *Journal of Autism and Developmental Disorders*, 33, 3–13.

Howlin, P., Goode, S., Hutton, J., *et al.* (2004) 'Adult Outcome for Children with Autism.' *Journal of Child Psychology and Psychiatry and Allied Disciplines*, 45, 212–29.

Konstantareas, M.M. and Hewitt, T. (2001) 'Autistic Disorder and Schizophrenia: Diagnostic Overlaps.' *Journal of Autism and Developmental Disorders*, 31, 19–28.

Kugler, B. (1998) 'The Differentiation between Autism and Asperger Syndrome.' *Autism*, 2, 11–32.

Leekam, S., Libby, S., Wing, L., *et al.* (2000) 'Comparison of ICD-10 and Gillberg's Criteria for Asperger Syndrome.' *Autism*, 4, 11–28.

McDougle, C.J., Kresch, L.E., Goodman, W.K., *et al.* (1995) 'A Case-controlled Study of Repetitive Thoughts and Behavior in Adults with Autistic Disorder and Obsessive Compulsive Disorder.' *American Journal of Psychiatry*, 152, 772–7.

McDougle, C.J., Naylor, S.T., Cohen, D.J., *et al.* (1995) 'A Double-blind, Placebo-controlled Study of Fluvoxamine in Adults with Autistic Disorder.' *Archives of General Psychiatry*, 53, 1001–8.

Newson, E., LeMarechal, K. and David, C. (2003) 'Pathological Demand Avoidance Syndrome: A Necessary Distinction within the Pervasive Developmental Disorders.' *Archives of Disease in Childhood*, 88, 595–600.

NIASA (2003) *National Autism Plan for Children (NAPC)*. London: National Autistic Society.

Nutt, D. (2003) 'Death and Dependence:Current Controversies over the Selective Serotonin Reuptake Inhibitors.' *Journal of Psychopharmacology*, 17, 355–64.

Powell, A. (2002) *Taking Responsibility: Good Practice Guidelines for Services – Adults with Asperger Syndrome*. London: The National Autistic Society.

Public Health Institute of Scotland (2001) *Autistic Spectrum Disorders: Needs Assessment Report*. Glasgow: Public Health Institute of Scotland.

Rimland, B. (1988) 'Controversies in the Treatment of Autistic Children: Vitamin and Drug Therapy.' *Journal of Child Neurology*, 3, 68–72.

Russell, A.J., Matrix-Cols, D., Anson, M., and Murphy, D.G.M. (2005) 'Obsessions and Compulsions in Asperger Syndrome and High-Functioning Autism.' *The British Journal of Psychiatry; The Journal of Mental Science*, 186, 525–8.

Scottish Executive (2000) *The Same as You? A Review of Services for People with Learning Disabilities*. Edinburgh: Scottish Executive.

Scottish Executive (2003) *Services for People with Autistic Spectrum Disorders*. Edinburgh: Health Department: Community Care Division 1.

Tantam, D. (2003) 'The Challenge of Adolescents and Adults with Asperger Syndrome.' *Child and Adolescent Psychiatric Clinics of North America*, 12, 143–63, vii–viii.

Towbin, K.E., Dykens, E.M., Pearson, G.S., *et al.* (1993) 'Conceptualizing "Borderline Syndrome of Childhood" and "Childhood Schizophrenia" as a Developmental Disorder.' *Journal of the American Academy of Child and Adolescent Psychiatry*, 32, 775–82.

van Krevelen, D.A. (1962) 'Early Infantile Autism and Autistic Psychopathy.' *Journal of Childhood Autism and Schizophrenia*, 1, 82–6.

Volkmar, F.R. and Cohen, D.J. (1991) 'Comorbid Association of Autism and Schizophrenia.' *American Journal of Psychiatry*, 148, 1705–07.

Willemsen-Swinkels, S.H.N. and Buitelaar, J.K. (2002) 'The Autistic Spectrum: Subgroups, Boundaries, and Treatment.' *The Psychiatric Clinics of North America*, 25, 811–36.

Wing, L. (1981) 'Asperger Syndrome: A Clinical Account.' *Psychological Medicine*, 11, 115–29.

Wing, L. and Shah, A. (2000) 'Catatonia in Autistic Spectrum Disorders.' *British Journal of Psychiatry*, 176, 357–62.

Wolff, S. (1995) *Loners: The Life Path of Unusual Children*. London: Routledge.

5.

Being told or being told off?

Reciprocity at the Diagnostic Interview

Michelle Dawson

This is dedicated to The Impossible Figure,
Dr Laurent Mottron, whose courage I hold in awe.

forethought re the distinction

The autism / Asperger distinction is the result of the best scientific evidence now available. This distinction is evident in differences in peaks of ability. These differences measure consistently so long as the diagnostician has not, as some have, arbitrarily adopted diagnostic priorities – like social reciprocity, or "empathizing" – to suit himself. Other observations related to development, and to what scientists rudely call co-morbidities, tend to confirm the distinction shouting from the peaks, so to speak.

Of course this subject is a quagmire in which remaining upright is practically impossible. Acknowledging the distinction does not disrespect the importance of similarities, but here's a small sample of the scientific fallout of making autism and Asperger's interchangeable:

1. *Consistencies in the developmental course and the abilities of autistics across all levels of measured intelligence are erased.*

2. *Peaks of ability, and their role as precursors for splinter and savant abilities, cease being characteristics of a specific diagnosis and unparsimoniously become the random and incidental quirks of individuals.*

3. *"Low-functioning" autistics are classified by level, rather than kind, of intelligence; they are then segregated and relegated to behaviourists, while*

> *cognitive scientists blithely pursue their social deficit theories (come to think of it, this one has already been afoot for more than a decade).*

4. *Intelligence in autism/Asperger's, now shorn of all striking consistencies and distinctions, remains always and only a matching variable which nobody has any cause to study.*

the interview

I need to be told what my diagnosis is and why this diagnosis. If I didn't care about why I wouldn't be here.

If you diagnose me as an undifferentiated Asperger/autistic, I need to be told *why* all the more. If I'm not aware that scientists have taken up sides on this issue, I need to be told about this and again told why. What's the problem? Why can't you guys figure this out? And if you very firmly are in the no-significant-difference faction, I may ask you not just about your science but about your ethics and priorities. Usually, I've noticed, when Asperger/autistic merges, "low-functioning" autistics are jettisoned into oblivion with a shrug. Since I identify totally with the cast-offs, I need to be told why you are setting them – or is it us? – aside.

If you differentiate – maybe having noticed that the similarities across all "levels" of autism are significant, and that discarding them in order to lump in Asperger's insults parsimony and ethics both – I need to be told all of this. You will be letting me know that I am worthy of this information. If I start with accurate information, I am less likely to be pushed around. I am less likely to have my mind and my diagnosis recruited by autism's hundreds of hungry and greedy agendas.

I need to be told that autism versus Asperger's is not a value judgment or a contest. It is not better/worse or us/them. And if my diagnosis is Asperger's or if it isn't, I need to be told that Asperger's is not and has never been a "mild" form of autism.

It might help for me to know that while prevalence rates for the spectrum as a whole are in recent studies consistent, the prevalence rates for each diagnosis – autism, Asperger's, and that none-of-the-above phenomenon of PDD-NOS (pervasive developmental disorder – not otherwise specified) – are anything but. While I would never accuse you of improvising, I need to be told that many diagnosticians are winging it.

I need to be told that my diagnosis is great news. Whether autism or Asperger's, I'm among some of the best and most fascinating human beings who ever existed. I have a lot to live up to and this I need to be told.

And I need to be told that my diagnosis is terrible news. I may risk my employment or my liberty by honestly stating who I am. I will as a matter of course be left out of the entire public, legal, political, and scientific discourse about myself. If I object to this, my character and sanity will be called into question. After all, I'm autistic. My role is limited to telling my story then leaving the room while the real people get down to business. I need to be told that all the work I do will always be completely compromised by my diagnosis. My work will only be used to verify my symptoms. Then it will be dismissed. If I should have any ideas in areas that count, like research and the law, I will need to have them promoted by persons who are not so ruthlessly disabled by prejudice, intolerance, and ostracism.

I need to be told why this prejudice and intolerance and ostracism are not censured, prosecuted, and punished as they would be were they applied to persons who are non-autistic. I need to be *told*.

Also I need to be told that autism research and treatments have been developed and designed to fulfill the needs of a wide array of non-autistic persons. If I have this accurate information, I will better be able to read the research and assess the treatments. In fact, I need to be told that I have a positive obligation to be conscientiously critical of autism research and treatments which are shoddy in their conception, execution, and/or ethics. There is no shortage of shoddiness in these areas. I need to be told that peer review sometimes fails, and that these failures have been most flagrant in the research and treatment of atypical persons judged by society and scientists to have no rights or worth. So autism research will tell me more about autism researchers than about autistic people, and this is unlikely to change any time soon.

As for autism societies, I need to be told with emphasis that, in spite of their names, they will neither represent nor welcome me. Unlike other disability organizations, autism societies practice and promote the intolerance and exclusion of those they are mandated to serve. The situation varies from country to country, but there exists no autism society that is about autistic people. Don't tell me about FEAT groups and CAN and

DAN and Safe Minds and so on, I will get emotional and I know that's not permitted. There also exist specific groups for Asperger's. If I look, I'll find not one solitary Asperger's person in the very fancy governance of the one Canadian organization claiming to represent them.

In view of this, I very much need to be told about what happens to a group of people who are entirely at the mercy of decision-making processes that exclude them. Autistics and Asperger's people, among themselves, show clearly the pattern of futility lived by persons helpless to influence their own lives in any significant area. We are treated like small, stupid, unruly children, not bright enough or responsible enough to know who we are and what we need. No group of persons treated this way has ever had good social or economic outcomes. We are doing better than we should be, given our matching straitjackets of denigration and ostracism.

And you must remind me that regardless of the extraordinary against-all-odds accomplishments of Asperger's people and autistics, we are still invariably considered to be a devastating burden on society. I need to be told that I am not a burden. I am not another sad and tragic statistic requiring endless expensive services. I will, however, be used this way by dishonest non-autistics who, honestly, should be denounced for their irresponsibility then treated for their emotional problems.

I need to be told that every message directed towards me as an autistic will inform me that my only hope is to train myself – my thoughts, my actions, my life, and my soul – to conform properly to the needs and expectations of non-autistics. And I need to be informed that I should reject all such messages while smiling at the bigots who emit them.

I need to be told that if I think things are hard for me, instead of whining, I should consider what autistic children have to contend with. They are called hollow shells by their own parents. They are said to have no personality, no soul. Their parents go to court to get monetary damages for not having the proper "consortium" with their children, because their children, being autistic, are the wrong kind of children. Yes, I'm aware that autistic children would be alert to their parents' views, you don't have to tell me.

Then I need to be told that I can't just wait around for Rosa Parks to materialize. After all, she was prepared for her role and had an organization behind her. This is not going to happen in autism, so it is up to me entirely. I have to think this way, and yes it is, for sure, not fair. Every day I'm going to have to get on that damn bus and sit down and *not get up*. Even though I'm not fit to tie Ms Park's shoes, and nobody seems to learn from what I do, I must every day get on that *goddamn* bus and refuse to give up my seat and get dragged away, humiliated. I cannot wait for someone else to do this. That is not allowed. And you don't want to be obliged to tell a whole other generation what you are now having to tell me.

Then I might ask you why you are not doing anything yourself. *I thought you would ignore that question.*

I need to be told why Asperger's people and autistics are judged the way ballerinas would be if you looked only at their feet. You would see deformity, pain, ugliness. You would refuse to consider the strength, determination, and beauty that resulted in those feet. The feet must be like non-ballerina feet! And so the treatment begins. Every increment of improvement in the feet is recorded and praised. The strength, determination, and beauty of the ballerina, always having been considered useless and worthless, are neither missed nor mourned as they are corrected into extinction. Can you explain why it is that we who are autistic or Asperger are judged this way? Because I need to be told.

But mostly, and always, I need to be told why it is wrong to be autistic. *And don't avoid the question.* Because if there were nothing wrong about being autistic, this whole business – diagnosis, disclosure, whatever – would be a piece of cake.

afterthought re the question

Not having an official diagnosis may be risky, resulting in the non-diagnosed Asperger's person or autistic being drugged and incarcerated. Both trying to get an official diagnosis, and finally having one, also pose risks. My experiences in these areas have been extreme. And I have been diagnosed seven-and-a-half times – don't ask. One of my diagnoses resulted eventually in the demolition of my career and the successful prosecution of the destructive diagnosing "professional", in that order – so caveat autistic. I have also been diagnosed by the most thoughtful and diligent diagnostician anywhere. Failing to notice this at the time of the interview, I instead criticized this scientist's science, and if I remember properly, his ethics as well.

Then, in an effort to be followed at a centre geographically accessible to me, I went through yet another diagnostic interview, this time with a scientist famous in his field.

"You do demographics," I said brightly.

"No, no," he said, "I do epidemiology."

And he explained the difference in clear and simple words. So then I asked my question. "Why is it wrong to be autistic?"

He replied that no, he doesn't see it that way, as autism being something wrong.

I said, "If that were true, then you would be doing demographics, and not epidemiology."

6.

Mental health issues surrounding diagnosis, disclosure and self-confidence in the context of Asperger syndrome

David N. Andrews

To the memory of David Hawker, my much-missed list-mate;
a young Aspie man who decided that life was not worth
living any more and acted on that decision. No matter how
much I can understand exactly why he did it, I can't help
wishing that he hadn't. We all felt the same.

Some time ago, just after he left us all, I promised David's parents to dedicate the next appropriate piece of work I did to his memory. So when I was asked to contribute this chapter it seemed right to use it to mark his memory and to leave the reader in no doubt that – no matter how we describe, delineate or construe the experience of those who would qualify for this diagnosis – life for such a person can very often be a mental health nightmare.

Introduction

My own experience of the Asperger-autistic life is very difficult to describe straight out. I do not propose to give my life history here but to use events from it to illustrate my text, which is also informed by my 'sometimes' role as a 'reflective practitioner'. Part of my training at the University of Birmingham deals with the assessment process and with diagnosis: the use of psychological test materials and other investigative methods in order to identify behavioural, affective and cognitive characteristics in a client who would fulfil the criteria for any of the diagnostic labels scrutinised in any reasonable text on the unreasonably named subject of 'abnormal' psychology. Of course, there are ramifications for the client who receives any such diagnosis: this is not a process without implications, happening in isolation. For this reason, any diagnostic agent must consider fully what the diagnosis may mean in the context of the client's life. I hope that this chapter will shed a little light on some of these issues.

Most of us who have an autistic spectrum diagnosis prefer to think of ourselves as 'autistic' as opposed to 'with autism', the unspoken message in the latter terminology being that – were it not for the autism – we would be complete people (Sinclair 1999). But we are complete people anyway, with 'our autism' as an integral part of who we are. I also use the masculine indefinite personal pronoun for general cases, which shall here be deemed to include the feminine.

In 1998, as part of my undergraduate studies at the University of Leeds, I researched and wrote up a project – a sort-of mini-thesis. The topic was mental health issues in Asperger syndrome, and it examined the relationship between Asperger syndrome and mental health problems (Andrews 1999). This chapter takes up those themes, focusing on the causes of anxiety and depression, which are the most commonly occurring. The main idea is that current clinical paradigms tend to be inappropriate ways of understanding and working with the Asperger-autistic person. A better understanding of such a person might be achieved if a social psychological analysis were made. Clinicians typically depend on the medical model of Asperger syndrome: the 'sufferer' has a 'deficiency' or an 'abnormality', which, upon 'treatment', can be 'cured'. A working treatment has not been found in medicine. Instead, there are so-called 'therapies' that fail to account for the states of mind that brought the unfortunate Aspie to the attention of the mental health services. Anxiety and depression are long-standing problems for many Aspies before they finally get a diagnosis (Tantam 1991, p.170).

Anxiety and depression, I argued (Andrews 1999), are responses to two main problems in society: societal pressure to conform and societal hostility toward those who are 'different'. I suggested then that societal expectations and demands for conformity are significant parts of what

could bring about chronic depressive states. Failing to conform convinc-
ingly to society's demands for a behaviourally, affectively and cognitively
homogeneous group, the ensuing outgrouping of the Aspie results in a
reduction of his self-esteem. In essence, the mental health problems come
(in large part, at least) as a product of the society in which the Aspie in
question lives. I further suggest that society – far from being the "all-
embracing group" that it is purported to be – has very subtle ways of
excluding certain individuals from its midst. The expressed emotions in
society impact on self-esteem and eventually perpetuate (or even cause)
mental health problems. Much of what is seen as autism may well be an
autistic response to reduce self-awareness (about failure of competence in
social contexts), which would in turn reduce the likelihood of damage to
one's sense of self-efficacy – a subset of self-confidence (DuBrin 2000; p.88).

The rationale for therapies aimed at 'normalising' the Aspie – things
like behaviour therapy and so on – seems to be aimed more at reducing
society's discomfort (about 'autistic behaviours') than the client's discomfort (about his difficulties in 'shaping up' to society's expectations).
Clinical perspectives are inappropriate, since essentially they pathologise
and then outgroup the person; they use 'normalising' therapies to enforce
conformity and, in so doing, increase the risk of mental health difficulties. Such cases of therapeutic failure often seem to occur unbeknown to
the practitioners involved. I suggest that there should be 'a radical
shaking up of the system…individuals [being] respected for who they are
and what they can do [with] less emphasis on the clinical obsession with
statistical norms' (Andrews 1999).

My rather strong disdain for the clinical way of seeing things is due
largely to the effect that clinical practitioners had on my early life. I was a
curious wee chap it seems. At age three, I 'didn't speak well', 'was easily
frightened' and 'would not play with the other children in the neigh-
bourhood' (paediatrician's notes, 1966). In 1969, I was seen by a psychiatrist and this, as far as I am concerned, is where it all went wrong. I was
seen by this man intermittently for eight years. During that time, nothing
concrete was done to help. Some tests were done, and a lot of letters went
between the psychiatrist, the psychologist and some headteachers, but
very little else. The testing was limited to Wechsler Intelligence Scales for
Children (WISC, WISC-R) and a couple of spelling and reading tests;

none of the results was tracked back to events in my school life. However, upon review as a practitioner nowadays, I can see these results in the context of my life – more than the professionals at the time did – and my training affords me the ablity to see clear evidence supportive of the diagnosis of autism. But would the diagnosis of autism have been useful at this point?

Well, although the knowledge on autism at the time was not very extensive, there were some people working in the educational field whose work was sufficiently good to be noticed and recognised as groundbreaking, and there was a school in London to which I could have gone. Further research on this possibility suggests that the school in question may have been the first school in the UK set up especially for autistic children – the Sybil Elgar School – a point that suggests that the notion of my being autistic was actually being entertained before being dropped in favour of saving money (ultimately at my expense). The results of the teaching done at this school were made evident on a BBC television programme on autism many years later, and I cannot see how it would have been detrimental to my development to have been there. Even if I didn't go there (and I ended up not being given the chance to go!), the schools in Barnsley that I attended could have been given on-the-job training in order to help the teachers to teach me better and identify what I was good at and use those skills as leverage for learning, in order to circumvent my learning difficulties. Even with only a little money being spent, a lot could have been done to make my life in school less like hell than it ended up being.

At this point, I should mention that the diagnosis of autistic spectrum difficulties can be a godsend and it can also be a curse. I elaborate on this later.

My difficulties were sufficiently severe that my schools were concerned about them enough to call in the educational psychologists. But they were not deemed severe enough to warrant doing anything substantive about them, apart from to drug me up, as was also done in Wendy Lawson's case (Lawson 2000). In my case conferences (such as there were any), my parents were seen as uneducated and were not present (as far as I can tell). I know I was never present. In sum, the test results were used indiscriminately to, essentially, declare me neurotic and lazy.

When I say I was 'drugged up', I mean that I was prescribed and treated with neuroleptics. First chlorpromazine (Largactil), and later trifluoperazine (Stelazine). My GP records two instances of my being on this particular medication: once when I was round about nine or so (in about 1971) and the other at age 13. In one year. I was prescribed a heavy dosage – 25 mg three times daily – an adult maintenance dose for schizophrenia. As a 13-year-old, I was thought to be '…developing a schizophrenic disorder'. Similar errors are common. For example, Wendy Lawson (who was also misdiagnosed as schizophrenic) and numerous other less-well known individuals were inappropriately diagnosed and drugged, and some (but not all) are being rediagnosed.

The psychiatrist I was seeing – after receiving a referral letter in which I was said to have a 'history of aggression', 'twitching of face' and 'occasional withdrawal into a world of fantasy', and my mother was said to be 'very anxious' about me (letter from School medical officer, 1968) – had tried previously to psychoanalyse my mother through me! When he began to observe me as *me*, instead of as an extension of my mother, he managed to collect some information. By 1975, in addition to mentioning an 'outburst', he had gathered that:

- '…his problem is his lack of awareness of other people around him…'
- '…his eccentricities…'
- '…no one can get through to him and he cannot give out adequately…'
- '…he is seen as eccentric…'
- '…he has been withdrawing from his family a bit and this makes everything calmer…'
- '…he admits he is doing badly at school…'
- '…he is withdrawn from others at home and at school…'
- '…contact annoys him … disrupts what he is thinking about…'
- '…he is very rigidly still thinking about aeroplanes…'
- '…his parents very anxious about his increasing withdrawal and rigidness in his approach to life…'

At this point, in June 1975, this psychiatrist wrote to my then-GP, saying '…it might be worth putting him on Largactil again'.

The 'outburst' to which he referred is what is commonly known as a nervous breakdown – a sometimes insidious and sometimes sudden phenomenon that is a very frightening experience. One feels increasingly uncertain about one's grip on reality, one loses control of one's emotional reactions to events. In my case, I can remember becoming seriously hyperventilated. I was crying and I could not do anything about it. The trigger: my mother asked me, noticing my return from grammar school to be a very subdued event, whether I was alright. I cannot honestly say whether I gave a sensible answer. One might imagine trigger and cause to be related, but here that would be the wrong thing to assume. The rather nasty behaviour of my peers on the school bus, although definitely not pleasant, did not cause the breakdown. The hanging outside the school, in which two boys pulled me up against the school gates such that my feet left the ground, although definitely a horrible experience, was not the cause either.

In 1973, I had passed the 11-plus examination and was selected to go to grammar school in Normanton, West Yorkshire. Since my entry to that school, it was noticed that my writing was not very good, that it was very untidy and almost unreadable sometimes. I was placed in the lowest set, but I was always being told that this didn't matter: I had got into a good school.

It was in this 'good school' that my life became hell. I was subjected to what the head of lower school called 'relatively mild teasing'. Maybe to her it would seem so, but you know what happens to concrete when it is subjected to repeated small shocks many times a day for hundreds of days. It crumbles. Day in, day out, the 'relatively mild teasing' took its toll and, just like concrete, I crumbled.

This led to two things. One was that this 'good school' requested that my parents not say anything about the hanging incident, lest the good name of the school suffer. Eventually, Normanton Grammar School became a comprehensive school (apparently breaking the headmaster's heart; served him right really, and it was some sort of poetic justice for me in the end … just as well, because the English legal system never gave me any justice on that). The other thing that happened was that I was prescribed that horrible and totally inappropriate medicine, chlorpromazine.

The effect of this drug was impressive to the psychiatrist, sure; but my mother became concerned about the child she had that was an avidly interested young boy (music and aeroplanes being the main two long-term interests), and she was concerned that he had disappeared and been replaced by a zombie for a year. During my attempt to get some legal remedy for this, much later in life, the psychiatrist consulted by my solicitor mentioned this phase of treatment in his report and put down that I was on chlorpromazine for an undetermined period of time, essentially with no apparent ill effects. Among these 'no ill effects' were loss of interest in anything, including my main interests – music and aeroplanes; loss of ability to feel any emotions whatsoever; loss of ability to concentrate on things, especially school work (oddly enough, my school work during this time was the worst it had ever been and nobody put two and two together and suggested it might be down to the medication); and, further down the line, I now have a pronounced thyroid problem, possibly due to the medication.

So what did this wonderful medication do for me? Did it solve the problems I was having? Did it stop the teasing and the bullying? No. That carried on, both at the grammar school and at the next school that I went to. It certainly didn't stop one of my new classmates from – and this was in front of the whole class – ejaculating all over my trousers while holding my neck in a lock with his left arm. Wonderful drug, chlorpromazine, don't you think?

So, there is me as a 13-year-old boy, on medication that has effectively lobotomized him. His former head of lower school has described him as follows: '…a boy of considerable ability [who] finds it extremely difficult to express himself in writing, which prevents him from achieving full potential…a quiet introvert…made increasingly unhappy partly through his failure to succeed in his work and partly by the attitude of his contemporaries…different from the average thirteen year old boy and… subjected to a certain amount of relatively mild teasing…seems…quite incapable of learning to live with this…now…loath to come to school… recently has made himself physically ill with fear.'

Being blamed for my difficulties, as I very clearly was (by just about all my teachers and by an educational psychologist), does not help to instil a sense of self-efficacy.

No constructive support was forthcoming. Nothing was done (no diagnosis, no help given), and I would say there was no real intention of doing anything. My development was effectively sacrificed to save money. And I was not the only one. Let's face it: an autistic child costs a lot to educate and fund care plans for, and it is so very cheap to fund a diet of chlorpromazine for a year. I honestly believe that what happened to me was an unmitigated case of wilful negligence on the part of the local council.

Let's have a look at what my former lower school headmistress said.

- '…considerable ability'. Yes, even as a nine-year-old, my IQ was 129. My reading quotient was a massive 153. And still I had difficulties with reading and writing as well as generalising from specifics. The test results were used indiscriminately to essentially declare me neurotic and lazy. Not once did an educational psychologist ever ask me what my experience of school work or school attendance was like.

- '…difficulty in expressing himself in writing'. My handwriting is not, and never has been, easy to read. In the years since I was at school, and with considerable practice, my handwriting has never improved. On the purely physical level, the act of holding the pen and causing it to move over paper, maintaining an even-ish pressure and forming clear letters, can be very hard for some people, and it is not made easier by practice. As time goes by, having to coordinate these actions to produce long tracts of prose gets painful and exhausting. Your hand cramps up and it hurts to move, and you are expected to keep on going with the same sort of clarity you manage at the start of it all. But you try and you can't, and then you get told off by your teacher for poor presentation. Being blamed for this difficulty, as I very clearly was (by just about all my teachers and by an educational psychologist), does not help to instil a sense of self-efficacy. On a cognitive level, as you are trying to keep the physical act of writing going to the teacher's liking, you are also trying to marshal your thoughts. But they are fast, because you think very much in a pictorial style, and it is hard to convert the pictures you see in your mind into words that you can see on paper. If you try to keep up with the thoughts, you lose the clarity of the written prose you're writing; if you try to keep the clarity, you lose track of the thoughts in your mind. An upshot of this, of course, is that the overall quality of your work goes down after a while, as you get more and more exhausted (and yes, the educational psychologist who assessed my work did, indeed, note the loss of quality in my work as my writing approached the end of the essay; and he saw it as a 'progressive relaxation in standards' without asking me a single thing about my experience). What that psychologist called 'a neurotic reaction to writing' actually has a more accurate name: graphomotor dyspraxia. This is a component of many specific learning difficulties clusters, what we refer to in the real world as dyslexic-dyspraxic syndrome, which may also include constructional dyspraxia, a type of cognitive dyspraxia in which there is difficulty in constructing sentences and other communicative structures – quite common in autism, so I hear. I blame the British Psychological Society for this: their ban on using the term 'dyslexia' in their Educational and Clinical Division in the 1960s and 1970s (Meredith 1972, p.19) was the basis of a wholesale wilful negligence against many thousands of dyslexic children throughout Britain, and I should know – I was one. The result of this whole thing was that I was stripped of whatever self-esteem I might have had and was left with a feeling of being guilty for my own difficulties in my school work. Well done, BPS! Incidentally, the current working definition for dyslexia put forward by this organisation is less than satisfactory in terms of usefulness and workability (Reed 2005, pp.268–72).

- '…quiet introvert'. Yes. I had admitted to the psychiatrist that I did not play with anyone, and he knew of my being 'aloof' and 'unresponsive' as a long-standing matter. He had made a diagnosis of autism in a neighbouring town some years previously, and it never struck him that my long-standing 'aloofness and unresponsiveness' might suggest that I could well be autistic too. As opposed to, say, schizophrenic.

- '...failure to succeed in his work'. Well, isn't that a convoluted way of saying I wasn't doing well? At the time that this letter was written, I was some weeks into a course of quite heavy sedative medication for a not-quite-teenager...and this experience had effects that I still live with today, regarding my ability to feel competent in anything. My sense of self-efficacy is damaged pretty badly, and I really am not sure it will ever be as strong as it ought to be for a man of my age and with my training. Even when I hand in very good work as a postgraduate, I still worry about it. The school experience, in which essentially I was left to fend for myself, robbed me of my developmental opportunities and gave me nothing to make up for it. And the educational psychologist's input definitely did not help.

- '...the attitudes of his contemporaries'. Yes, they sucked. They hated me. I wanted to learn. They didn't. So I ended up paying for their laziness. And my own difficulties were ascribed by a psychologist to laziness, without his making a direct inquiry to me.

- '...different from the average thirteen year old boy'. Oh, yes! We have seen long-standing aloofness/unresponsiveness, social withdrawal and rigidity of approach to life, communication difficulties (of an albeit specific type), and...oh, wait a minute... doesn't this look like something familiar? When I was doing my specialist modules, I saw this very cluster of specific difficulties. As I said to my GP when looking for evidence of being dyslexic, 'That's Asperger syndrome, that is!'

And I was right. This diagnosis was confirmed by a psychiatrist on 7 January 1997.

Even so, as a result of my experiences from school days and work days, without the benefit of a diagnosis to help me to understand myself, I have a strong sense of self-non-efficacy. Stops me getting too big for my boots, sure enough, but at what cost to my mental health?

From my background of training in psychology, I can begin to suggest what went wrong and how my life could have been influenced for the better, even in those 'dark ages'. The first thing I notice is the psychologists having not actually asked me anything: I remember no questions about school or home life. There is nothing linking the psychological testing to my school and work circumstances or difficulties, and this is what the testing *should* be done for. Otherwise, doing them was a complete waste of my time. An IQ of 129 is not much good to a person who has difficulties using it, and it is never enough to quote that sort of number with no indication of where it came from or what it really means (Meredith 1972, pp.21–3). The psychiatrist who used the results of these tests, and the reports made by the psychologists, in his deliberations actually had a degree in psychology, an MA in child psychology, and so there are things he himself should have known about how to use test results, and how to understand a psychological report. However, his conduct towards me failed to take into account accurately what the tests meant: he assumed that my fundamental difficulty in life was 'largely emotional', simply because my IQ was too high and I spelt too well.

A third thing I notice is that, instead of recommending anything to work around or with the writing problem, it was recommended that I '... be given long-term psychotherapy to develop more realistic attitudes'. Nothing was ever mentioned of any strengths, or special interests or anything positive at all; it was all negative and essentially blaming me for my own difficulties. Given that if a child in school is failing, then so is the school (Meredith 1972, p.26), why were the schools not criticised as much as I was? I was, as a fourth point of criticism, given heavily sedating neuroleptic medications.

All this malpractice and/or negligence (which it is) has left me in a horrible position, and one from which I never really managed to get away: the 'you'll never make anything of yourself' position. Even now, as a man of 43, living in Finland – opposite my ex-wife and our daughter, and backed up by some excellent comments from my supervisor (Dr Glenys Jones, one of the UK's foremost practitioner psychologists in the autism field) – I still feel less than competent, despite the fact that I have shown myself to be more than reasonably able to do the job I have been training for: applied educational psychologist. Since I moved here, the system has slowly worn away at what feeling of ability and competence I had until it depressed me enough to consider suicide again. The message one gets here, with the diagnosis of Asperger syndrome, is that one has – effectively – had a bilateral hemispherectomy, i.e. no brain of which to speak. Nobody takes me seriously here if I say anything regarding my specialism.

The struggle is still very much uphill. When I applied to a Finnish university and my diagnosis was mentioned, the university officer in question said to my ex-wife: 'How does he think he'll be able to study – to become a psychologist – with all that?' Happily for me, Glenys Jones and Rita Jordan in the University of Birmingham in the UK seem to have thought I'd do fine. This year (2005), I shall be graduating from there with my required master's degree and probably far more knowledge, competence and understanding of my specialism than any other Finnish psychologist currently has.

In a bleak future for an Aspie psychologist, that is all I have going for me. I am seen as successful by many: postgraduate psychologist in a very good university (actually the best in Europe for the training that it offers); ex-wife (still a valued colleague and friend); a child (more precious to me than anybody in the world); almost savant musical ability; associate editor in Finland for *Good Autism Practice* journal; chairman for an autism-related political pressure group, Autistic People Against Neuroleptic Abuse (APANA) (www.apana.org.uk). I speak two languages, one of which I have known for only about five years. And I am a singer-songwriter–musician of serious ability. Yet *still* I have to feel like a complete incompetent because my skill and knowledge are unrecognised in Finland where I live. And it struck me while writing this chapter why I have been so depressed and angry for the past five years: just like when I was a child in school, I am not allowed to feel competent. The whole system tells me I know nothing, all because I am autistic. Like I say, the future is very bleak. The thesis I wrote in 1999 concluded with a few lines, which I shall use to close this chapter: after half a decade of no change in societal attitudes towards autistic people, I think they have taken on a certain poignancy:

> There needs to be more reliance upon the practices and findings of social psychologists, and less emphasis on the clinical obsession with statistical norms. There must be a shifting of values within clinical and educational psychology to take into account the autistic individual's right to be himself and to determine his own life. Humanistic principles might, alongside the social psychological understanding of individual difference, facilitate such a change. The problem is that – whilst ever it is a system run by the so-called 'normal' individual (and for that sort of individual) – that change will never come. (Adapted from Andrews 1999.)

Epilogue

The sad fact is that the above is not a set of experiences that only I experience: there are things in that set of life events that are common to the lives of many people who are (or would be, if clinicians were astute enough) diagnosed as being autistic, especially at the Asperger end of the spectrum, and it does not take genius to figure out these common experiential factors. It does, however, take honesty on the part of mental healthcare professionals (something, from the collective experiences of many people with whom I have been in contact in one way or another, that is sadly lacking when 'we' are the patient/clients of such professionals). The honesty is required for the practitioner to come to terms with the extent to which his or her discipline has let us down. All too often, I hear from other autistics about how practitioners have played on the social naiveté aspects of their being autistic in order to 'Delphi' their clients (e.g. see www.iror.org/control_guide.asp). As a practitioner myself, I often feel as if I am also on the spot for this. Ultimately, however, I cannot and do not identify with many practitioners since most do not accept my ability and/or competence. And I at least was trained in a way that implies the taking of responsibility for one's actions. No skin off my nose, then, to join in the condemnation of practitioners who repeatedly fail to put the mental health needs of their clients uppermost in their minds.

I mentioned, in an article published in the journal *Good Autism Practice* (Andrews 2002) that mental health problems for the Asperger autistic person do not arise from the biochemistry of autism but that, rather, they arise from how he or she experiences society. Society, as yet, is not an inclusive organisation. As an example, the backlash against Michelle Dawson's paper on the misbehaviour of behaviourists (Dawson 2004) was not directed at the paper so much as against her personally. One of the more prominent psychologists working in intensive behavioural intervention in the USA was seen to have personally attacked the diagnosis given to Michelle by a competent practitioner in her own country and even suggested an alternative from the so-called personality disorders. If society was as inclusive as it likes to make itself out to be, then this could never happen. It could not happen, because the interests of so-called neurodiverse minorities would be protected or even valued, unassailable by those less charitable or humane. What happened in the Dawson situation was a clear example of how the majority attempts to silence the minority: to call into question the quality of the information put forward by the minority person purely on the basis of the diagnosis that he or she has, and in some cases even question that person's diagnosis. How can a society that allows this sort of 'social' behaviour (which is, in fact, *antisocial* behaviour) be seen as inclusive?

And how can autistic people *not* fall prey to mental health difficulties when constantly faced with that sort of 'social behaviour'?

References

Andrews, D.N. (1999) 'Mental Health Issues in Asperger Syndrome: A Short Theoretical Paper.' Unpublished mini-thesis. Leeds: University of Leeds.

Andrews, D.N. (2002) 'Mental Health Issues in Asperger Syndrome: Preventive Mental Health Work in Good Autism Practice.' In *Good Autism Practice*, 3, 2, 2–8.

Dawson, M. (2004) 'The Misbehaviour of Behaviourists.' www.sentex.net/~nexus23/naa_aba.html

DuBrin, A.J. (2000) *Applying Psychology: Individual and Organisational Effectiveness.* Upper Saddle River, NJ: Prentice Hall.

Lawson, W. (2000) *Life Behind Glass: A Personal Account of Autism Spectrum Disorder.* London: Jessica Kingsley Publishers.

Meredith, G.P. (1972) *Dyslexia and the Individual.* London: Elm Tree Books.

Reed, C. (2005) 'Reading and Dyslexia.' In A. Esgate and D. Groome (eds) *An Introduction to Applied Coginitive Psychology.* Hove: Psychology Press.

Sinclair, J. (1999) 'Why I Dislike "Person-first" Language .' web.syr.edu/%7Ejisincla/person_first.htm

Tantam, D. (1991) 'Asperger's Syndrome in Adulthood.' In U. Frith (ed) *Autism and Asperger Syndrome.* Cambridge: Cambridge University Press.

7.

One that got away

Dinah Murray

For a few years now I have been tentatively checking with/disclosing to my growing number of autistic friends the possibility that I might myself belong somewhere on the autism spectrum, and I have been honoured by near-universal acceptance. Yet there are reasons why I do not entirely feel I deserve the accolade: I am flexible, even slippery; I proceed insouciantly, with generally well-founded confidence; I am *acceptable*. A couple of years ago, Jane Meyerding found, from the online group ANI-L (Autism Network International, www.ani.ac) a useful category for me, 'autistic cousin'. She also told me a story about how, on becoming a Quaker and thus a pacifist, William Penn sought advice about continuing to carry a sword, which as a male aristocrat he had always previously done. He was told he should wear his sword for as long as he could, i.e. for as long as his conscience would let him. So I've divulged my highish 'autism quotient' score (Baron-Cohen *et al.* 2001) to my main professional autism forum[1]; I've used it to indicate to my friends that I might be a bit odder than they thought. My husband and sons had earlier intimations and seem unperturbed. Now I'm going into print for the first time, now I have taken off the sword, will I be both more immediately vulnerable and no longer a person of status?

There follows a narrative I have made of my life. I have made it the way it is to illustrate an argument. It could have been a completely different story and yet just as true. If, as you read it, dear reader, you keep

---

1   That is, people attending the Durham conferences organised by Sunderland University's Autism Research Unit.

thinking, 'Hang on! That could be me...', then think on. Perhaps your life could be told this way too?

The story is about a person growing up soon after Kanner (1943) and Asperger (1944) first published, a person who has hardly ever had any problems getting her meanings across, whose presentation of self-skills have almost always been sufficient unto the day, who has always had all the support she needed. It is a story about how easy it is to stay out of trouble if you're good at what society likes, and about how that has the knock-on effect of building confidence, i.e. positive expectations of self-efficacy, without which the potential for exploration and discovery may be crippled. It also shows how even someone with massive confidence in some realms can lose it comprehensively in states of emotional meltdown with tiny apparent triggers. On those rare occasions when her meanings are taken amiss or not understood, and an assumed smooth encounter is engulfed by mismatched expectations and negative assumptions, she can become a person incapable of communicating, of socialising, of thinking – and she can be strongly drawn never to expose herself to such risk again.

Most of the people Dinah knows who are on the autism spectrum tell her they regard her as 'one of them'; the same applies to her 'normie' friends. Most of the time, she passes muster in either camp. This uncertainty is reflected in her scores on the Baron-Cohen parlour games for identifying one's position on various characteristics relevant, his findings suggest, both to 'male-brainedness' and the diagnosis of autism spectrum conditions (Baron-Cohen 2003). On the autism quotient (AQ) test, the systemising quotient (SQ) test and the empathising quotient (EQ) test, she scores between a typical male and a person likely to have an autism spectrum diagnosis. She also scores at just subclinical level retrospectively on Tony Attwood's (1997) short questionnaire in his book on Asperger syndrome. Just for good measure, she also has ring fingers longer than index fingers, apparently another indication of both maleness and autistic disposition (Baron-Cohen 2003).

Contrary to those indications, she scores at the top of the normal range in the remaining Baron-Cohen test, 'reading the mind in the eyes'. She seems equally good at reading emotions in voices. Those skills may have contributed to sparing her from all but a tiny handful of the social catastrophes she would otherwise have experienced. However, those skills were probably not developed until she was well into her twenties, so we must look elsewhere for why Dinah escaped diagnosis and, indeed, why she should. The next sections of this chapter will summarise the evidence that she belongs to what is sometimes called the broader phenotype of autism. After that, we shall look at reasons why, in spite of that, she has never attracted any formal dysfunctional label.

Being rather weird

Dinah was on the beach with her family when she was 15 months old. Her family were socialising with another young family. Parents were talking to each other, kids were playing. Suddenly, they realised that Dinah was missing. Rather than playing with her peers, she was off climbing precipitous rocks. Brought back to cries of relief, she went straight back up the rocks again. A fondness for climbing often led her up doorways, walls, cliffs, trees and even rooftops until she was in her early twenties.

Although generally easy-going and good-natured, she would occasionally flare up very rapidly into extreme rage, misery, or panic. Things that struck her as grotesque were the main sources of panic. She can remember panic at her teddy bear's lost eye, terror at carnival figures with giant papier mâché heads, fear when her mother told her she had snake hips. Dolls horrified and repelled her with their distorted pink tinted heads and limbs and their rolling eyes. Her favourite object for years was a strip of fur, which she called Scilly the snake.

It was, presumably, rage, or some desperate need for freedom, that made her fight so hard against the boys in playground wars between the sexes at primary school. It took four boys to catch her and keep her because she struggled so hard. Apart from jacks and yo-yos, that was the only playground game she ever joined. She remembers watching the other children doing 'one potato, two potato, three potato, four' with their fists and feeling completely unaware of the meaning of it all, and yet having no inclination at that age to find out. In her late teens, she read her way through the Opie collections of playground chants (Opie and Opie 1959), which used to mean so little to her and to which she was so little drawn as a child.

She did not initiate pretend games herself. She remembers being at a party for five- and six-year-olds in which everybody was supposed to pass through a pretend guillotine of children holding their arms to make an arch while chanting fiercely about heads being chopped off: no way was little Dinah going to do that, however firmly pressed. She owned her toy knights for their beauty, and she loved to line them up according to their colours and admire their gorgeous shininess; they were never used in mock fighting. She loved playing with bubbles in the bath. She loved to go through her mother's drawer containing coins and pins. She loved spinning coins, but probably never for more than a few minutes at a time, often trying to get as many spinning at once as possible. She loved skimming stones, which she might do for an hour or more, with or without company. Climbing trees was intrinsically fun and had the desirable result of hiding her.

She learned lots of games of patience, including some extremely challenging ones in her late teens, and she invented various card games to play with an imaginary opponent. She suspects a significant motivation in much of this behaviour was avoiding competitive situations in which she might lose. At about the age of ten, someone she'd just met told her that it 'stands out a mile that you're scared to death of failure'. She was taken aback at the time but has come to realise the near-truth and great importance for her of that statement. She believes that fear stems from the hideous futility of wasted time and effort. One of the expressions that always puzzzled her was 'could try harder': how could she? Either she was trying with all her might, or she was not trying at all. Later on, she got a bit braver and learned several card games of moderate difficulty, which she played against other people with pleasure. Building houses of cards was also a special favourite activity: Dinah was very good at this balancing act.

At about the age of nine, Dinah discovered that she enjoyed something the other children regarded as torture – a 'Chinese burn': hold the wrist tightly and revolve hands in opposite directions pulling the skin with them. She went round the playground inviting people to engage with her by giving her Chinese burns. To this day, she finds a light touch very uncomfortable and is likely to startle violently at one if not expecting it – this has occasioned some inappropriate attributions of meaning in her life. Twice while watching tennis on television she has injured herself – once a cut foot, once a broken finger – without being aware she had done so until the match was over.

As a child, Dinah had marked sensory issues around touch. She required to be tucked into bed firmly, with a heavy eiderdown placed over her, otherwise she felt floaty and unsafe. She would not tolerate tight clothes around her neck, but she insisted on things being done up tight around her waist, otherwise she felt loose. And nothing prickly! She still tends to cut out the labels from garments because they annoy her. She hated wearing shoes and went barefoot whenever possible, including going barefoot into London's West End at the age of 18: why not?

At night, the sound and feel of her blood rushing and pounding in her ears were intolerable, so she had a loudly ticking clock to drown it out, the intrusive sound of which she dealt with by fitting words of songs into its ticks until she fell asleep.

Her clothes are chosen either because they are comfortable, cheap, easy to look after and visually acceptable, or because she finds them inherently beautiful – they are not chosen because of how she looks in them. She tried shaving her armpits once (yuk!) and may have tried lipstick twice (yuk again!). She has been to a hairdresser only two or three times in her adult life, her mother always having cut her hair as a child. Now she cuts her own hair, mainly 'blind', by feel. The results don't usually get her into trouble.

The tactile qualities of various foods, such as figs, tapioca and peach skins, would provoke retching. Smells are also important to Dinah. Because she threw up as a toddler every time when offered her cod liver oil with added vitamins, she developed a pre-rickets condition by the age of three (caught just in time). She still frequently retches when dealing with cat food or, still worse, dog food – both the smell and the texture affect her badly. Pencils, paper, and the white glue paste in little tubs at primary school were all favourite munchies; she also discovered that young lime leaves, the nectar in fuchsias and honeysuckles, and the stalks of wild garlic flowers were delicious. At secondary school she more or less stopped eating the stationery but she continued uninhibitedly to pluck and eat the wild treats.

Dinah used to do lots of looking at the world through her fingers, an activity that her mother discussed with her as giving one very interesting views of things. She would fiercely squeeze and press and work her eyeballs, loving the sensation and the patterns created; this she still does. She sucks the roof of her mouth. She has permanent creases around the base of each of her index fingers, from a lifetime of bending them hard away from her hands and enjoying the intense sensation in the knuckles. There is also hard skin on the inside of the first joint of her right-hand index finger from a habit of rubbing it hard against its next-door finger. She likes to crick her neck first to the right and then to the left, feeling her head's connection to her body. Most of these are easily hidden: the world need not know about them. She loved making spit bubbles on her hands but she learned early on that this drew disgust from other people, and so she kept the habit private.

Despite the minor oddities described, most of Dinah's behaviour, both at school and at home, was socially acceptable. Her pleasure in her own company and her tendency to long words and difficult questions were seen as evidence of a philosophical disposition. Her very early reading was greeted with joy and not seen as dysfunctional, her memory for birthdays and phone numbers was seen as a desirable asset; her excellent spelling won her the school spelling bees. Only sibling relationships gave her any early training in expecting things sometimes to go wrong. When things did start to go wrong at secondary school, Dinah progressively stopped trying to succeed academically, focusing some effort still on art (at this school, everyone could succeed at art) and lots of effort on staying out of trouble and not drawing attention to herself. Being identified as 'A Problem' would have counted as being in the worst sort of trouble, of having failed completely. After years of constantly trying to 'get it right' and succeeding, suddenly at secondary school doing so was no longer effortless. That might have crushed her. Instead, having always been good at hiding disapproved traits, Dinah now added challenge-avoidance and mirroring to her rather limited repertoire of social skills.

She wrote this poem in her early twenties:

> Cut a flower, it does not bleed
> The sap withdraws
> So from your blade – your love –
> Does my self turn

I build myself a house of glass
You look, and thinking you see me
You see yourself
You smile, murmur love
And call it union
That I would call
The coldest separation.

Her attempts to hide in this way through mirroring are subverted when the heat of her emotions glows through, sometimes with catastrophic results. Mostly, such extreme intensely emotional upsets occurred not at school but at home, until part way through secondary school. During these phases, Dinah becomes completely inarticulate (this remains true), sometimes for as much as an hour, during which she does not want human contact until her equilibrium has done some self-restoration. She experiences very brief very violent impulses when she loses her temper, which typically dissolve fast into the tears described above. It may take her weeks after such an event to work out what was really going on in the situation that triggered it. It can be vital for Dinah to remove herself from other people at such times, because her inability to explain anything then gets rich interpretation from them and tends to generate responses likely to drive her further into inarticulate miserable helplessness and rage.

When she was 18, Dinah's class teacher, who had known her for seven years, was displeased because she'd forgotten to request advance permission for some time off. The next day, the teacher told her, in front of the class, that she had 'told the class, the trouble with Dinah is, her world is just Dinah and The Others'. Dinah's reaction to this at the time was a characteristic meltdown, floods of unstoppable tears and rapid escape from the presence of other people. But in retrospect, she can see the teacher's point. Here are a few more examples of what Dinah supposes was meant:

- Not realising people typically identify with characters in books they read. She learned this in her late twenties from someone who expressed surprise when Dinah said she never did.

- Assuming that her fairly steadfast concern to contribute constructively to the current common interest is obvious, at least to her friends, without her having to maintain it with verbal cues and general 'phatic communion', i.e. the contentless bits of talk that help people to feel pleasantly connected. This parallels stories of Asperger syndrome partners thinking that saying 'I love you' once should be adequate forever. Correcting this requires vigilance on her part, it does not occur effortlessly.

- Stating her views without remembering to remind listeners in some way that they are merely her views, and that she does believe other people have an equal right to their opinions (these propositions seem self-evident to her).

- Not realising that one person's expressed wants might make another person feel obliged to further those wants, whether or not they were personally disposed to do so, and without any authority relationship (this shocking revelation came to Dinah in her late thirties). Remembering and allowing for this requires vigilance on her part – it does not occur effortlessly.

- Not realising that typical people 'strategically display emotions to influence other people's behaviour' (Rieffe *et al.* 2000, p.195) – Dinah thought until very recently that doing this was a rarity, not the norm. Even if she had understood that she was meant to develop this capacity, her feelings often burst forth faster than she can rein them in and make it impossible to hide or disguise them. This has been a key source of many social difficulties that she has encountered or created.

Dinah applied (as she still tends to) a rough all-purpose other-modelling indifferently to everyone. That included the assumption that we are all equal, which meant, for example, that she treated teachers as the same as – not superior to – everyone else. Here is what Asperger (1944, p.81) said about his case studies:

> They follow only their own wishes interest and spontaneous impulses, without considering restrictions or prescriptions imposed from outside.... They treat everyone as an equal as a matter of course and speak with a natural self-confidence. In their disobedience too their

lack of respect is apparent. They do not show deliberate acts of cheek, but have a genuine defect in their understanding of the other person.

She strongly recognised herself in this passage. If rules strike her as arbitrary, then unless she is contractually bound to obey them she will tend to ignore them. She reaches her own conclusions.

In her late twenties, probably thanks to having children, Dinah began to tune in to other people's emotions directly, started to feel what they were feeling. Before that, her feelings were affected only by other people's through reason, and her sympathy was all-purpose and universalist, as above. Now the 'on switch' has been thrown, her empathy is unfortunately equally universal, and hence she can't cope with, for example, the kind of exposure to people's pain that watching most television news entails.

Dinah was born before the statistical methods of twentieth-century psychology had established developmental timetables, generated the absurd idea that 'normal' was desirable, and pathologised atypicality. At no point in her life has any catastrophe made her the responsibility of psychiatrists or psychologists. She has always been flexible about accepting changes and surprises – she's just no good with failing to 'get it right'. Although she did lots of things as a child that are typical of children who these days attract a diagnosis of Asperger syndrome, so do most children to some extent. As Hutt *et al.* (1965) observed in the 1960s, and the diagnostic criteria confirm, the odd behaviours in autism are odd in quantity rather than quality. She probably did fewer of the other things that children do, but she did not do anything obsessively. She did not keep doing odd things that attracted unfavourable attention: she stopped skipping but kept smiling. So is Dinah really a normie? Or is she just good at staying out of trouble? Or are those the same thing?

Dinah has repeatedly found that her monotropic disposition can be turned to good account. If she knows what the task is, and she believes the task is hers, then she sets to with a will. She is capable of getting far more done than most people if she sees cause. Even though we have painted a picture of fear-driven avoidance, which she believes is perfectly correct, it is usually so succesful in keeping her away from the violently dreadful feelings that she very rarely experiences those. Hence, in practice, her general approach to life is one of bouncy confidence and get-up-and-go. But it follows that among the factors that have kept her away from diagnosis has been concealment, the opposite of the disclosure contained in this chapter and discussed elsewhere in this book. The mirroring technique clearly caused her some disquiet when she was running her social life with it. But it had important advantages: it kept open channels of communication with other people; it was a good way of learning about people and their feelings; it maintained her acceptability. Eventually, the mirror melted away, and other people got right into her head and heart and stayed there – as they are meant to.

So, am I saying 'I am an Aspie'? or even 'I am someone with Asperger syndrome' – or not? If it is a simple categorial distinction, the answer can't be yes *and* no – but it is. Tony Attwood (1997, p.145) says: 'It is recognised that the condition is on a seamless continuum that dissolves into the extreme end of the normal range. Inevitably, some children will be in a "grey area"'. I am in that grey area. As Tom Berney remarks in his learned chapter, diagnosis is an attempt to impose a categorial distinction on a multidimensional reality. So, each dimension offers a different point at which a boundary may be drawn, and it is the nature of the diagnositc criteria that each demarcation will have 'acceptable' or 'normal' on one side of the line and 'unacceptable' or 'abnormal' on the other. In the introduction to this book, Mike Lesser and I have set out a proposed analysis of these dimensions: I am here going to apply that analysis to myself.

Depth of interest

Being steeply attention-tunnelled with all your awareness narrowly focused can be a great way to learn about those objects that seize your interest. I have very rarely paid attention as wholeheartedly as that as far as I am aware. Certainly, I have always been able to switch attention as required, albeit sometimes with discomfort. Being steeply attention-tunnelled means that other people-ness may pass you by and that if other people do impinge, then it is likely to be in a loud, insistent and potentially shocking manner. My own childhood was not dogged by people trying in vain to get my attention. I thought people were interesting and I was not demotivated by how they treated me. So although my ability to focus tightly is probably greater than most people's, it is neither so great as to make me behave unacceptably nor so great as to give me any highly unusual capacities.

Breadth of focus

Sometimes I can slow myself down enough to home in on the details, to notice the light refracting through a dew drop, to notice the riff running through a piece of music, to notice the tiny fungi among the grass blades. Small intense pleasures like these are intrinsically and immediately satisfying, but for me they are rare and short-lived. People whose interests tend *always* to be detail-focused will tend to miss the bigger picture, and they will tend to behave in ways that other people find puzzling and unacceptable. The two main interests that have dominated my life – first, language, and then the relation between it and thinking – have been of immense scope. And those broad interests have not provoked behaviour that other people found puzzling or unacceptable.

Action threshold

Level of action threshold affects rate of cycling from one focal interest to another. When not driven by a topic of personal interest, I tend to move on rapidly. Even when personally engaged, I tend to switch back and forth between the leading interest and some other less demanding one. When not so engaged but needing to stay on task, I self-stabilise in various inconspicuous ways that might be thought of as 'hidden stims', e.g. trying to divide the visual field into a number of rectangular sections that is a multiple of five. Although very inattentive in class, that was so well disguised that having what my mother called a 'grasshopper mind' – and might get an attention-deficit/hyperactivity disorder (ADHD) label these days – never got me into trouble. It contributes to my making lots of connections and not missing too much of what's going on.

Rapidity of arousal

Distress arousal is so rapid and out of control that it shocks other people, disables social presentation and forces disclosure of my unacceptable face. The desire to avoid this has motivated mirroring techniques and reduced social contact. On specific occasions of meltdown, time to regain composure is the only strategy that works; without that the situation worsens.

Overall available quantity of attention

This rarely seems problematic for me during waking hours. At times of meltdown, processing capacities are overwhelmed and usable attention is dried up. Loss of confidence more generally involves a retreat into whatever seems safe and, thus, a reduction in distributed attention. Most of the time, high levels of confidence are maintained and with them plentiful attention, including extrafocal attention.

Capacity to maintain functional arousal outside the focal interest

At times of meltdown, it stops being automatic and subjectively effortless to be aware of what's going on outside my focal interest, including monitoring and adjusting to other people's behaviours and reactions. Scarcity of attention also reduces this capacity and may result either from extreme processing demands or from loss of will consequent on depression or loss of confidence. However, most of the time, my high levels of self-confidence result in a high capacity to maintain arousal outside the current focal interest, which in turn has an impact on my capacity to adapt and adjust.

Degree to which interests are socially approved

The environment I grew up in welcomed and respected my intellectual turn of mind and universalising egalitarianism and accepted such oddities as I revealed: this certainly minimised disaster and strengthened confidence. My specific interest in language and its relation to thinking has propelled me through three university degrees. The egalitarianism fitted right into family traditions and translated into political activism, which has found me many comrades over the years. Even my keen interest in fungi of all sorts is socially acceptable!

Whether or not interests have included language early in development

This is key to being socially acceptable in one's formative years, since learning to talk by a certain age tends to be seen as the *sine qua non* of proper development. I learned to talk very early and appear to have rapidly acquired a large vocabulary, confidently and competently deployed. It was not until about the age of 30 that I realised there was more to my thinking than the attention-grabbing words with which I logic-chopped; until then, I missed out completely on the potential of visual thinking, and this remains poorly developed in me.

Emotional quality

Anger and misery are disabling. Except in states of meltdown, my temperament tends to be sunny and easy-going. Generally, I have a confident and positive orientation, which is probably significantly influenced by the fact that I do only things that I expect to be good at; I almost never try again something that has gone wrong; I have minimal specific expectations on any given occasion; I repeatedly note the things and events that make me happy, seeking such in every situation. Vis-à-vis other people, I smile a lot and people tend to smile back.

Along every one of these dimensions, a small difference in temperament or circumstances could have caused a major shift in behaviours. And that shift in turn would have meant that I received the sort of negative message that tends to provoke total social shutdown in me. In declaring my status as an autistic cousin, I am acknowledging kinship not just with what Ralph Smith calls 'the shiny Aspies' but equally with those judged to be 'low-functioning'.

I was never enough of a problem as a child to be identified as needing special help or treatment. I hated drawing attention to myself unless I was perfectly certain how to proceed without 'crashing'. Being noticed as problematic was the last thing in the world that I wanted – or anticipated – and I very rarely experienced or experience that. I'd rather just be able to get on with my own projects without interference. My main, usually succesful, project for at least a decade was not getting into trouble. I would have experienced being seen as a problem or, worse still, being given a dysfunction label as catastrophic. People only started worrying about me when I was 16, and thankfully only lightly. Of course, there are lots of things I need help with, however reluctant I may be to accept that. But those gaps happen never to have precipitated the sort of crisis that would have meant my being seen as A Problem.

I did not have any awareness as I grew up of being personally distinctively different in contrast to other people, who were more 'the same' than I was. I knew it was unusual to be able to spell everything and to be able to remember whole poems, birthdays, phone numbers. Other people were unusually good at different things. In the social milieu in which I grew up, being the 'different' person who was Dinah never meant being left out, never meant being treated as alien. In this setting, nobody would have seen the goal of making children 'indistinguishable' as acceptable, never mind desirable. Later on in a wider social setting, potentially alienating differences from those around me emerged. Suddenly, I was not always welcome. I had to work out how to remain inconspicuous and continue being included; I had to work out new ways in order to avoid trouble.

As I grew up, any difference I was aware of contributed to, rather than undermined, my confidence. I knew I was a typical member of a distinguished family (Huxley) within an intellectual élite who could be eccentric to their hearts' content. I knew that the weirdest people may have the best thoughts. I grew up in a society of people with similar attitudes and values, and scarcely ever met any rebuff as I proceeded towards adulthood. My behaviour was seen as typical of a proto-philosopher, not as deviant. Even outside this narrow sphere, my areas of interest have been valued socially.

I suspect most 'autistic cousins', as well as those people more clearly on the spectrum, will have a similar sense of having grown up as members of an interesting and unusual family. With luck and care, that can give them a sense of being special in a good way and also a sense of belonging. Having my interests valued and feeling I belong seem to me the most crucial beneficial features of my life that can be duplicated. If people's interests and abilities include those that win social respect outside the family, then their confidence and motivation may be replenished rather than drained by encounters with social expectation. With these assets, they may have enough bounce to survive many more of life's blows without catastrophe.

As an adult, I do not think of myself as able to move between two worlds, the neurotypical (NT) world and the non-NT world. From where I am, no margin is apparent in the flowing tide of humanity. I generally feel as happy and comfortable with my clearly NT friends as I do with my clearly autistic ones. That said, the lack of social demand that is usual in autistic relationships is very relaxing and agreeable for me. There are all sorts of situations in which I feel rather detached from what is going on, but that does not make me feel sad or uncomfortable. It is often a good thing to be a bit detached. Those situations probably most often involve typical people doing things they find more socially rewarding than I do.

As I get older and more tired, the effort of maintaining a constantly appropriate social façade seems less and less worthwhile. So could I excuse my perhaps growing lack of social graces by referring to my autistic cousinhood? When I realise someone has been upset or put off by something I have done, should I 'disclose' that it's 'because I'm a bit of an Aspie'? That would be like claiming the right to use a wheelchair because one has occasionally twisted an ankle. I do not deserve any special consideration. However, within the world of autism studies, I'd like to see more practitioners acknowledging that they are as far from normal as I am and recognising their own kinship with the 'subjects' towards whom they tend to adopt such a superior stance. In that context, disavowing any superior status is the key to developing respect and recognition of equal personhood.

As Simone Weil put it, 'Our social personality, on which our sense of existence almost depends, is always and entirely exposed to every hazard … anything which diminishes or destroys our social prestige, our right to consideration, seems to impair or abolish our very essence.' (Weil and Raper, 1974, p.88)

If the protagonist of our story had had her social prestige destroyed, then how different her story might have been. Instead of being a carefree member of an élite, she might have been one of those embarrassing people who grunts or greets strangers inappropriately; she might have completely given up 'trying to get it right' beyond her narrow sphere of perfect control; she might have been an outcast with neither power nor influence.

The boundary that distinguishes the normal from the abnormal, wherever it applies, is always determined by the immediate previous history of the idea of normality. Every act of diagnosis and disclosure moves an individual to the officially unacceptable/abnormal side of the divide. This becomes part of the immediate history of the idea of normal and, therefore, has a potential impact on that boundary. Every instance of diagnosis in which the individual's autistic profile is etched that little bit less sharply shifts the boundary imperceptibly towards the centre; now, fewer people count as normal, although they may not know it yet. My image of this is of the great bowler-hat shape of the bell curve of normal statistical distribution. All around it, diagnosticians are wielding their expertise, excising the atypical rim. But lo! As they do so, the typical centre shrinks, and a new rim appears.

That is not a process I want to contribute to. But there is another way in which the boundary can change: instead of cramping in towards a more and more tightly delimited norm, it could be a different sort of edge. It could be a distinction between value sets. The route towards social acceptability by current standards is a route towards disguise, concealment and presentation: it's the bullshit route. It places the highest value on presentation skills; it devalues everything else in the process. We do not have to agree that those are the most acceptable values. We might see that being the sort of person who attracts an autism spectrum diagnosis is likely to mean having an honourable and scrupulous disposition and a concern for 'getting it right', which includes a concern for truth and may confer tremendous capacity for work.

If people declare themselves unable to accept the traders' values that underpin current norms, then the process is different from that of authorised diagnosis. It can be a process of acceptance rather than rejection, a process through which a cultural shift in what counts as acceptable may occur if enough socially acceptable people make this choice. If you would like to stand up and be counted as an autistic cousin yourself, please go and register your stance at www.autismandcomputing.org.uk.

References

Asperger, H. (1944) 'Autistic Psychopathy in Childhood.' In U. Frith (ed) *Autism and Asperger Syndrome.* Cambridge: Cambridge University Press.

Attwood, T. (1997) *Asperger's Syndrome: A Guide for Parents and Professionals.* London: Jessica Kingsley Publishers.

Baron-Cohen, S. (2003) *The Essential Difference: The Truth about the Male and Female Brain.* Reading, MA: Perseus Publishing.

Baron-Cohen, S., Wheelwright, S., Skinner, R., Martin, J. and Clubley, E. (2001) 'The Autism-Spectrum Quotient (AQ): Evidence from Asperger Syndrome/High Functioning Autism, Males and Females, Scientists and Mathematicians.' *Journal of Autism and Developmental Disorders,* 31, 5–17.

Hutt, S.J., Hutt, C., Lee, D. and Ounsted, C. (1965) 'A Behavioral and Electroencephalographic Study of Autistic Children.' *Journal of Psychiatric Research,* 3, 181–97.

Kanner, L. (1943) 'Autistic Disturbances of Affective Contact.' *Nervous Child*, 2, 217–50.

Opie, I. and Opie, P. (1959) *The Lore and Language of Schoolchildren*. Oxford: Clarendon Press.

Rieffe, C. Terwogt, M.M. and Stockmann, L. (2000) 'Understanding Atypical Emotions Among Children with Autism.' *Journal of Autism and Developmental Disorders*, 30, 3, 195–203.

Weil, S. and Raper, D. (1974) *Gateway to God*. Glasgow: Collins.

8.

'Why's it all so difficult?' Sharing the diagnosis with the young person

Philip Whitaker

Introduction

For many parents, the process leading to their child's diagnosis is protracted and stressful (Howlin and Moore 1997). Getting the diagnosis may bring a sense of relief and feel like the end of a difficult journey. But, of course, it is also the beginning of a different journey. As well as coping with their own reactions to the news, and continuing to carry out all their parental responsibilities, many parents will face the challenge of helping their children understand themselves and their diagnosis.

There is a growing body of research into parental experiences and perceptions of the process of diagnosis (Howlin and Moore 1997, Brogan and Knussen 2003). However, as Glenys Jones (2001) emphasises, the academic literature on autistic spectrum disorders (ASDs) contains surprisingly little about sharing the diagnosis with the young person with ASD. An extensive database search, using Medline and the Applied Social Sciences Index and Abstracts, identified substantial research into the process of informing youngsters with serious physical diseases of their diagnoses. Not a single study referring to autism was identified. We do not know the answers to even relatively simple descriptive questions, such as the proportion of young people who are told of their diagnosis, the age at which this occurs, or the considerations that lead adults to share this information. There is no objective evidence to guide parent or professional in deciding how best to undertake the task of telling a youngster with ASD about his or her diagnosis and what the possible impact will be.

Although research evidence may be in short supply, over the last several years, resources to assist those embarking on this process have become increasingly available. Based on clinical experience with children and parents, workbooks and detailed guidance have been produced by a number of writers (Vermeulen 2001; Faherty 2000; Gray 1993). The growing number of autobiographical accounts written by individuals with ASD provide significant insight into the potential benefits of sharing this information.

In this chapter, we explore the arguments in favour of sharing the diagnosis and go on to consider how this might be undertaken. Although not intended as a how-to guide, we discuss and summarise some of the key principles and strategies common to a number of the publications in this area. We also draw on the accounts of a self-selected group of 30 or so parents who met to share their experience of the process and on our experiences in Leicestershire's autism outreach team.

The challenge of explaining autism

The literature on sharing diagnoses of physical illness with young people shows clearly that this can be a complex process (Young *et al.* 2003), with significant potential for long-term psychological consequences. Arguably, the task of sharing a diagnosis of autism may be even more complex and challenging. Although ASDs are not life-threatening, the knowledge that one has a lifelong pervasive condition could certainly be viewed (and experienced) as life changing. Even before possible emotional and psychological responses are considered, there are a number of major challenges in helping individuals grasp the meaning of their diagnosis:

- Our understanding of ASDs has advanced dramatically over recent years, but uncertainty and debate persist over some very fundamental questions. When even the name of the condition remains contentious, what can be said to a child about the cause or what the future holds?

- The very concept of autism – the thing that is to be explained – is both complex and controversial in itself. It is generally accepted that it is not appropriate to think of it as an illness, but there is no consensus on whether it should be considered a disability, a difference – or even a culture (Mesibov 1997).

Personal experience and popular representations of illness provide a relatively accessible and concrete foundation for helping youngsters to understand physical conditions. They do not really pave the way for understanding something identified in terms of behavioural and psychological traits.

- Understanding the idea of the diagnosis and its personal relevance requires a relatively sophisticated degree of awareness of self and others, as well as the corresponding verbal and conceptual understanding. Youngsters need to have developed a sense of their own separateness and to have begun thinking about themselves and others in terms of the psychological qualities and characteristics that differentiate them from others. This level of social development is not generally regarded as emerging until at least the fourth or fifth year of life (Miell 1995).

- The 'autistic' way of thinking and of understanding the world also poses challenges. Jordan and Powell (1997) have argued that individuals with autism may have a very specific difficulty in developing a capacity for self-reflection, since this grows from awareness of how others see you. This limited self-awareness may make it very difficult for them to connect theoretical accounts of the nature of autism to their own experience. At a more basic level, it may be difficult to provide the level of certainty and lack of ambiguity that individuals with ASD often crave. Information may be interpreted in a very concrete way, leading to erroneous conclusions, e.g. 'People with autism like collecting things. I don't collect things, so I can't be autistic'.

These difficulties are not an argument against sharing the diagnosis. However, they do highlight the complexity of the undertaking and the importance of seeing it as an ongoing process rather than as a one-off event, with the adult gradually feeding information and ideas and helping to connect these to the individual's emerging sense of self.

Sharing the diagnosis: how can it help?

In planning this chapter, we originally intended to set out the arguments for and against sharing the diagnosis, without advocating a particular standpoint. With further thought and discussion, we have come to the view that, in all but exceptional situations, the diagnosis should be shared. At the outset, it should be noted that there are complex ethical arguments supporting youngsters' entitlement to this information (Kunin 1997), and this principle has been adopted by the British Medical Association, in relation to physical illness. However, it should be emphasised that our view is also based heavily on practical considerations – on the benefits that can result, and on the risks of not sharing this information. This is not to say that the process will necessarily be free of problems. Some individuals do react with significant levels of emotional distress. The temptation to protect an already vulnerable individual from what may be painful awareness is understandable. Nonetheless, over the longer term, it is our view that in most cases, the practical benefits of sharing the diagnosis substantially outweigh the counterarguments.

Making sense of your self and your experience

> If everyone feels like this, why am I the only one who can't cope? (Sainsbury 2000, p.126)

The majority of youngsters with ASD catered for within mainstream schools become increasingly aware of their difficulties as they move through the primary years. The challenges, failures and frustrations that they face can be compounded by a gradual realisation that their peers are coping, apparently effortlessly, with the same demands that are causing the youngster with ASD such a problem. Some will conclude that they must be stupid or crazy, while others may assume that more effort is needed, often echoing the feelings of adults around them. When this extra effort fails to make a difference, they may be led to more extreme conclusions about themselves, such as Clare Sainsbury's (2000) conclusion she must be on the verge of schizophrenia.

These experiences, and the reactions of peers (who may readily apply such labels as 'freak' or 'weirdo'), may lead some individuals to suspect that they are fundamentally different from their peers. Luke Jackson (2002, p.25) writes of 'feeling freaky on the inside'. Clare Sainsbury (2000, p.9) writes of feeling like an alien and of her childhood dream:

that one day a spaceship will fall from the sky onto the tarmac in front of me, and the people will step out and tell me, 'It's all been a dreadful mistake. You were never meant to be here. We are your people and now we've come to take you home.

Without any way of understanding this sense of being different, individuals may redouble their efforts to fit in. For some, this can feel like 'trying to be someone else' – a sense of not being true to who you really are. When this sense of discomfort is finally put into words (and only a small minority may ever articulate their experience), well-intentioned attempts to reassure can make matters worse. Clare Sainsbury writes of wondering why she was the only one not able to cope. Gunilla Gerland (2003) describes feeling 'violated'. She refers to her therapist's failure to hear what she was saying about her experience and insistence on reinterpreting what was being said in terms of her particular therapeutic outlook.

For many of the parents with whom we discussed this topic, the single most persuasive argument for sharing the diagnosis was the help it provided their children in understanding themselves and their experiences. A young man, not diagnosed until he was 24, told his father that he felt 'like he'd come out of a tunnel' when he learned of his diagnosis. Another young person talked of feeling as if he had been 'in a glass bubble' until then. Learning about the diagnosis can help make sense of the very particular and puzzling pattern of difficulties (and strengths) that are core features of ASD. One seven-year-old who had almost grown up with his diagnosis expressed the very matter of fact view that it was a useful thing to know because it helped to explain why he was distracted and distressed by too much noise. Those who have experienced difficulties over an extended period may experience a sense of relief – of no longer feeling wholly to blame for the problems they may have experienced or presented. This sense of relief may go deeper still. Gunilla Gerland writes of finally 'recognising herself' and of realising that her subjective experiences did have a basis in objective reality. Although other, less positive reactions may follow, knowledge of the diagnosis offers a way of organising what may feel like a puzzling and worrying jumble of experiences. Gerland (2003, p.238) wrote: 'One of my strongest defences … is the awareness of exactly where my problems lie: strategies, support and self-advocacy.'

The recognition that there is a pattern and a reason for one's experience and difficulties provides a foundation for the long process of learning to take responsibility for overcoming or 'working round' these vulnerabilities. Although self-management may be an ambitious and distant goal, knowledge of the diagnosis may help to shift a youngster's role towards one that is more active and (potentially) cooperative – understanding why certain things are being done in certain ways rather than being a passive recipient of 'help'. The seven-year-old referred to earlier now realises that he gets into trouble at school because he fails to recognise a particular tone in his teacher's voice – a tone that his classmates intuitively sense as a warning. He understands why his mother now works with him to help develop this skill.

Awareness of the diagnosis offers a shortcut to the growing arsenal of documented intervention and self-help strategies. It may also help the individual to identify their personal strengths and to use these to develop compensatory strategies. It offers understanding of why some situations are challenging and may allow some difficulties to be anticipated. In discussing what he terms 'affective education' for adolescents with Asperger syndrome, Tony Attwood (2004) describes helping teenagers to develop an 'emotional toolbox' – strategies that they can use to manage their stress levels. Dennis Debbaudt (2003) writes about the importance of teaching explicit strategies for reducing vulnerability and enhancing personal safety. Central to this teaching is the young person's awareness of the nature and source of their vulnerability.

With increasing age, awareness of the diagnosis can make a significant contribution to the individual's capacity to advocate for himself. Tony Attwood (2004) proposes teaching the individual to offer 'guidance' to those with whom they are interacting. The use of 'explanations' such as 'I find it easier to listen when I don't look directly at you' is suggested as a helpful way to avoid potential misunderstanding. The past several years have also seen a rise in more assertive and organised forms of self-advocacy and mutual support, undertaken by individuals and groups of people with Asperger syndrome, often making use of internet forums. Although these are made up of very diverse individuals, the shared experiences and perceptions that stem from their particular way of experiencing the world provide the organising and unifying thread in these networks.

A sense of belonging and identity

These groups also illustrate another of the psychological benefits that awareness of the diagnosis can offer – a sense of no longer being 'the only one'. Realising that there are others who share one's experience can come as a tremendous relief, and access to a real or virtual community of such individuals can be an important source of support.

Even without participation in such networks, the existence of this community and the active self-advocacy of some of its members is increasingly providing resources that may help individuals to build a positive identity. Rather than thinking in terms of 'disability' or 'disorder', it is increasingly argued that Asperger syndrome should be viewed as a 'difference' and that equal attention needs to be paid to the qualities and strengths that often typify those people with the diagnosis. This way of thinking has been carried to its logical conclusion in Attwood and Gray's (1999) reformulation of typical diagnostic checklists in terms of qualities and strengths. The autobiographical writing of those with autistic spectrum disorders, the contributions of people who speak eloquently about their experiences and the (often posthumous) diagnosis of the great and the good all offer potential for building self-esteem and sense of identity that is not dominated by notions of disability.

The difficulties of withholding the diagnosis

The majority of the parents we consulted had positive reasons for sharing the diagnosis. A number also identified practical and ethical obstacles to withholding this information. First among these was the fact that children were often aware of the assessment process and curious about its conclusion. When siblings and members of the extended family were likely to be informed of the conclusions, some parents felt very uncomfortable about concealing this information from the child and worried about the impact of this 'shared secret' on family relationships.

The prospect of 'accidental disclosure' was also a well-founded concern. The current emphasis on increased pupil participation in special educational needs processes in England and Wales makes this a real possibility. The growth of ASD-specific services for children and young people also creates an obvious risk of a youngster asking (or discovering) why they are being provided with a particular form of support. This becomes an even more important issue with the transition to adult services. The changed legal context and the prevailing ethos mean that participation on a voluntary and informed basis will be favoured, and parental rights to consultation about disclosure are likely to be very limited.

Anecdotal evidence suggests the possibility of strong reactions from adolescents and young adults who learn of their diagnosis accidentally, particularly if it becomes evident that this information has been withheld. By definition, the timing is unlikely to be ideal and no supportive process will have been established. Any emotional responses to the diagnosis are likely to be compounded by reactions to the fact that information has been withheld by the very people on whom the individual is most dependent.

Sharing the diagnosis: how

As mentioned previously, providing a young person with information about the diagnosis may be an extended process. The intellectual and emotional demands of assimilating such complex and significant information mean that selective retention, misinterpretation and misunderstanding are inevitable. Although an enormously difficult judgement to make, individuals will need to be given the type and amount of information that they are capable of processing. Their current understanding of themselves and their grasp of individual differences provide the starting points. Immediate questions and reactions may offer guidance about pacing the process and point to issues that need to be covered in more depth. It is difficult to write a detailed prescription of how to go about this, and there is no hard evidence to justify one approach over another, but there is an emerging consensus on the broad outlines of the process. What follows is not offered as a substitute for the valuable resources referred to earlier but is an attempt to distil the key principles and stages common to much of this work.

Creating a context

A number of parents reported that discussion was aided by already having created a context for helping their child think about him- or herself. Several parents of younger children described a process of what they termed 'drip feed'. This seemed to involve almost incidental reference to areas of difficulty and difference. This was often set in a wider context of deliberately trying to help their child think about his or her personal experiences and make generalisations about his or her own traits, strengths and difficulties. Where this process had been possible, the diagnostic label seems to have been treated as the final piece in a puzzle, tying together a pattern of which the child was already aware.

In *I Am Special*, Vermeulen (2001) provides guidance and worksheets to help develop the conceptual understanding that he regards as a necessary context for understanding the diagnosis. This includes awareness of differences between self and others (in terms of personal qualities and characteristics as well as physical features), some basic biological information, and ideas of disability and difference. Perhaps unsurprisingly, he suggests that a verbal developmental age of nine to ten years is required to cope with this material. In our experience, useful levels of understanding can be established with youngsters whose verbal skills are well below this level, typically by making use of the approach outlined by Carol Gray (1996) in *Pictures of Me*.

Talking about strengths and difficulties: putting the diagnosis in its place

As well as trying to give youngsters the understanding and concepts to think about themselves, Vermeulen (2001), following Gray (1996), places strong emphasis on initially exploring the individual's talents and personality. Lowe (personal communication, 2003) extends this approach by including pictures of the child at different ages and stages of his or her life, so that a sense of personal history is also fostered. This process, involving other family members and school staff, is intended to reduce the likelihood of the youngster defining themselves solely in terms of their diagnosis. The aim is to help the child to understand that having an autistic spectrum disorder is only a part of who they are.

Vermeulen in particular uses discussion of talents and strengths as a platform for then beginning to think about areas of difficulty. Depending on the child's capacity for self-reflection, these may also need to be referred to or identified in the contributions of others, set firmly in the context of positive features. From this point on, two approaches are outlined in the literature. Beginning with the specific details of the child's experience, it may be possible to draw out the strands of the triad and explain that this is a very special pattern found in individuals with ASD. Alternatively, and particularly if a youngster already has some awareness that they have a 'condition', the youngster is first given basic information about the diagnosis and the triad. There is then discussion of the light that this sheds on the individual's difficulties. Discussion of the diagnosis also opens the way to highlighting associated strengths and qualities.

Depending on the level of understanding, and interest, there is an increasing range of resources that can be used directly with youngsters. Some of these provide background information about ASDs and others enable exploration of particular difficulties. Catherine Faherty's (2000) workbook links each area of difficulty to a range of practical coping strategies. For some, the personal accounts, guidance and descriptions written by other people with ASDs may be an extremely useful source of further information, and foster a more positive image of those who share the diagnosis.

Youngsters who show limited initial reaction or curiosity will still need the opportunity to return to the topic. Spontaneous questions and expressions of concern may create an opportunity for further discussion, but individuals with ASD may be less likely to initiate this sort of dialogue. Parents will, therefore, need to be alert to distress or misunderstanding and to actively initiate further information-sharing and discussion. Even when the sharing has been initiated by a professional, parents will have a crucial and unavoidable role in a process that one mother described as 'discovering together'.

Sharing the diagnosis: when and who

In considering the difficult question of when to begin the process of sharing the diagnosis, first consideration needs to be given to the parent's readiness. Even if a professional is taking the lead in this process (and this should never be done without parental consultation and agreement), the involvement of parents in providing additional information and support is essential. In order to cope with these demands, parents need to have gone some way towards coming to terms with their own reaction to the diagnosis and to have acquired some basic information about the condition.

There is no simple formula to guide judgements about when to begin the process, but it is possible to identify some pointers:

- If a youngster has actually reached the stage of asking questions about themselves or is articulating concerns about 'being different', then this should be taken as a very clear indicator of the need to begin discussion of the diagnosis.

- Unfortunately, the absence of such questions cannot be taken as a sign that the child is not ready for, or does not need, this information. Some youngsters may be reluctant to air their concerns or, more typically, may not appreciate the need to share their distress or their questions. Others may simply be unable to articulate their concerns or experiences. As Gerland (2003) writes, 'How difficult is it to ask about something that you don't have words for?' For these reasons, it is important to monitor closely any signs that a youngster has a sense of being different from others or is experiencing stress and unhappiness that may derive from the core difficulties. Where this is apparent, it may be necessary to start the process by helping the youngster to begin talking and thinking about their experience and the patterns and threads that may run through it.

- On the basis of purely anecdotal evidence, it seems to be easier to begin the process well before adolescence. This reduces the risk of some of the more extreme reactions, when the youngster's response may be intensified by the other complications of adolescence.

- Vermeulen (2001, p.18) also highlights the need to share the diagnosis as part of preparing the individual to cope with unsupervised situations in which they may be vulnerable or with experiences where they may encounter rebuff or rejection. It could be argued that the individuals to whom he is referring (capable of a significant degree of independence) have an absolute need and right to know of their diagnosis and would probably benefit from this knowledge well before the point where they are likely to be exposed to such challenges.

- The question of whether there is such a thing as 'too early' is even more difficult to answer. Earlier, we referred to the levels of understanding that may be required to grasp fully what the diagnosis means. Youngsters without this level of awareness and understanding may simply ignore information and concepts that are beyond their grasp or have no personal relevance. The potential for problems is almost certainly less than when disclosure is left too late. Where problems do occur, they tend to arise from partial or overly concrete interpretation of complex ideas, e.g. assuming that the condition is an illness that can be caught and cured.

Almost all of the parents with whom we spoke had informed their child themselves. Some felt that this was an intrinsic part of their parental responsibility; for others, it was a natural culmination of the process of discussing their children's experiences with them. Some parents felt that they had little choice. Either circumstances had arisen that made it an immediate need, or access to professional support was not available. It is impossible to say how representative their experiences are. However, in the UK context, where appropriately experienced professionals are in short supply, it is virtually certain that very many parents take responsibility for this process.

Vermeulen recommends that parents do not undertake the task, describing it as 'a process of guidance', likening the adult role to that of therapist and arguing for this being a professional responsibility. With parents initiating the process, he claims, there is a danger of role confusion and of the person with autism coming to avoid their parents, as the bearers of bad news. The limited and obviously selective experience of our groups does not seem to confirm these worst fears, and Vermeulen certainly acknowledges the need for active, informed involvement by parents in providing ongoing support to their child. The arguments in favour of professionals taking a lead role seem much stronger in the case of adolescents, where emotional reactions may be much more intense and where there may be issues relating to earlier decisions not to disclose. Professionals will also need to take a lead where, for whatever reasons, parents feel unable to undertake this responsibility. Whether local services are resourced and organised to provide this type of input is clearly a moot point. Professionals and parents in the UK may well look enviously at some of the provision available in Sweden, where Svanfeldt (cited in Jones 2001) describes psychologists running groups specifically intended to help teenagers with Asperger syndrome come to terms with their diagnosis.

'Is there any more cheese?': coping with the aftermath

Parents and professionals often approach the business of sharing the diagnosis with understandable anxiety. There may be a desire to protect an already stressed individual from a further burden, anxiety about how the individual will react, and self-doubt about being able to provide the necessary support.

The range of reactions to news of the diagnosis is predictably wide, and individuals vary greatly in the extent and nature of the support they need. It is essential to bear in mind that the process is not simply one of factual explanation. As Vermeulen (2001, p.22) emphasises, 'this information will stir up thoughts, desires and feelings', and those undertaking this task also have a responsibility for helping the young person cope with these emotional repercussions. Several patterns emerged in our discussions of parental experience:

- Where parents had fed their child information gradually and had encouraged their child to talk and think about the kinds of difficulty typically experienced, news of the diagnosis was sometimes accepted in a relatively matter-of-fact way. The words quoted in the title of this section were one youngster's immediate response to his mother's carefully prepared explanation.

- A period of denial also seems common, sometimes lasting more than a year. Parents who had coped successfully with this situation described adopting a low-key approach. This might entail making occasional, oblique references to the difficulties (without insisting on using the term), and providing relevant written material to be read or ignored as the youngster saw fit. As children got older, there was sometimes a willingness to concede that the diagnosis had applied 'back then', while insisting that things were now much better and not actually denying the relevance of the label.

- Distress, anger and blame are not uncommon reactions, even if there is also a sense of relief, and can be intensified if the young person feels that information about the diagnosis has been unreasonably withheld. Providing the time, space and words to express what is being felt and experienced, while avoiding messages about what should and should not be felt, is at the core of providing support. This may be an impossibly demanding challenge for parents who are the focus of these powerful feelings.

- News of the diagnosis can be experienced as a damaging blow to an individual who may already have a shaky sense of self-esteem. Creating a positive context for information about the diagnosis in the way described earlier in the chapter may help to reduce this negative impact. However, as Chris Slater-Walker (2003) describes, it is important to be aware that the diagnosis may be a trigger for depression and professional help may be required.

Many parents and professionals fear that once an individual learns of their diagnosis, it may come to be used as an excuse for avoiding responsibility or demands or may contribute to lowered expectations. Indeed, this is sometimes put forward as an argument against sharing the diagnosis. Many of the parents with whom we spoke had certainly had experience of this happening, sometimes in a touchingly naive form, as with the youngster who claimed his Asperger syndrome prevented him from washing up. Parents had often developed a small repertoire of stock responses that they used to challenge this sort of thinking, and most seemed to view this danger as a minor occupational hazard rather than a fundamental reason for not sharing the diagnosis.

Who else needs to know?

Popular awareness of ASDs has developed massively over the past few years. Although the experience of many parents suggests that knowledge and understanding in schools are still very patchy, very many more teachers are at least aware of the existence of this condition. It is our experience that sharing the diagnosis with the school is always helpful, provided that school staff also have access to information, advice and support in how to cater for the particular needs of a given youngster. Not surprisingly, the benefits to school staff of knowing the diagnosis have close parallels to those experienced by parents:

- Knowledge of ASDs in general, and the particular profile of strengths and difficulties displayed by a specific child, provides crucial guidance for devising teaching and management strategies.

- Knowledge of the diagnosis enables schools to access the growing literature about autism-specific educational interventions and provision. It may also help the school to access appropriate local support services, and in some areas may be a prerequisite for doing so.

- When school staff know that a youngster has an ASD, and when this is accompanied by some understanding of the condition, it can often help them to make sense of behaviour that may be both worrying and challenging. Being able to make sense of the child's experience and difficulties can contribute enormously to successful management. Equally importantly, it may reduce the temptation to blame and the tendency to see the child as choosing to behave in a challenging or demanding way.

Youngsters with ASD often need management approaches, provision and resources that are visibly different from those required by the majority of their peers. This may particularly apply when it involves management of behaviour and can be a significant concern to mainstream staff. Anxiety about how the majority of the class will perceive any form of 'special treatment', particularly if this is framed as 'tolerating' lower standards of behaviour, is often at the root of resistance to implementing required management strategies.

These anxieties are not without foundation. However, our experience in setting up 'circles of friends' for youngsters with ASDs (Whitaker *et al.* 1998) suggests that teachers may overestimate the extent of this potential problem and that the risks can be minimised. Discussion with whole class groups (an early step in establishing a 'circle of friends') typically reveals that classmates are very aware of the ways in which youngsters with ASD are different from themselves. Other youngsters may well find the individual with ASD challenging and will sometimes express resentment about their impact on the class's activities. Particularly with older pupils, there is often a high level of recognition that the youngster with ASD may be very unhappy and highly stressed. In our experience, there is usually recognition that these individuals do need different forms of management and that different standards need to apply.

Where parents have given permission to talk openly about ASDs, or social and communication difficulties, this has helped significantly in discussing and making sense of the common threads that underlie a particular child's difficulties and needs. Needless to say, these discussions are more productive (and carry fewer risks) in schools where there is an ethos that promotes awareness of, and respect for, difference and disability. Such discussions are also helped enormously if there is a culture of open communication between staff and pupils. Directly and indirectly, pupils with ASD can make substantial demands on their classmates. Understanding why their classmate is as he or she is, combined with the experience of being listened to and having concerns acknowledged, can make a very significant impact on the levels of acceptance and support offered by the rest of the class too.

Conclusion

Some of the parents with whom we spoke, whose children had reacted negatively to news of their diagnosis, experienced periods of severe doubt about the wisdom of their decision to share this information. In the end, however, all felt that the advantages had outweighed the disadvantages. In our discussions and thinking about this issue we were repeatedly struck by the parallels between the experience of the parents and of their children. When parents talk about what drives them to seek diagnosis, or the benefits they feel this information brings, they typically refer to the help it offers in making sense of their child and in signposting the way to intervention, management and support. The opportunity to make connections with other parents in similar circumstances is also a highly valued by-product of the diagnosis. There are striking similarities between these benefits and those that individuals with the condition can derive from learning of their diagnosis. The parallels may also extend to reactions to news of the diagnosis. Many parents experience a barrage of feelings that often resemble those that follow bereavement or loss. The anger, need to blame and depression, which some individuals experience on learning of their diagnosis, can be viewed as an equivalent and entirely normal part of the process of adjusting to a life-changing experience.

The growth in practical guidance and resources and the gradual accumulation and sharing of clinical experience are to be welcomed greatly. Research is now needed to evaluate the different approaches to sharing the diagnosis, to inform the development of new strategies, and to provide guidance as to how and when to begin this process in any given case. Among professionals, there has been a necessary and understandable focus on the process of making diagnostic decisions. Professionals now need to be very much more aware of the need for information and support for those with the diagnosis. We would argue that it is often appropriate for this sharing of information to be undertaken by parents. However, it is essential that professionals are available to offer guidance and support and are able to become more directly involved when parents seek this or when individual circumstances dictate.

Acknowledgements

We are very grateful indeed to those parents who generously gave their time and shared their experiences with us. Particular thanks are due to Lindy Hardcastle and Sue Harrison of the Leicestershire Autistic Society for organising this opportunity, and to Billy Howard and his mother Ruth for sharing their insights.

References

Attwood, T. (2004) *Exploring Feelings: Cognitive Behaviour Therapy to Manage Anger.* Arlington, TX: Future Horizons.

Attwood, T. and Gray, C. (1999) *The Discovery of 'Aspie' Criteria.* www.tonyattwood.com.au

British Medical Association (2001) *Consent, Rights and Choices in Health Care for Children and Young People.* London: BMJ Books.

Brogan, C.A. and Knussen, C. (2003) 'The Disclosure of an Autistic Spectrum Disorder.' *Autism* 7,1, 31–46.

Debbaudt, D. (2003) 'Safety Issues for Adolescents with Asperger Syndrome.' In L.H. Willey (ed) *Asperger Syndrome in Adolescence: Living with the Ups, the Downs and Things in Between.* London: Jessica Kingsley Publishers.

Faherty, C. (2000) *Asperger's ... What Does it Mean to Me?* Arlington, TX: Future Horizons.

Gerland, G. (1997) *A Real Person: Life on the Outside.* London: Souvenir Press.

Gray, C. (1996) *Pictures of Me.* Jenison, MI: Jenison Public School.

Gray, C. (1993) *The Original Social Story Book.* Arlington, TX: Future Horizons.

Howlin, P. and Moore, A. (2003) 'Diagnosis in Autism.' *Autism* 1, 135–62.

Jackson, L. (2002) *Freaks, Geeks and Asperger Syndrome: A User Guide to Adolescence.* London: Jessica Kingsley Publishers.

Jones, G. (2001) 'Giving the Diagnosis to the Young Person with Asperger Syndrome or High Functioning Autism: Issues and Strategies.' *Good Autism Practice* 2, 65–74.

Jordan, R. and Powell, S. (1997) *Understanding and Teaching Children with Autism.* Chichester: John Wiley and Sons.

Kunin, H. (1997) 'Ethical Issues in Pediatric Life-Threatening Illness: Dilemmas of Consent, Assent, and Communication.' *Ethics and Behaviour* 7, 43–57.

Mesibov, G. (1997) Unpublished communication during 3-day TEACCH training.

Miell, D. (1995) 'Developing a Sense of Self.' In P. Barnes (ed) *Personal, Social and Emotional Development of Children.* Oxford: The Open University /Blackwell Publishers.

Sainsbury, C. (2000) *Martian in the Playground: Understanding the Schoolchild with Asperger Syndrome.* London: The Book Factory.

Slater-Walker, G. and Slater-Walker, C. (2003) *An Asperger Marriage.* London: Jessica Kingsley Publishers.

Vermeulen, P. (2001) *I Am Special: Introducing Children and Young People to their Autistic Spectrum Disorder.* London: Jessica Kingsley Publishers.

Whitaker, P., Barratt, P. and Joy, H. *et al.* (1998) 'Children with Autism and Peer Group Support.' *British Journal of Special Education,* 25, 60–64.

Young, B., Dixon-Woods, M., Windridge, K.C., Heney, D. (2003) 'Managing Communication with Young People who have a Potentially Life Threatening Chronic Illness: Qualitative Study of Patients and Parents.' *British Medical Journal* 326, 305.

9.

Telling peers at school about Asperger syndrome: thoughts on how and why

Heta Pukki

There is no single answer for all schools and all children when it comes to telling peers about Asperger syndrome (AS) or any other autistic spectrum diagnosis. For one thing, you have to accept that some very sick environments exist, and that there may be very little you can do if you and your child are dealing with one. It always seems to me that in course materials and books people are talking about an ideal world; that teachers and other children just need to be told, and they will automatically be nice and reasonable. I would suggest a thought experiment: imagine yourself there, whether you actually are on the autistic spectrum or not. Imagine the worst bully you knew at school, the most stuck-up, selfish kid you ever encountered, one you could never get on with. Imagine someone in your adult life – a difficult boss, a jealous colleague, a suspicious neighbour. Imagine a situation in which you have done something embarrassing and need to explain it somehow. Place yourself face to face with one or more of these people and start telling them. Try looking a completely unreasonable person in the eye, and starting with: 'I have a neurological condition.' What is their reaction? Can you easily think of words to explain further, in such a way that the person will listen and understand, will not think you've gone insane, will not think you're asking for sympathy? If you put some thought into this, you will probably come up with different words to use with each person, depending on how you perceive their attitude and level of comprehension.

While studying autism-related special education, I read about one approach in which the whole class is given a lesson on different learning styles (Winter 2003). It's the only suggestion I've seen so far that I feel I can wholeheartedly recommend, without reservations. All pupils in the class get to think about their own preferences, strengths and weaknesses, and the distributions of these are visualised. The autistic child will be seen as a fairly extreme case perhaps, but still as just another child who can be described in the same terms as everyone else. The words 'autism' or 'AS' do not need to be used. I think this approach would cause no harm in most situations and groups, because the autistic child is not made a target by subjecting him or her to things that others don't have to go through. Everyone is being observed.

This does not mean that I think an autistic spectrum diagnosis is something to be ashamed of, something we should hide from the world. I'm all for autistic adults' right to diagnosis – independent of any current perceived or assumed 'clinically significant' level of suffering or dysfunction – and for wearing the label proudly to resist negative stereotyping. I just don't think that anything can be gained by forcing a person to take a similar stand. A young child cannot make an informed decision on this, and I feel that giving the diagnostic term to the peers early on actually takes away an important chance to make a choice and learn assertiveness later. Using the labels as such with peers can only lead to them becoming nasty names to call someone. They have no informative value for children. What children do pick up, however, are subtle implications and associations of inferiority, loss of status and disease, which tend to go with anything defined medically. Pointing out concrete differences – that this kid draws better than you but is not as good at catching a ball, that he or she prefers quiet games while you prefer noisy activities – is something children will understand intuitively. This kind of approach communicates something of the real meaning of the difference, instead of vague and faulty associations. I might add one thing to the lesson on learning styles and preferences if the child with AS is very obviously different and already a focus of attention in the classroom: point out that this child is somewhat unusual, but there are others like him or her and it's nothing to worry about – it's just a relatively rare combination of talents and preferences.

I've done systematic observation of two school-age children with ASD in school environments, in addition to my own daughter (five years old, day-care/preschool situation, as is common in Finland at that age). One realisation I gained from those experiences, something I never saw mentioned in special education materials is that we have to consider the *other* children's rights. It's in everyone's best interests, in the long run. The children who face an autistic peer are confused. I saw the kind of confusion I must have caused as a child, and I felt that this was not something that autistic children would consciously choose to do to their peers. Both sides need to be given ways to process the differences they see and feel but cannot name. I've written some social stories and made attempts to use them, but during that process I kept thinking that this should really be done with the whole class too. The problem is in the group, not in the individual, so they should all be allowed to contribute to the story, which may become a solution. I felt like I was trying to ask questions and solve problems that were really theirs to ask and solve.

Usually, children get to know a peer and define him or her as safe through social play. If they can't find other ways to do this, they will tease the autistic peer until they get a response that they understand, until a description or definition has been produced that makes that child an integrated part of their culture. I tend to think in terms of sociological theory here, particularly that of Corsaro (1997), who describes play as a way to reshape and re-create cultural meanings and practices. As I see it, an important implication of this theory is that it can be beneficial to offer children descriptions that they can use to process the things that are hard to grasp. This should be a subtle, ongoing process of naming situations, feelings and actions arising from and supporting the children's own attempts to do the same; it should not be a one-off passing of information from those who know, i.e. authority figures, to those who don't know, i.e. the autistic child's peers. Information that is just handed down will be misunderstood, forgotten or resisted. In fact, the child's peers, more than anyone else, possess important insider information about how this particular autistic child fits in with this unique group of children. Ideally, they should be observed, and from the observations – collected as notes, perhaps, over long periods of time – the adults should gain the knowledge of exactly what the children need to be told and when. One book with a TEACCH (Treatment and Education of Autistic and related Communication handicapped CHildren) style approach outlines one way to do this effectively for the autistic child (Faherty 2000). The question of friends being told is presented, but it is limited to *whether* the friends should know or figuring out *which* friends should know, not *how* to provide them knowledge in an individual and meaningful way.

How do you know *when* to approach the peers at school? I feel that the timing can be crucial. I've done a relatively small amount of observing, but I had the advantage of not having any other duties to attend to. I could pay really close attention to the interaction between the autistic children and their peers. In these situations, I got the impression that, essentially, you just have to keep your eyes and ears open. Sometimes the children will simply ask; sometimes they look confused and go quiet; sometimes they act out when they feel confused. This is when clarification could work best, the abstract information becoming a solution to a practical problem. Are you allowed to react if the autistic kid licks things at lunch and you think it's gross? Are you allowed to tickle the autistic child if it produces really funny results? After all, tickling is play. Is it acceptable to tell off an autistic friend for intruding on your private chat with your new best mate, when everyone else has already learned to obey subtle unspoken signals? These kinds of questions were obviously in the air but not voiced. The children were not sure whether they were acceptable questions, or they could not pinpoint the cause of their own confusion, or they could not put the question into words. It's these details that children need to learn. These little situations give the terms content and meaning. They determine whether autism, AS or other clinical terms, when they are learned, become synonymous with scary, incomprehensible, annoying, idiot, generally someone to be avoided – or simply someone interesting who requires a different mode of communication.

I feel that all information that is given to peers should be given to the autistic child as well. If it seems that it's over the child's head or could be taken as an insult, I'd say rewrite it. The children construe their meanings together. No matter how withdrawn the autistic child may seem, there is always interaction. It does not help if they have different vocabularies, or the peers feel superior, in league with adults in order to control a 'difficult' peer. It only leads to them taking authority roles, which is not likely to go down well with intelligent autistic children. I have some reservations about approaches like the 'circle of friends' (Whitaker *et al.* 1998) because of this, although I can see that they can bring great benefits too if used in a sensitive way.

Reading about other people's experiences in special schools, and having seen my credibility sink almost visibly in some people's eyes when they learn about my diagnosis as an adult, I'm profoundly grateful that I was not diagnosed as a child. It could have taken so much energy to fight against condescending attitudes, conscious or unconscious. I'm not going to expose my daughter to that if I can avoid it. I instruct the nursery staff the best I can, but I tell them not to even try to explain autism to the other children without me being there to advise them how to do it. In our case, this has not even been attempted yet. It's not always easy communicating what I want to be done. I haven't always met eye to eye with special education professionals or well-meaning social workers. To some of them, I think, I'm forever a suspect. They have gone to a couple of short courses on ASDs, perhaps, and have learned that I lack common sense, that I have difficulty recognising emotions (maybe they assume this applies in my relationship with my daughter) and, most importantly, that children with ASD need regularity and structure. So they worry about me not bringing my daughter in at the same time every morning. They do social play in the mornings. Can't I see that it's important? Of course, but she is an irregular sleeper, often very slow getting dressed in the mornings, and throws tantrums when pushed to go faster than she feels comfortable. Can't they see I have to balance several things, not just stick to a single rule? Don't they understand that a child who kicks and screams is not in the right state of mind to learn social skills? Such questions do not always seem to reach them or do not seem to be considered important enough to require answers. It's a familiar feeling I get in many other situations too, like I'm speaking a foreign language. I feel I'm making sense, but it's just so incredibly slow to get the point across. They keep repeating how very important structure is. A plan that was written to define my daughter's support needs at the daycare setting states that she 'will be brought to the nursery at the agreed time'. It's hard not to get stuck in a defence position, an attitude of constant opposition, when you feel your words are not getting heard because people have some superficial stereotypical view of what you are. It's a long work of diplomacy. I have to somehow communicate who I am before I can trust them to work with me, to teach other children who my daughter is.

With children, I think the whole matter of telling should not be just one big revelation, coming out of the closet and that's it – things have suddenly changed. Adults can choose to do that if they like. Some may even enjoy such drama, or it may serve some practical purpose. Adults in the workplace can be expected to take some responsibility and be active in learning about the autistic spectrum, working on their misconceptions. With children, however, I feel it should be a number of parallel processes. You wait and observe. You coach and prepare a child to understand the differences, to have a strong sense of self, to recognise and defend against teasing, condescension and prejudice, without resorting to aggressive means. You look for situations where the staff and peers might be open to receiving new information. You prepare to repeat yourself endlessly; you redefine, explain, give concrete examples, keep breaking the stereotype. There's no point in giving a name to a misperception and leaving it at that. It doesn't help to just say it's a disability or a neurological difference, if the person receiving this information has no real sense of what these actually mean. It's best to be prepared to do a lot of talking, if you intend to do any at all. For me, allies have been invaluable. I've learned to let people with professional credibility back up what I say, instead of stubbornly expecting everyone to learn to take me seriously despite my own peculiarities. This has saved some time and effort with professionals who have a lot of faith in authority figures and who expect meaningful information only from people they perceive as being above them. It's not an ideal situation, but I would recommend that parents use the help of sympathetic experts whenever possible, rather than stress themselves out unnecessarily.

References

Corsaro, W.A. (1997) *The Sociology of Childhood.* Thousand Oaks, CA: Sage Publications.

Faherty, C. (2000) *Asperger… What Does it Mean to Me?* Arlington, TX: *Future Horizons.*

Whitaker, P., Barratt, P., Joy, H., Potter, M. and Thomas, G. (1998) 'Children with Autism and Peer Group Support: Using Circles of Friends.' *British Journal of Special Education* 25, 60–64.

Winter, M. (2003) *Asperger Syndrome: What Teachers Need to Know.* London: Jessica Kingsley Publishers.

10.

Disclosure at secondary school: sharing the news of Asperger syndrome with a young person's peer group

Penny Barratt

It is sometimes suggested that school life, and in particular secondary school life, must be the most difficult time in the life of a person with Asperger syndrome or autistic spectrum disorder (ASD). Why might this be? If we consider what it might be like for a person with Asperger syndrome in a theoretical secondary school environment, then we might be provided with some of the answers. There are a very large number of people in close proximity who accidentally push or touch in corridors. They make a lot of noise. You come into contact with a wide range of different people – adults who have differing standards and each one treats you differently (what one thinks is funny, another tells you off for) and peers who often vary their attitude towards you based on their mood. Even if they are consistent in their own behaviour, this varies from peer to peer – one might be consistently nice, one consistently not nice (and this is not just associated with gender, which would make it easier to understand). There are some really stimulating displays on the walls, but they are so interesting and attractive that it is difficult not to focus on these and instead to focus on what the teacher is saying. A lot of the time, you exist within a general sense of chaos. This profile is provided as a suggestion of how things might be for a person with Asperger syndrome, based on personal discussions with young people with Asperger syndrome and autobiographies such as those by Grandin and Scarieno (1986), Williams (1992), Sainsbury (2000), Gerland (2000) and Jackson (2002).

It is into this hotbed of experiences and feelings that we might be looking to share the news of a young person's Asperger syndrome. Are we wise? Is this the right thing to do? How can we ensure a positive response to the information?

This chapter will look at the issues surrounding the timing for informing the peer group, what information should be shared, and how. There is surprisingly little literature on this. In recent years, work has been published on discussing diagnosis with the young person (Jones 2002) and how to best support families (Randall and Parker 1999). There seems to be an underlying assumption in the general literature on supporting youngsters in schools that discussing their needs with their peer group might be beneficial, but there is no real discussion about when or how this should be done.

In practice, I have found that sharing the news with peers usually takes place in a secondary school setting. One reason for this is that the label of Asperger syndrome is often not given until the young person is in their early teens.

I do not argue about whether or not the peer group should be informed, as I will present the case that in all situations work should be undertaken with the peer group on understanding each other better. This is the beginning of sharing the information, but at its 'softest' edge. This metaphor is borrowed from Dennis Debbaudt, a fellow contributor to this book.

Points for consideration before sharing the news

The topic under discussion is that of sharing information with a young person's peer group. If we use terms with negative implications, such as 'disclosure' and 'diagnosis', with young people, then we may be setting ourselves hurdles to overcome in the young people's understanding, which would not be there if we avoided these terms. I therefore prefer to use the term 'sharing the news'.

There are a wide range of strategies that can be used for sharing the news, and the news can be shared with and by a number of different people. However, there are stages to this process. The first is to consider how much should be shared. Once the decision has been made to share some information with the peer group, there are further factors to be considered in order to decide the most appropriate strategy to use and who should do it.

Parents'/carers' views

I agree with Jordan and Jones (1999) when they suggest that the timing for sharing this information with the peer group must be determined by the young person with Asperger syndrome and their parents/carers. They may be informed by discussions with staff from school or other professionals involved with the young person, but the decision on sharing the information and when it takes place must, ultimately, be theirs.

There are a number of considerations to make from the parents'/carers' point of view. If they are new to the terminology themselves, they may be developing their own understanding, and they will need time to do this before passing on the information to others. Once the parents/carers know, they may feel the need to share the information with those around them who can support them in the first place. This may be family and/or close friends.

The young person

It is particularly important that a young person with Asperger syndrome is given time and appropriate support in order to understand what Asperger syndrome is and what it means for them before this information is shared with their peer group. It should not be assumed, just because they have been told of the term, that they understand its implications. I have found that once young people are informed of the label applied to them, they are often expected to deal with it and take it on board very quickly. In fact, however, given the difficulties that having Asperger syndrome means they will have, they are likely to have greater difficulty understanding the terminology and need a longer time to adjust and develop an insight into what it means. They may well need support in doing this from either their parents or professionals, or both.

If you or I were diagnosed with cancer, we would expect to be the ones to decide who was told and how and when they were told. We are likely to involve those closest to us, for example our parents, in this decision-making process, but in conjunction with us. Imagine how you would feel if your parents or the doctor told others of your cancer before you had been told yourself or been given time to come to terms with what living with cancer meant for you.

I see the decision to share the information of Asperger syndrome in the same way. It requires informed consent from both the parents of the young person with Asperger syndrome and the young person themselves. Some would argue that it can be difficult to gain informed consent from some young people with Asperger syndrome. I agree that it can be difficult, but that time and effort must be put into developing their own understanding of their difficulties, and true informed consent must be gained before one proceeds to share any information with the peer group.

Community

Schools are large social institutions that sit within the communities they serve. Information shared in a school will automatically be information shared with a community. It would be illogical to assume that information can be shared in a school and remain only with the personnel involved in the school. Information, such as the application of the term Asperger syndrome, once shared in school becomes public shared knowledge within the community. The young person with Asperger syndrome and their parents/carers must be aware of this and make a conscious decision to make this information public. They must consider the repercussions of the information becoming public, because once shared the information cannot be withdrawn. It is impossible to return to how things were before sharing the news.

Informed consent of both the parents and the young person means that they will have thought about, and discussed the likely outcomes of, sharing this news with peers and the effects this may have in the community. They need to have considered what might happen and how they will deal with potential outcomes. This means considering how to handle responses ranging from the parent of another student who comes up to them in the street and says 'I've heard, I'm so sorry', to potential taunts of others.

The community can do a lot of good. They can provide a lot of support. They can also do a lot of damage. In sharing the information with the peer group, we have to ensure we utilise public good will and not alienate members of the community.

The school perspective

It is likely that personnel from the school will have their own perspective on whether the information of Asperger syndrome should be shared with the students. Some may feel that all children should be respected for who they are and may not be in favour of sharing of labels. Others may see the identification process as an answer to some of the problems that are being presented in school. In practice, the sharing of the information alone does not lead to long-term change in the way other young people see or interpret the behaviours of the young person with Asperger syndrome. This needs to be followed by other processes that are integrated into the working life of the school and, hence, requires a commitment from school staff, which should be explicit and understood before the information is shared.

The history of the young person within the school, and the empathetic response of the peer group

At this point, I am assuming that the decision has been made to share some news with the peer group. It is now very important to consider the history the young person has within the peer group. Is the person very withdrawn, and do they avoid social contact? Are they prone to self-harming behaviour such as banging their head against their desk in front of others? Do they present challenging behaviours? If so, are these aimed at inanimate items, adults or the peer group? Does anyone get hurt during these episodes? Can odd or challenging behaviours be understood easily by others, or do they appear to be extremely bizarre? Does the young person have special interests that they talk about? Do they make social gaffs?

I do not wish to portray a negative picture of youngsters with Asperger syndrome in asking the above questions, but it can be seen that there are many different presentations (only some of which have been suggested above), and the way in which the news is shared must in part be based on the presentation of Asperger syndrome that other students are party to in this particular circumstance.

It is unlikely that news of Asperger syndrome will be shared blind. This does happen on rare occasions, such as when a student is moving to a new school and the peer group is told of their Asperger syndrome before the person arrives at school, but this is the exception rather than the rule. It is far more likely that the young person already has a history within the school. The peer group is likely to have some expectations of the young person's behaviour and to have developed certain attitudes about that young person. What this history is, and how the peer group respond, is very important when considering how to share the news. Responses of peer groups to the same presenting behaviours vary tremendously, and so the planning for how to share the news must also take into consideration the natural response of the peer group before hearing the news as well as the presentation of Asperger syndrome in this case.

Some peer groups are very understanding and empathetic. They interpret behaviours as being a reflection of a difficulty that the young person with Asperger syndrome is having and in some circumstances go some way to trying to support them through their difficulties. In other situations, because behaviours appear odd and different, the young person with Asperger syndrome is mocked and taunted or ignored. The strategies employed in order to share the information need to take into account the natural empathetic response of the peer group. Some strategies encourage empathy and set up systems to develop this further. These may be needed in situations where there is little empathy at present. Other strategies just share information and rely on natural empathy to prevail. In my opinion, it never hurts to encourage the empathetic response of the peer group.

School systems and culture

Readers who have visited a range of different schools will appreciate not only that they are all physically different but also that they all feel different. Some are very curriculum-focused, while others place a really strong emphasis on pastoral support and student welfare. In some schools, you get a sense that the teachers are very much in charge and there is a strong overtone of discipline; in others, there seems to be an air of mutual respect between staff and pupils, and there is clear evidence, perhaps through displays, that the students contribute to some of the decision-making processes within the school. These are features of the school culture and will be reflected in the systems operating in the school. Schools that have a strong emphasis on pastoral support and student welfare often have systems in place to support this. This may include a very strong tutor system with opportunities for personal discussion and target-setting and a strong personal, social and health education (PSHE) curriculum, with a focus on understanding a range of learning styles and a real celebration of diversity and understanding of citizenship, which pervades all curriculum areas and is written into all schemes of work. Some schools use teaching approaches that encourage this sort of work, e.g. 'circle time'. It is important to know whether schools are using such strategies, as these are useful mechanisms through which to share the news.

It is easier to use a strategy that encourages an empathetic response in schools where, through the pervading school culture, students are encouraged to be empathetic and tolerant. These strategies can also be used in schools where students are less used to discussing emotions and empathy openly but here they may need to be presented in a different way.

It is important for the person who is going to share the news with the peer group to have visited the school on several occasions and considered which strategy to use for sharing the news and how to use this strategy based on these visits. If students are used to circle time or group discussion, then it is sensible to use these. If they are not used to these strategies but rather are used to receiving information from the front of the classroom, then an adaptation of this teaching approach may need to be employed. It is important for the young people to get the message and hear the news, and so the strategy for passing on the information should be fairly familiar to them, otherwise they will focus on the mechanism for sharing the news rather than on the news itself.

Strategies for sharing the news

In his chapter in this book, Dennis Debbaudt refers to 'soft disclosure' and 'hard disclosure'. Using this phraseology, the strategies suggested here vary in their softness and hardness. Because of many of the issues relating to the wider community, which I discussed earlier, my preference is for a softer disclosure where this is feasible. However, this is not always possible, and in some situations a hard disclosure is necessary. The strategy used, and its degree of softness or hardness, should be determined by consideration of all of the factors discussed previously. Softer strategies should include those that do not require the disclosure of the label, just some of the features of Asperger syndrome. There are a range of strategies that address this requirement, including:

- buddy systems (Cumine *et al.* 1998; Hughes and Carter 2005)
- circle of friends (Whitaker *et al.* 1998; Newton and Wilson 2003)
- assembly on difference
- assembly on social and communication difficulties
- lessons on learning styles
- circle-time sessions on differences (Mosley 1993; Mosley and Tew 2001).

Another consideration should be how often the students need to hear the message. Should this be part of an ongoing programme or a one-off event? This should, again, be informed by the discussion above, particularly with consideration of the school systems and culture and how much support school staff are likely to give to this sharing of the news. Strategies that spend more than one session on the issue of sharing the news are:

- circle of friends (Whitaker *et al.* 1998; Newton and Wilson 2003)
- lessons on learning styles
- circle-time sessions on difference (Mosley 1993; Mosley and Tew 2001)
- tutor sessions referring to a booklet on social and communication difficulties (Barratt and Thomas 1999).

If only one session is likely to be given, then some careful thought needs to be given to how follow-up can occur through systems already operating in the school – questions and answers during tutor time and follow-up PSHE lessons are examples of how this might happen.

In situations where hard disclosure is necessary, strategies that might be used are:

- an assembly on Asperger syndrome (I have seen this work extremely successfully, where the assembly was taken by the young person's brother)

- a talk about what Asperger syndrome is, describing the full range of potential strengths/difficulties/behaviours and using the young person in question to illustrate points

- a talk given by the young person with Asperger syndrome.

It is not within the scope of this chapter to provide lesson plans and scripts for each of these strategies, but to illustrate the points I have made previously I will briefly describe a few case studies and the strategies that were used to share the news in each of these cases.

Maria

Maria attended a local secondary school that used circle time on a regular basis during tutorial sessions. After discussion with her, her parents and the staff at the school, it was agreed that we would do some work with her tutor group in the hope that they would be more empathetic when situations arose. At this time, Maria was involved in a few 'incidents', but the biggest issue was her lack of friends. She wanted friends but didn't know how to go about getting them.

Three sessions were delivered through circle time with the whole tutor group. The first focused on our own strengths and difficulties; the second on difficulties and disabilities, naming people with disabilities who the students knew, what these disabilities were and asking any questions to clarify concerns; and the third on what you could do to support someone with difficulties or a disability. Maria was part of the group. She chose not to declare her Asperger syndrome. Despite this, when the students looked at what they could do to support someone with difficulties, two of the groups chose to talk about difficulties that Maria had and how they could support her.

This was an extremely 'soft' and subtle approach, but at the time it worked and did not necessitate the hard disclosure.

Shortly after these sessions, there was an incident involving Maria misinterpreting a social situation, which upset some of the members of the tutor group. In the next tutorial session, the tutor dropped what she was going to do and a circle-time session took place, where every member of the group, including Maria, was given the chance to say what was bothering them – those who wanted to could then suggest solutions.

This worked very effectively and was accepted by all, including Maria, as a resolution to the problem.

During adolescence, Maria's difficulties became more pronounced, challenging and different in the secondary school setting. A group of girls who had been part of the tutor group during the earlier sessions stuck by her and continued to try and support her, even when her behaviour became extremely challenging. It was agreed by all the concerned parties that in order to maintain their support, it was time for the hard disclosure. This was done through a presentation on what Asperger syndrome is using some of Maria's behaviour to illustrate points. The girls were extremely empathetic, appreciative that the news had been shared with them, and wonderfully supportive following this session.

This case study provides an example of the degree of softness or hardness of the information shared being varied according to need, even with the same young person, and that there is not always a need to go in hard to start with.

Nathaniel

Nathaniel attended a school where a buddy system was already in operation. Older students in the school had volunteered to become buddies to support some of the younger students in the school. The students to be buddies could self-nominate or could be nominated by their tutor. The buddies received six hours' training and had to pass a role-play situation before being awarded a certificate stating their competence as a buddy. This training was generic and was not linked to disability in any way. The buddies learnt listening skills, how to approach young people who may be distressed, and how to encourage students to talk to them. They also learnt about confidentiality, child-protection issues and when they must refer on to adults. The buddies were provided with group supervision sessions once a week.

Nathaniel was assigned a buddy. Staff were aware that Nathaniel was described as having Asperger syndrome. However, this information had not been shared with Nathaniel's peers. Nathaniel himself was only just developing an understanding of this term. Nathaniel's behaviour was extremely withdrawn. He did not choose to talk to his peer group and only initiated conversations with adults or much older peers. Aside from this, he did not appear particularly different to his peers.

Nathaniel met with his buddy at a prearranged time twice a week. It took quite a while for Nathaniel to discuss anything other than facts about school or his particular interest (time zones around the world) with his buddy. This was frustrating for his buddy, who would raise this at supervision meetings. Nathaniel seemed to gain something from this 'special relationship', even though it was not obvious at the time. He later talked about being different and even later still discussed having Asperger syndrome with his buddy. His buddy was aware that this was not something to discuss during group supervision and went to the adult facilitator of the buddies for support. Nathaniel and his buddy were able to learn together about Asperger syndrome.

In Nathaniel's case, further sharing of the news was not felt to be necessary. He needed support to understand his disability. But once this was provided, although he could not overcome his difficulties, he learnt to develop strategies that masked many of the difficulties in front of his peer group.

It is questionable whether the buddy system could even be counted as a mechanism for sharing the news. If so, it is at the softest end of the continuum. However, I have included it as an example, as it can often be a place to start, particularly if the young person or his or her parents are not ready for the news of Asperger syndrome to be shared. The buddy system can provide some support in the interim.

A brief note for those reading this chapter who are keen to initiate buddy systems in their schools or schools they know of: the initial training and the weekly supervision meetings are essential. This is a system of support that requires support. It is not the same as matching one peer to support a youngster with Asperger syndrome. This in my experience does not work – the supporter becomes fed up of supporting and not getting much back in return. They also need supporting.

Usman

Usman was aware of having Asperger syndrome but did not want others to know about it at this point. He was still learning to understand it for himself. His behaviour in school was odd. He would make frequent social gaffs, but despite this he was well liked by the other students, who wanted to help him but didn't know how to. Usman liked talking to others.

It was decided to establish a 'circle of friends'. This required informed consent from both Usman and his parents but did not require the term 'Asperger syndrome' to be used. The adult doing the initial talk does not declare the features of the young person's disability: these are named by the fellow students. The young people were asked to identify Usman's strengths and areas of difficulty. They were extremely positive about his strengths, coming up with the most obscure strengths. They were also extremely perceptive about his areas of difficulty. They named many of the difficulties associated with Asperger syndrome but did not need a label to pin them on. As part of the session, the whole group came up with some strategies and ideas that would help with Usman's areas of difficulty. Staff at the school had predicted that the students would suggest that Usman change some of the things he did; however, the students seemed to understand intuitively that this was not always possible and made suggestions for things they could do to make things easier for Usman. Some of the students then volunteered to be a part of Usman's 'circle of friends', which met weekly during lunch time. Six students met with Usman and an adult facilitator from the school to discuss what had been going on and to make suggestions for how things could be improved. The peer group made suggestions that only they could implement – they were not things an adult could do easily, e.g. play football at break time, and they were not things an adult could easily request the peer group to do. Because the ideas came from the peer group, they stuck to them and implemented them. They made tremendous changes for Usman at school.

In this case, acknowledgement of Usman's difficulties and drafting in peer support were all that were necessary as far as sharing the news went. They did not need a label to explain Usman's behaviours at this point.

If you would like to implement circles of friends, please see Whitaker *et al.* (1998) and Newton and Wilson (2003). I would not suggest using this strategy for a young person who does not already appear somewhat different to the peer group, as the process of establishing the circle does identify them as different.

Deon

Deon was transferring from primary to secondary school, and considerable difficulties were predicted. He had a history of challenging behaviour and complaints from other parents at his primary school. Deon's parents had not yet told him of the label applied to him, so it was not thought appropriate to share the news in full with the new peer group.

In this situation, a booklet was written to provide a reference point for the peer group (Barratt and Thomas 1999). It was not a booklet on Asperger syndrome; nor was it a booklet describing Deon's difficulties. There were other students in the school with Asperger syndrome, and the booklet was used with their tutor groups as well. It was a generic booklet. It was written based loosely on Davies (1993), written to explain the diagnosis to siblings. Davies writes in language appropriate to the audience and with suitable and amusing illustrations. This model was adopted. The booklet was written referring to students with social and communication difficulties, explaining their difficulties and suggesting ways in which peers could help. The parents of Deon and the other students with Asperger syndrome were consulted on the use of the term 'social and communication difficulties' and all agreed. There were also suggested activities to help the peer group to understand the difficulties and to come up with suggestions for support. These were put in the booklet in particular to support the tutors.

These booklets were used as part of PSHE (personal, social, health and education) lessons initially, during the delivery of a module on understanding differences and disabilities. The students identified for themselves that Deon had social and communication difficulties. However, because the information was delivered in a sensitive way, this was not used against him. When incidents occurred, the youngsters were encouraged to re-look through the booklets and ask any questions they had during tutor time. This helped them to understand better the difficulties Deon had and also to come up with strategies to support him in the future. A request for a tutor session looking at the booklets could be made by either the tutor or the students. The booklets were kept by the tutor in the tutor room and were always available.

This strategy supported Deon well during his transition and first year at secondary school. Later, other, 'harder' strategies were implemented.

Final thoughts

It could be asked why are we telling the peer group anything? Why should they respond positively? Why should they support their peer? What's in it for them?

I have a couple of responses to these questions. One is located firmly in an argument surrounding the purpose of schooling. If we feel that the purpose of schooling is about producing the workforce of the future, and solely this, then we are not likely to be very sympathetic to ideas of sharing news such as this, as there is no obvious benefit. However if we hold that 'education should help individual students to develop their personal potential so that they are prepared to be creative, self-motivated lifelong learners who are effective problem-solvers, able to communicate and collaborate with others, and to meet the varied challenges they will encounter in their adult lives' (Fink and Stoll 1998, p.310), then it can be seen clearly that supporting young people with Asperger syndrome through the varied strategies suggested and discussed previously can be of benefit to all students.

My second response is based on the way we view disability (Mittler 2000). If we identify with the medical view of disability, then we locate the problem in the young person with the disability, Asperger syndrome in this case. It is their problem. However, if we identify with the social model of disability, then we acknowledge that people with disabilities, including Asperger syndrome, are part of our society, and it is everyone's responsibility to look at any difficulties they face and address them.

References

Barratt, P. and Thomas, B. (1999) 'The Inclusion of Students with Asperger Syndrome in a Mainstream Secondary School: A Case Study.' *Good Autism Practice*, September, 65–71.

Cumine, V., Leach, J., and Stevenson, G. (1998) *Asperger Syndrome: A Practical Guide for Teachers.* London: David Fulton Publishers.

Davies, J. (1993) *Able Autistic Children – Children with Asperger Syndrome: A Booklet for Brothers and Sisters.* Revenshead: Early Years Diagnostic Centre.

Fink, D. and Stoll, L. (1998) 'Educational Change: Easier Said than Done.' In A. Hargreaves, A. Lieberman, M. Fullan, and D. Hopkins (eds) *International Handbook of Educational Change.* The Netherlands: Kluwer Academic.

Gerland, G. (2000) *Finding out about Asperger Syndrome: High Functioning Autism and PDD.* London: Jessica Kingsley Publishers.

Grandin, T. and Scarieno, M. (1986) *Emergence Labelled Autistic.* New York: Warner.

Hughes, C. and Carter, E.W. (2005) *Success for All Students: Promotion Inclusion in Secondary Schools through Peer Buddy Programmes.* London: Allyn and Bacon.

Jackson, L. (2002) *Freaks, Geeks and Asperger Syndrome: A User Guide to Adolescence.* London: Jessica Kingsley Publishers.

Jones, G. (2002) *Educational Provision for Children with Autism and Asperger Syndrome: Meeting their Needs.* London: David Fulton Publishers.

Jordan, R. and Jones, G. (1999) *Meeting the Needs of Children with Autistic Spectrum Disorders.* London: David Fulton Publishers.

Mittler, P. (2000) *Working Towards Inclusive Contexts.* London: David Fulton Publishers.

Mosley, J. (1993) *Turn Your School Around: A Circle Time Approach to Developing Self Esteem and Positive Behaviour in the Primary Classroom.* Cambridge: LDA.

Mosley, J. and Tew, M. (2001) *Quality Circle Time in the Secondary School: A Handbook of Good Practice.* London: David Fulton Publishers.

Newton, C. and Wilson, D. (2003) *Creating Circles of Friends.* Nottingham: Inclusive Solutions.

Randall, P. and Parker, J. (1999) *Supporting the Families of Children with Autism.* London: John Wiley & Sons.

Sainsbury, C. (2000) *Martian in the Playground: Understand the School Child with Asperger Syndrome.* Bristol: Lucky Duck Publishing.

Whitaker, P., Barratt, P., Joy, H., Potter, M. and Thomas, G. (1998) 'Children with Autism and Peer Group Support: Using Circle of Friends.' *British Journal of Special Education* 25, 60–64.

Williams, D. (1992) *Nobody Nowhere.* London: Doubleday.

11.

The Conversation[1]

Jennifer Overton

J: Nic, are you finished with your breakfast?

N: Yes, I'm done. I don't want the rest of my Cheerios.

J: OK, take your pills, and then I want us to have a conversation in the family room.

N: What about?

J: Well, um, about you.

N: Yeah. I'll take my pills.

J: OK. I'll sit here. Where do you want to sit?

N: Here on this green spot. This green cushion.

J: OK. How old are you?

N: I'm the big nine. I'm going to put my head behind you. Lean back. Tighter. Tighter.

       (*Thirty seconds pass. Nicholas sits up*)

J: OK. Now can we talk?

N: Yes.

J: So, I want to talk to you about...

N: About what?

J: Well, about you.

---

1   This chapter was previously published in Overton J. (2003) *Snapshots of Autism: A Family Album*. London: Jessica Kingsley Publishers.

N: OK. That's fine.

J: OK? Now, you know that we sometimes go to see Dr. Hawkins.

N: OK.

J: Yeah. Why do you think we do that?

N: I'm not sure.

J: Do you think… Do you know other kids that go to see Dr. Hawkins?

N: I think we're the only people.

J: Yeah?

N: Because since I don't see other kids at Dr. Hawkins or maybe they do but I don't see them do it? (*sneeze*)

J: Gesundheit! Maybe you're allergic to being nine years old!

N: No, that's silly. (*sneeze*)

J: Gesundheit again! You are Mr. Sneezy this morning. So you think that maybe other kids go to see Dr. Hawkins but we just don't see them there?

(*Nicholas nods*)

J: Yeah? Maybe. So, what kind of doctor is Dr. Hawkins?

N: A regular doctor. Or is she a normal doctor?

J: Well…

N: It means the same thing.

J: Yeah. She's a… she's a doctor for special kids. Ummm, what about…let's talk about school for a minute. What about school? What about Ms. Williams? Does she help just you in the classroom, or all the kids in the classroom?

N: I believe all the kids.

J: Yes, that's true, but she mostly helps you, doesn't she? She sits beside you in the classroom doesn't she?

N: 'Cause that's the most time she has.

J: And what kind of things does she do for you? What are the things she helps you with?

N: Spelling and math.

J: Yeah? I thought you were great at spelling and math. Maybe there are some other things she helps you with.

        (*Nicholas nods*)

J: Like what?

N: Ummm, I'm not sure.

J: Like what about when Ms. Ferguson reads a story to the class. Do you have trouble listening to that?

N: Yes.

J: Yeah.

N: Do you think it's because I don't think hard?

J: Well, no... I think, I think that...

N: Is it a tough one?

J: Yeah, it's tough for you. To listen to things, isn't it?

        (*Nicholas nods*)

J: Because...

N: Because I have my earphones on because I have sensitive ears?

J: You have sensitive ears – that's exactly right.

N: That's true.

J: Now, do you think all the kids in your class have sensitive ears or just you?

N: No, I think I'm the only one.

J: You're the only one. So, there's a reason why you have sensitive ears. And there's a reason why you don't like to be touched.

N: 'Cause they can knock me.

J: Yeah, and you don't like that do you?

N: 'Cause that hurts.

J: Yeah. And what about when I just touch you like that – does that hurt?

N: No.

J: No. Well. Ms. Williams is in the classroom to help you with some things you have difficulty with, and we go and see Dr. Hawkins, and sometimes Dr. Orlik.

N: Yeah.

J: Because…you are a very special boy. Remember how we talked about how your brain is a little bit different from other people's brains? Remember we talked about that because you sometimes get frustrated when I don't remember things as well as you do, right? And I told you that what is in my brain might be different from what is in your brain, right?

N: Right.

J: You have an excellent memory. You remember everything, don't you? Not everyone can remember things as well as you can. What other things are you good at?

N: I'm not sure.

J: You're great at spelling. You've always been great at spelling.

N: I'm great at math.

J: And yes, you're great at math.

N: Am I great at language arts?

J: Yes.

N: And was I great at copying my homework from the board?

J: Yes, you still are.

N: Yeah!

J: But I want to tell you why you're so great at some things and you have some difficulty with some other things.

N: Like…how about autumn shoes and spring shoes? I have difficulty with them.

J: You have difficulty with that?

N: Tying them up.

J: Oh yes, that's true. And you have some difficulty with riding your bike.

N: Yeah.

J: Yeah. That's why we have to practise that. So, you think maybe you're a little bit different from some of the other kids at school?

N: (*long pause*) Yeah.

J: Because your brain works a little bit differently from the other kids'. It's a great brain. You have a very special brain. But you have…ummm…and your friend Tommy has…autism. (*pause*) Have you heard that word before?

N: How do you spell that?

J: A-U-T-I-S-M.

N: What does it mean?

J: Well, it means…it's a word that describes…

N: A place, a balcony.

J: No, it's a word that describes how your brain is different from my brain and Dad's brain and the brains of the kids at school. It describes what makes you special. You have autism.

N: Yeah.

J: And it means that you're really smart at some things, but you have some difficulty with other things.

N: Yeah.

J: And that's why Ms. Williams is there to help you at school —

     (*Nicholas gets up and starts to leave the room*)

J: Nic, we've not done yet, buddy. Why are you leaving?

N: Because I feel like it.

J: Well, we've not finished our conversation yet. Come back and sit on the couch beside me.

N: No. I want to stay here.

J: You won't be able to hear me from there.

N: Yes I will.

J: Well, I'm worried I won't be able to hear you from here.

N: Yes you can. I'll talk louder.

J: OK.

N: I'll pretend that I'm standing on the blue spot right there.

J: OK. So. Autism. Uh, so that's why Dad and I help you practise certain things —

N: Are we finished?

J: No, and that's why we're so proud of you —

N: You mean embarrassed! Be embarrassed!

J: — sorry, I forgot you didn't like the word P-R-O-U-D — we're happy that you're doing so great at swimming —

N: (*getting anxious*) Are we done now? How many minutes — how many more things do we have to say?

J: About seven.

N: Yes. Can we do ten, or is that too much? Can we do ten or is that too much?!!!

J: That's fine. We can do ten if you like. So...

N: Let's do three more.

J: Yeah, that's fine. So. Autism.

       (*Nicholas cringes*)

J: Are you frustrated?

N: Yes, I've had enough.

J: Have you? Is it upsetting you that we're talking about this?

N: Yes, I really want to go play Super Mario.

J: Well, in three minutes you can go play Super Mario, OK?

N: Two minutes now! Two minutes please! OK, two minutes!
       Say two minutes!!!

J: OK.

N: Or four minutes! Can I have four minutes?!!!

J: Yes.

N: Whatever, my choice?

J: Whatever, your choice. What's your choice?

N: Zero minutes.

       (*Jennifer shakes her head*)

N: OK, I hope the conversation's not for long!

J: No, it won't be long.

N: Not for long!!!! Not for long!!!!

J: Can I just explain a little bit more about autism?

N: Yes.

J: OK. Autism means... Having autism or being autistic means
       that you have difficulty learning how to have proper
       conversations, yes?

N: Yes.

J: And that you have very sensitive ears.

N: Yes.

J: And it means that you don't like to be touched.

N: Right.

J: Right? You don't like to be hugged or kissed.

N: Right.

J: And it also means that you're very smart, and
       that...ummmmm, sometimes you need to learn about proper
       behaviour.

N: What does that mean?

J: Well —

N: Time-outs?

J: Yeah, well, it means that we use time-outs to teach you how to behave and learn what is good behaviour and what is bad behaviour. So that you can learn how to behave properly. What is appropriate behaviour and what is not appropriate behaviour. And you need to learn how to have great conversations and play with friends. Yes?

(Nicholas nods his head)

J: So, if somebody asks you, "Nicholas why don't you like to be touched?" What could you say?

N: I don't know!!

J: Well, you could say, "Because I have autism."

N: Mom, can I go play Super Mario downstairs?! I really need to! Now I'm done!

J: OK, buddy. Our conversation's done. Do you want to get dressed first?

N: No! Or do I have to?

J: No, you can get dressed after you play Super Mario.

N: I'm not going to play Super Mario!

J: Oh. All right.

N: Mom, is Dad going to be in the bathroom for a short time or a long time? Which do you think? What does he usually tend to do?

J: We'll have to wait and see. He tends to be in the bathroom for a short time.

N: What about yesterday?

J: Oh, was he in there for a long time yesterday?

N: Do you think so?

J: Yeah, I guess so.

N: How come? 'Cause it was what?

J: I think it's private what goes on in the bathroom, so I didn't ask.

N: Because it was his birthday, is that why?

J: Yes, that must be why.

N: Do you think he had a relaxing time in there?

J: Yes, I'm sure he did.

N: Yeah. See ya. I'm going downstairs.

J: OK, sweetie. Love you.

       (*pause*)

J: What do you say?

N: Love you too.

J: And remember, Nicholas, you are special. And if you have any questions about autism or being autistic, you come and ask me or Dad. OK?

N: See ya.

       (*Nicholas goes downstairs*)

J: (*whispering*) Or maybe Dad and I should ask you questions about autism and being autistic.

12.

Disclosure: talking about what makes us human

Stephen Shore

In memoriam: Eileen Torchio.

The disclosure process often begins with an awareness of our physical and/or psychic (more mental, not extrasensory) being, with all of their benefits and limitations. Sensing differences from expectations and misunderstandings with others often results in searching for the source of relational dissonance. A reorganization of self occurs as we see ourselves more realistically as we affect others. A need to tell another person wells up from within and it's time to talk.

The act of disclosure involves telling another person potentially damaging information about oneself in order to build better mutual understanding and fulfillment (Shore 2003). With disclosure comes uncertainty. We don't know for certain how that other is going to react to this information. Perhaps even more importantly, how will we interpret and respond to their reaction? What challenges does that create for people on the autism spectrum who have difficulty in reading non-verbal and other subtle communications from the non-spectrum world?

Disclosure is common to humanity. Everyone at some time has had to tell someone something about themselves that could have negative consequences in the relationship with that person. However, that other person is told of our human difference, which is often considered as a frailty, in an effort to engender better mutual understanding, trust, and sharing of humanity. In summary, in this type of sharing, the three separate, and yet simultaneous, worlds comprising of the physical being, a consolidation of self, and a you–me relationship with another person (May 1983) play a vital role in the disclosure process.

This chapter will examine the role of disclosure as a way of sharing humanity and strengthening relationships for people on the autism spectrum. Some of the relationships examined will include family, significant other, friendship, employment, and education.

Disclosure is a choice we make on two levels. The first concerns *whether* we will disclose. The second level deals with *how much, when, to whom,* and *why.* The goal of this chapter is to lend insight into the disclosure process in order to help you make the best *informed* set of choices about disclosure. Proper and careful thought to disclosure is so important, because everyone, at some time, has had to tell another person something about themselves that could damage their reputation with that person. The engine propelling the act of disclosure forward is the need to develop a better mutual understanding with another person (Shore 2003).

Disclosure can be especially challenging for people with autism, because autism is considered as an invisible disability or condition. Visible disabilities effectively make themselves known on contact, whereas invisible conditions require active disclosure. Suppose your niece Suzanne meets a distant cousin with amyotrophic lateral sclerosis (ALS). Although the technical name of the disorder may escape her, she immediately knows this cousin, who can move only his wheelchair and communicate only by sipping and blowing into a straw, will not go jogging with her before dinner. In fact, he looks rather disheveled, is drooling, and is not a pretty sight. A general sense of limitation and negative assumptions about this cousin's capabilities often forms, reducing the life chances of a person with this visible disability – this is called stigma (Goffman 1963). These negative assumptions quickly come to a halt when Suzanne finds out that her drooling cousin's name is Stephen Hawking, arguably one of the most brilliant scientists ever to grace the earth.

What about the person with an invisible difference or disability? At the same family gathering, another relative brings a handsome young child, Lawrence, who refuses to make eye contact, maintains a death grip on an old toy cat, and tantrums at seemingly random intervals. An older relative tries to take the cat away and the child screams. "Gee! He's so good looking… but what dreadful behavior! A firm hand and some discipline will take care of that," someone remarks. Not only is the child implicated with poor behavior, but also the parents are accused of spoiling their son. In addition to Lawrence's invisible disability creating even greater stigma than the cousin's visible ALS (Goffman 1963), Lawrence bears an additional weight. For those who know Lawrence but not well enough to perceive his condition, he passes as a "normal" or typical person. A disclosure at this point may be greeted with "Why have you waited so long to tell me?," causing damage to the relationship (Shore 2003).

This very type of damage occurred when I disclosed to my wife after six years of marriage. While we were dating, my mother and I showed her pictures of me as a very autistic-looking toddler along with descriptions of my behavior. However, she had only moved to the USA from the People's Republic of China about two years previously, and there was a language barrier. Her take on the matter at that time was that I had "closing disease," which in retrospect is a very good layman's diagnosis, considering that the direct Chinese translation of autism is "self-close." Like me, at that time, she considered this difference to be very much in the past and not worthy of more attention than reporting on a broken bone in childhood.

My second disclosure attempt, six years into our marriage, occurred after my coming to the realization that autism was not "all done" and was still very much a part of my life. This time, I printed out several pages of introductory information on autism that was translated into Chinese from an Internet web page. I left it on her pillow, only to wake up to a very confused, concerned, and angry spouse in the morning.

Having a name for my condition, she was amazed at how far I had come. However, she was angry that I hadn't told her of my placement on the autism spectrum until this point and was terrified that others would find out, causing loss of face in the community. Both reactions are under-standable. In the first case, I should have taken the additional step to find a doctor or other qualified professional to translate what my mother and I told her. In the second case, growing up in the People's Republic of China during the Cultural Revolution would cause a person to be wary of releasing information of a condition such as autism to the community. Fortunately, those times have passed, and now my wife completely supports my activities in the autism community.

Sam

Your brother Sam, the black sheep of the family, finally arrives. He earns a good living as a computer software engineer but is a complete flop when it comes to social graces. Recently, Sam relocated to a new cubicle in his workplace, with fluorescent lights, making it hard for him to concentrate and see his computer screen. Additionally, Sam's new supervisor has been chiding him for not joining his fellow workmates for a pint at the bar on Friday evenings. Before the end of an hour at this family gathering, Sam's been interrogated on his lack of having a girlfriend, had a miserable time, and left slamming the door… again. Sam sighs, hopes dashed at having a "normal" family gathering where this time he could bring up the news of his nine-month-old relationship with Alice.

After much consideration, Sam brought up his difficulties with his doctor, resulting in a neuropsychological examination four months ago. Upon receiving the results, Sam was simultaneously relieved and devastated. The diagnosis mentioned something about Asperger syndrome, which the examiner explained was a sort of high-functioning autism. Autism? Wasn't that for little kids who rocked, screamed, and banged their heads all day? No… oh… *Rainman*? That guy in the movie who spoke in a flat tone and could multiply big numbers in his head but couldn't talk sense to a woman? Sam wasn't either of *those* people. Sure, he had some problems getting along with other people, kids teased him in school, and the environment seemed to overwhelm him at times. Otherwise, Sam was a pretty regular bloke who just had some problems understanding how people "worked" and often felt that they didn't understand him either.

At this time, Sam is at the crossroads of needing to take the risk of telling his employer, members of his family, and perhaps others about his placement on the autism spectrum in search of better mutual under-standing. Before that happens, Sam needs to understand how autism affects his interactions with the environment and perception of himself. The autism spectrum is listed in the American Psychiatric Association's *Diagnostic and Statistical Manual of Mental Disorders* (2000) as a disability, listing all of the things the person on the spectrum *cannot* do and giving a very negative viewpoint. The negative connotations of the word "disability" make me think it's better to consider the autism spectrum as a *different* rather than a *disordered* way of being (Shore 2003). That said, instead of taking a more eugenicist's viewpoint of eradicating autism, we should focus on alleviating some of the sensory and other issues that make it very difficult or impossible for people with autism to lead fulfilling and productive lives. The next section will look at a framework of three simultaneously functioning domains that factor in deciding to disclose and, eventually, executing an act of disclosure.

Rollo May's three worlds of being as related to disclosure

What if a disclosure was to take place? How do the "three worlds of being" (May 1983) come into play? What are some likely responses by Sam's mother, father, siblings, and other family members? His friends? The bank he works for? Would it be different if Sam was a college instructor of special education? What about the woman he's been dating for the past nine months? He has not mentioned this new relationship with his family because he does not want to subject himself to family interrogation. Most importantly, how does Sam reconcile his placement on the autism spectrum with himself when he first finds out? Let us suppose Sam is considering disclosure to his family and later on, to his supervisor. What implications do Rollo May's 'three worlds of being' have?

The work of May (1983) describes three simultaneous worlds of being – biological self, being with myself, and with others – where thought, action, and reactions with oneself and others occur. The "biological self" world pertains to Sam's physical being. Sam has always been about average for physical milestones, but he has always been rather clumsy when it comes to catching a ball. In fact, when playing catch with his Dad, Sam would run away because it always looked like the ball was going to hit him in the face. He was just never any good at team-oriented sports. Sam could not tolerate fluorescent lights as a youngster, and he still finds them very distracting at work and elsewhere. Sam was always mystified as to why he could visualize, take apart, and repair almost any mechanical object, no matter how delicate, but at the same time the small motions needed for good handwriting weren't there. In short, the biological self refers to Sam's physical/mechanical being. As Sam comes to know how his physical self impacts his interactions with the environment, he draws from the "being with myself" world.

Being with myself involves how well Sam knows himself on the physical plane as well as on the emotional and cognitive planes. Sam needs to consider how being on the autism spectrum affects his relationships with others as well as himself. He needs to consider his strengths and challenges as "an effective working model of [him]self" (Gardner 2000, p. 43). Developing this *intrapersonal intelligence* requires self-examination and reflection, usually involving talking with other trusted people and, possibly, a counselor familiar with the autism spectrum. In learning about himself, Sam may come to understand that he is much better at computer programming than most people. In fact, he is better at coding and debugging programs than anyone else at work. Sam never thought about this strength as being a gift, and he is quite pleased with himself.

Other realizations may be more difficult. Sam avoids pubs, because he finds them too loud, causing him to get this funny, fuzzy faraway feeling in his head. It's just about all he can do to handle those lights at the workplace. Plus, Sam almost never gets the jokes his co-workers tell when they are in the bar. Part of this consolidation of self includes Sam's review of his own diagnostic report and Asperger syndrome as the characteristics mentioned in the document line up with life experiences. Initially resistant to the idea of being on the autism spectrum, Sam realizes quickly that this diagnosis finally helps him makes sense out of his life. The understanding of how Sam's physical self affects his interactions with the environment and other people is contained within the world of being with myself. Sam's interpretation of how others respond to him is the third world of "being with others".

Being with others is often the most challenging of the three domains because it requires Sam to interpret another's response. Specifically, Sam has to figure out what that other person is thinking and feeling as he makes his disclosure. Referred to as "theory of mind," the documented challenges of people on the autism spectrum understanding the minds of non-spectrum people (Cohen 1997) make this domain particularly difficult.

Irving Goffman (1963) writes how one of his research subjects, Ray, had to very quickly process incoming data in order to assess accurately what the other was thinking. The subject, a Caucasian, spent much time fishing with a group of black children. He noticed that they called each other "Negro" and then "nigger" as they became more comfortable in his presence. One day, during horseplay, the words "Don't give me that nigger talk" popped out of the research subject's mouth. The immediate response was "You bastard!" with a big smile (Birdwhistell 1956).

In the situation described above, Ray had to process incoming information about his playmate's response to what normally is a racial slur. Did Ray have to prepare to get beaten up, or worse, for these words? Alternatively, would the members of this black group of children ignore or make light of the potential faux pas? In less than a second, all of this information and more had to be processed – hopefully accurately. In fact, in employing the same words that this group of children used on each other, Ray suddenly deepened his acceptance within the group as a "wise" person, where, although he was of a difference race, he was accepted as one of them (Goffman 1963, p.29).

Sam now decides that discussing one aspect of his being on the autism spectrum is a good way to open the disclosure with his mother. Realizing that his neurological wiring allows him to perceive and be overwhelmed by the cycling of fluorescent lights, causing sensory overload leading to tantrums as a child, he has covered both the biological self and being with myself worlds (May 1983). The biggest challenge will be the being with others, where he has to determine accurately his mother's reactions and how they make him feel.

Sam starts the disclosure process by saying to his mother: "Remember when I used to spin around in circles and would run away screaming when you put on the fluorescent light in the kitchen"? His mother responds: "Yes, I do remember those times. Now after so many years and thousands spent on psychotherapy, you are finally telling me what went on in your head?" Not a very encouraging response and, like many times before when trying to explain himself, Sam almost decides to drop the whole matter because he feels his attempt is being discounted by his mother. However, this time, and armed with the adult diagnosis of Asperger syndrome helping to validate his experiences, Sam presses on. "I probably won't be any worse off as a result of this disclosure, and I think I can bring more understanding and mutual trust to this relationship with this information."

"You are autistic?" his mother continues. "You had many difficulties as a child. However, if you believe you have autism, you really need to see a psychiatrist and work this out." Pushing back clouds of doubt, Sam describes how the results and suggestions of his recent diagnostic assessment explain many of his difficulties. Sam also "checks in" with his mother to make sure he is interpreting her signs of beginning to understand his situation by asking her whether his explanations are clear.

Not wanting to overwhelm his mother at this emotionally stressful time, Sam made a conscious decision not to immediately show the entire 18-page neuropsychological report and risk information overload. Reluctantly, his mother agrees to review the few pages of the document that Sam has with him, and the two become fascinated with their different interpretations of Sam's childhood events and characteristics. Sam and his mother slowly come to a place of better mutual understanding and trust as he interprets accurately his mother's emotions towards his disclosure and him as a person. That makes Sam feel good.

Disclosure, when to tell, denial, and acceptance

Much angst is expended on the appropriate time to inform a person of their differences. Earlier is better than later, where consideration of disclosure ideally begins as soon as you know that person has a difference. If Sam had awareness of his autism as a young child, then he may have had an easier time coming to grips with his condition as a difference rather than a disordered way of being when he found out later in life. Finally, the act of disclosure must be planned out carefully as soon as the person becomes aware of their difference from the greater society. In brief, "disclosure must be considered when the effects of autism significantly impact a relationship with another person and there is a need for greater mutual understanding" (Shore 2003).

> I was lucky in terms of disclosure since my parents freely used the word "autism" around the house for as long as I can remember. Instead of being something shameful, "autism" explained why things were difficult for me in school and why I saw special doctors once a week (to root out the demon of autism). (Shore 2003, p.162)

Consideration of developmental level rather than age when deciding when to disclose to a child their autism should be the focus. It is when a child becomes aware of their difference that they must be informed. For example, if a child comes home from school questioning why she gets pulled out of class a few times a week for speech or other therapy, or why it is so difficult to make friends, then the time to disclose has arrived. Talking about strengths and needs, or challenges, as well as likes and dislikes is a good way to begin. Commonly, the strengths and likes will align together with the needs and dislikes making their own group.

These discussions with the child sensitize them to how their own capabilities can be best used to their advantage and is the beginning of building skills in self-determination. In other words, given my strengths, needs, and preferences, where can I be most fulfilled and productive? The next step is further discussion on how these strengths can be used to accommodate for needs. At this time, it may be helpful to bring in positive role models of others with, or suspected of having, Asperger syndrome and having similar strengths as the child. *Asperger and Self-esteem: Insight and Hope through Famous Role Models* by Norman Ledgin (2002) is a great source to find people with similar profiles to people on the autism spectrum. Only after the child firmly grasps their identity as a valued person with unique strengths and challenges is it useful to wrap up their condition within the words "Asperger syndrome" or "autism spectrum". In this way, the diagnostic term becomes a way of summarizing a person's condition rather than a set of limitations that must be overcome.

A larger challenge exists when a person has reached adolescence without a disclosure of their difference due to ignorance or a fear of societal stigma (Goffman 1963). A split from reality occurs as the person perceives themselves differently from how they actually present to the world. In fact, everyone has this difference, as discussed by Goffman (1959). It's just that difference is much greater for people living with an undisclosed autism spectrum or other condition.

An adult diagnosis can be particularly difficult: as the person grows older and continues to build their sense of self, there is a greater chance of denial because a way of life is given more of a chance to solidify. Two common responses to disclosure to an adult, whether to the person with the condition or to another about a person with a difference, are denial and acceptance. Again, as with all disclosure, it is important to focus on how a better knowledge of the strengths and needs of the person significantly impact their interactions with the surrounding environment, moving them in a direction of leading a more fulfilling and productive life.

How much to disclose?

For the most part, disclosure should be done on a need-to-know basis, with as little information being revealed as possible. Sam wisely did this when he chose to initially show his mother only the last few pages of his report containing results and recommendations. Disclosure should be considered only when the effects of autism significantly impact a relationship or the individual on the spectrum. For example, with a younger child interested in the causes of his or her differences, then you may want to restrict the conversation to people's needs, and how sometimes those needs need accommodation, while refraining from using the diagnostic label "autism" or "Asperger syndrome". In a workplace situation, proper disclosure is especially important as employers are often reluctant to retain employees who they feel will require extra attention, inconvenience, and additional costs in making accommodations. However, many accommodations can be effected with little or no additional expenditure of resources.

For example, fluorescent lights make it difficult for Sam to work productively in his cubicle to such a point that his supervisor has suggested strongly that much greater output is necessary for retaining his job as a computer programmer. Sam now *needs* to *advocate* for his needs, *disclose* the reasons for providing this information, and *gauge* his supervisor's reaction as Sam strives to build *better mutual understanding* and *trust*. To maximize the chances for a successful disclosure, Sam may offer to bring in his own incandescent or other non-fluorescent lighting after discussing his need for different lighting.

Disclosure can be especially anxiety-producing for people on the autism spectrum due to the uncertainty as to how others will interpret the information. An amount of risk is involved because contrary to what people on the spectrum desire, there is a degree of uncertainty of outcome when making the disclosure, requiring processing of non-verbal cues and, possibly, complex emotions from the other person in real time. An accommodation for this challenge requires that Sam "checks in" with the supervisor by asking clarification questions as he advocates for different lighting and makes his disclosure. A possible question could be: "Have I been clear in explaining how the type of lighting has a significant impact on the quality of my work?" It may also be appropriate to say: "I work best if people are very direct with me instead of trying to mince words on a subject they might think would be upsetting to me." In short, like with everyone else, clear and direct communication makes for better understanding all around.

Conclusion

This chapter has peeked into how some of the dynamics that go into disclosure can assist in making informed choices on telling another about one's own, or their, placement on the autism spectrum. Conceiving of autism as a profile of characteristics to be assembled in a way that maximizes a person's chances of directing their own fulfilling and productive life is much more positive than considering the condition as a horrible disability. Understanding how autism affects us in terms of the biological self, being with myself, and being with others can aid in disclosure to oneself and others as we work towards building greater understanding and acceptance of self, others, and society as a whole in what it means to be human.

References

Birdwhistell, R. (1956) in B. Schaffner (ed) *Group Processes. Transactions of the Second (1955) Conference.* New York: Josiah Macy, Jr. Foundation, p.71.

Cohen, S. (1997) *Mindblindness: An Essay on Autism and Theory of Mind.* Cambridge, MA: MIT Press.

Gardner, H. (2000) *Intelligences Reframed: Multiple Intelligences for the 21st Century.* New York: Basic Books.

Goffman, E. (1959) *The Presentation of Self in Everyday Life.* New York: Doubleday.

Goffman, E. (1963) *Stigma: Notes on the Management of Spoiled Identity.* New York: Simon and Schuster.

Ledgin, N. (2002) *Asperger and Self-esteem: Insight and Hope through Famous Role Models.* Arlington, TX: Future Horizons.

May, R. (1983) *The Discovery of Being: Writings in Existential Psychology.* New York: Norton.

Shore, S. (2003) *Beyond the Wall: Personal Experiences with Autism and Asperger Syndrome.* Shawnee Mission, KS: Autism Asperger Publishing Company.

13.

Disclosure: a parent's perspective

Jacqui Jackson

Telling our child

When my son Luke wrote his book *Freaks, Geeks and Asperger Syndrome*, (Jackson 2002) he was very particular about allowing me to edit it. Although I helped to structure his writing and made sense out of the reams of words he had frantically churned out, as far as changing any of the actual wording or making any amendments or even suggestions, Luke was extremely unreceptive. He takes the view that if I were to contribute to his work other than to edit it, then he would not be entitled to be called author of the book.

Although this is a very commendable characteristic and perhaps typical of someone with Asperger syndrome (AS), it was not without its drawbacks – the main difficulty being that in one chapter in particular, a lot of what he wrote was not suitable for small children to read. He used rather strong language and it took a considerable amount of discussion before Luke would agree to keep the general gist of the chapter but maybe tone it down a bit.

The chapter that to me, as his mum, was most poignant was that entitled 'To Tell or Not to Tell'. Reading this chapter as he wrote it was certainly a revelation to me. As I read on, the knot in my stomach pulled tighter and tighter. Luke wrote with anger, upset and resentment at how he had muddled through his primary years with the notion that he was a 'freak'.

As parents, we do our best to bring our children up in the way that we see fit, disciplining, teaching and protecting in accordance with our own particular values and belief systems. The majority of parents do what they do with the best of intentions.

As I wrote in *Multicoloured Mayhem*, my reasons for not telling Luke that he had AS were deep-rooted, and I had managed to convince myself that the words I spoke were actually true. I told the few people who did know that Luke has AS that the reason I hadn't yet informed him was because I was worried that, being an avid reader, he may read up on it and start to exhibit 'symptoms' that ordinarily would not have been a problem. I argued that I was waiting for him to become old enough to understand and for the right time. If I am brutally honest, the real reason was that I was scared. I didn't know how he would react, didn't want him to feel different (boy, little did I know!), didn't know what to say. Maybe I hoped that one day it would go away – deluded, I know, but…

I worried that my husband, members of my family and some of my friends who didn't believe in 'labels' and thought that he was merely a bit eccentric would criticise and disapprove. At that time, I didn't have the strength of character or the confidence in my own parenting skills to ignore them and release them to think what they like.

The issue of telling my oldest son Matthew he had dyslexia didn't seem to be such a worry, as it was clear to him that he had great difficulties with reading and spelling and was having extra support at school. He also regularly saw an occupational therapist (those were the days!) who gave him exercises to do and came into school, and so it was fairly easy to explain that he also has dyspraxia, as dyspraxia was a term that referred to his difficulties in motor skills.

Luke, however, was different. Regardless of the numerous assessments that Luke had, and regardless of the fact he had differentiated work, occupational therapy in school time and numerous hospital tests, he never asked why and never seemed to think there was anything unusual about all this. Happy to be left alone in his own little world of dinosaurs, technology, batteries and pencil-tapping, Luke seemed oblivious to the fact that there was anything different about him (note I said 'seemed') and so I left things as they were.

As I made my regular trips to school to try to stop the endless bullying, and as I attended Individualised Education Plan (IEP) meetings and spoke to the local autism team, I began to convince myself that maybe they were wrong. Maybe I was wrong. I decided that as he was nearing secondary school age, he could possibly leave all the autism stuff behind.

For all you parents pondering over whether to tell your child that they have AS and what to say, here is what Luke has to say on the matter:

> I had finally found the reason why other people classed me as weird. It was not just because I was clumsy or stupid. My heart lightened instantly and the constant nagging that accompanied me all my life (not my mum) stopped immediately. I finally knew why I felt different, why I felt as if I was a freak, why I didn't seem to fit in. Even better, it was not my fault!...
>
> So my final word on this subject is *get them told!* (Jackson 2002, pp. 34–37)

That is Luke's take on the issue of disclosure, and it certainly seems as if children with AS or other differences begin to realise that they are different from others. Luke says that he thought that everyone else was weird and watched them sometimes, intrigued as to why they behaved in the way that they did. Only as he reached the age of nine or ten years did he begin to realise that these other children behaving in their own 'weird' ways all seemed to understand each other, smile together, pull unfathomable faces at each other and have their own particular way of talking. He tells me that the realisation that it was him that was different and that they were all the same was a real shock, and he spent a long time questioning whether he was an alien, an outsider from another planet or maybe playing some bizarre part in a play, rather like the *Truman Show*. He will speak of how thoughts of whether he was real and others weren't – or, indeed, perhaps he was the one who was unreal – bounced through his waking and sleeping hours. Even though this is still the case, and he does still think such thoughts, he can now also apply logic and realise that this is part of having AS and it is something he has to deal with.

'Why would you want to give him a label?' 'I'm sure he will grow out of it.' 'He's just a bit eccentric.' How many of you have heard such things said about your child? I know I certainly have.

In an ideal world, there would be no need for labels, and everyone would be accepted for who and what they are without question. In an ideal world, the right amount of care and support would be given to those who need it, regardless of the disability or area of need. However, we are not in an ideal world, and society is governed by economic, political, cultural and social factors, and 'labels' are needed to act as signposts in order to point people in the right direction for services and to provide an insight and a name for the collection of behaviours that people on the spectrum exhibit.

There is never a right or wrong time to tell a child that they have AS or some difference that they do not know about. Each parent can only go on their own knowledge of the child. I think we know our children's own understanding and what they are capable of. Each child, however, is very different, and when to tell a child that they have AS or another spectrum difference is not a question with definitive answers. As parents, all we can ever do is to watch our child, learn from others' mistakes (like mine) and hope to recognise the fact that they are aware enough and able enough to understand. One thing to remember is that there is no need to give the full details of the triad of impairments and how it affects your child, unless of course they are desperate to know. It is enough to start with the fact that their brain works differently to other people's and that although their brain is just as good, they may need help in some areas. Often, easy books on the subject can be looked at together and the child given opportunity to ask questions.

Telling others

Years ago, when I was undertaking my degree, I was required to write an essay arguing the pros and cons of the human genome project. This was a long time ago and I am a social scientist rather than a biologist, and so I will not go into the ins and outs of the human genome project (mainly because I don't know that much). The crux of the argument, however, was that we would all have our DNA taken at birth and kept on file so that the information could be used for a variety of reasons. Of course, genetic disorders such as cystic fibrosis could be pre-empted, and maybe many lives could be saved or made easier as a result of anticipating genetic diseases. On the other hand, however, who was going to keep these records and how accessible would they be in reality? Would insurance companies be able to check records and refuse insurance knowing that someone had the genetic predisposition to a disease that characteristically struck in middle age? Would it be ethically acceptable for a doctor to withhold or disclose the knowledge that someone had inherited a disease that didn't manifest for many years?

As I said before, biological science and medicine are not my fields but yet these questions really struck a chord with me. The reason such issues seemed so poignant to me was that there seemed to be stark parallels between the issues of disclosure for my sons and the issues I was writing about.

At that time, my son Joe had just been born very early and was very ill, Matthew had been diagnosed with dyspraxia and dyslexia, and Luke had been diagnosed with AS. I had not told Luke about his AS or been particularly forthcoming with information about my sons' differences compared with others. Writing about whether a doctor should disclose information to a patient made me consider my own situation. When did I tell the children that they had their own particular brands of difference? Is there a particular age? Is it up to me to tell them, or a 'professional'?

Even after I had told them about their own differences, there would still be disclosure issues. If they filled in an application form and disclosed immediately that they had dyspraxia, dyslexia, AS or attention-deficit/hyperactivity disorder (ADHD), then would that automatically mean the application was discarded?

How would Matthew fill in an application form? Do I do it for him and hope he isn't asked to undertake a written test later, or do I leave him to fill it in himself in the knowledge that he is unlikely to pass the first hurdle?

If they did disclose the information about their differences and were accepted for an interview and even got jobs, would they feel that they were filling an employer's quota of disability and not earned it on their own merits, and would they be treated differently for disclosing their differences?

If they did not disclose their differences, then what would happen next? Go for an interview, have poor eye contact, fidget in their seat, misinterpret questions and take a long time to process their answers? Not ideal!

Years later, we have just been given a poignant example of the need to disclose in certain situations. Matthew has applied recently to join the police force. He has received his results and achieved exceptional grades in all of the categories apart from written communication. It transpires that he decided not to disclose that he was dyslexic, presuming that he would be discriminated against, and so hoped that there would not be a significant amount of writing. But there was.

After discussing this, he argued that although he knew that legally they are not allowed to discriminate, he presumed that it would be quite easy to fail his application if they didn't want a dyslexic applicant and so decided not to declare his differences.

This situation reinforced the fact that disclosure in formal situations such as interviews or assessments is important, and I suppose we can only take the attitude that if the potential employee is discriminatory then it is their loss. He has since discovered that if he reapplies and declares his dyslexia and dyspraxia, then concessions will be made.

A hidden 'disability' is often not quite as hidden to others as it is to parents, who naturally adapt their language and environment in order for their child to feel secure in their own surroundings. As parents, we build safety nets around our children, adapt our homes to cater for their physical difficulties, and change our language to accommodate their own unique way of interpretation. Thus, in turn, things run smoother than pre-diagnosis and sometimes we may even doubt whether the original diagnosis was accurate in the first place.

Nevertheless, there are often times when we catch other parents sneakily snatching a sideways look at our child or surreptitiously moving their own child away from ours, and it becomes plainly obvious that others, particularly other parents, are aware of – and sometimes even fearful of – our child's differences.

My own personal attitude to disclosing my younger children's differences to others is that if there is going to be any length of time spent together, maybe in a play area, then I will quietly talk to the parent or carer and tell them that the boys have autism/ADHD and are trying their best. I am naturally altruistic, and so I would like to think that although the majority of people do not understand about autistic spectrum disorders, they are more than willing to try and accommodate our children and their ways. Of course, there are always the grumpy exceptions to this rule, but I prefer to focus on the majority and see the human race in a better light.

To see these obvious differences between our child and typically developing children can often bring about that familiar knot in the stomach, and I try to avoid making comparisons at all costs. Standing in the playground, mothers huddle together chatting about their beloved offspring. They talk with pride about their achievements and exchange endearing anecdotes of their daily antics. Listening to such conversations can often prove painful; to fight off the dreaded wave of self-inflicted pain when comparisons begin, I have often smiled to myself inwardly as I contemplate how to join in such conversations.

When Luke was younger, maybe I could have said 'Well, I really am so proud. Luke went a full day without hitting anyone yesterday.'

Or perhaps 'Something really amazing has just happened. Luke has just come out of school with one sock slightly rolled down.'

To feel like shouting from the rooftops because your child has eaten one pea, been to the toilet without stripping naked or made some exchange with another child about something other than their own specialist subject is a feeling that parents of autistic children are all too familiar with.

However, such things can be conversation stoppers and somehow I suspect that the other parents may not understand the significance of such achievements and think I am slightly peculiar for considering them worth a mention! In fact, do parents of typically developing children really want to hear about such achievements or even about the fact that our children have a diagnosis of autism, ADHD or AS? Judging by the embarrassed looks and the rapid subject changes, I sometimes wonder.

So, when is an appropriate time to tell other people about our child's differences?

I must confess that there have been times when I have been faced with a less tolerant member of society and have taken a perverse delight in disclosing the boys' autism (my youngest son Ben has autism). On days where I have been up since 4 a.m., been weed on and kicked, had doors slammed in my face and refereed a number of teenage altercations, the disapproving stare of a casual observer or a misplaced comment about my parenting skills is often the proverbial straw. To thrust a card stating 'My child has autism!' at a wagging finger and watching them flush with embarrassment has been known to give me some degree of satisfaction.

I personally think that disclosing our child's differences to others depends on many factors, the child's age being one of them. I am more likely to readily explain to another parent that Ben has autism or that Joe has ADHD than to explain to others about Luke and his differences.

Often, because of Luke's book and the circles we move in, people already know that Luke has AS, but in times where they do not, I believe that unless Luke is getting into serious difficulties with communication and is likely to alienate himself when he doesn't want to do so, it is best to take a back seat and let him find his own way.

How much information?

As a parent of more than one child with a different way of thinking and behaving, it has always been imperative that each and every one of them knows that they are valued for who and what they are as individuals, whether they have a 'label' or not. Teaching the children that difference is something to be celebrated and diversity in society enriches all of our lives is something that is fundamental to our household. However it does have its drawbacks.

All those years of coaxing, encouraging and teaching my youngest son Ben to talk, and now I am ashamed to admit that I cringe for the majority of the time we are out – although it does give me some perverse amusement too.

Comments like 'Your teeth need cleaning!' or 'Yuk, he has a horrid face!' happen on a daily basis. Ben hasn't got the understanding just yet for me to explain about politeness other than at the very basic level of needing to say please and thank you, and so he says exactly what he thinks. This ability to talk more clearly now is also causing his poor brother some problems too.

We will be chatting casually with someone at a park or at the sports centre, when Ben will suddenly pipe up with 'Luke has Asperger syndrome.' This is followed by hysterical laughter and lots of flapping. The reason Ben likes to repeat this to as many people as possible is that it gives him the opportunity to say the word 'Ass' – something he and Joe find highly amusing. Fortunately, as yet, Ben's speech is not quite clear enough for most people to understand many of his words, and so I usually whisk him away before he can be asked to clarify.

One lesson that is difficult to explain is that although they are, quite rightly, proud of who and what they are, it doesn't necessarily mean that after just a few minutes of meeting someone, they have to disclose their 'disability' to all and sundry.

Indeed, if Mat knocks over a cup of coffee while chatting to someone, it is hardly necessary to explain that he has dyspraxia and all that that means. However, in the workplace, where he is constantly getting into difficulties for his clumsiness or his difficulties with spelling and writing, then it is wise and only fair to explain that he has dyspraxia and dyslexia if that hasn't occurred already before being given the job. Issues such as when and who to tell are not answered easily.

A golden rule of disclosure that I try to instil in Luke is that if it will make him feel more confident and better about himself in the long run, then go ahead and explain that he has some differences and describe briefly what they are.

If he is likely to feel alienated and is in a situation where he doesn't have to have deep personal contact and can run an effective emulator for a short while, then there really is no need.

Simplistic advice, which I am sure has its short-fallings. The truth is that there is no golden formula when it comes to human interaction. Humans are complex; therefore, trying to predict how someone will act and react in any given situation is nigh on impossible, and all we can do is advise to the best of our ability and pool together the depth of knowledge and experience in the hope that some will be useful at any given time.

One thing I do tell my children and other parents is that there is no need for all the information to be given at any time. Often, it is enough for a sibling, potential friend or another parent to know that the child has a different way of thinking and behaving, and there will be time in the future to expand on this as situations arise. If the person is going to be significant in the child's life then there is a lifetime left for them to learn.

Sometimes, however, as we discovered recently, there is a definite need to disclose the fact that you, your child or your partner has a 'hidden disability'. A situation arose for us that could have turned out very differently – a situation that made me grateful that Luke is so unpredictable in his reactions and understanding of others.

Full of the joys of spring and euphoric at finally being deregistered from school, Luke had decided that the issue of 'socialising' needed to be taken very seriously. When he heard that his sister and her friend were going to Heaventeen, a teenage disco, he decided that he was going to spike his hair (or, rather, let his sisters do so), have a shave and go out 'on the pull'. Every credit to him, I have to say, as Luke's ideal scenario is not to join 200 teenagers in a noisy, overcrowded and badly lit environment. He was determined, and so I had to make do with dampening down my natural protectiveness and encourage him along as he brimmed with excitement at doing 'normal' things. After all, surely AS was only a problem in a school environment, so now it wasn't an issue, was it?

An hour later, an extremely trendy looking Luke was escorting two very pretty young girls to the disco. The trouble was, on arrival, the queue was half a mile long. At least 300 teenagers were pushing and shoving in a bid to get in the club. Luke, who loathes queuing at the best of times, was still insistent that he wanted to join it and in fact seemed quite eager to do so. It transpired that to Luke, the queue looked like a tidal wave; he didn't see it as being made up of individual people but rather an opportunity to amuse himself by leaning backwards and shoving forwards and making 'ripples' of people.

Eventually they got inside, and Luke soon discovered that his dislike of crowds and groups of teenagers was not reserved solely for school after all. Struggling to cope with the situation, he decided that the best course of action would be to analyse the popcorn machine. Minutes later, a security guard came and asked him what he was doing and, of course, Luke proceeded to tell him how the popcorn machine worked. Not impressed, the security guard looked around and noticed a wheelchair, positioned next to a large hole in the wall. Deciding that Luke was looking shifty – no eye contact, fidgeting and moving from foot to foot – he came to the conclusion that Luke was a vandal and the popcorn-machine analysis was an attempt at diverting the guard's attention, and so a bemused Luke was carted off to an office and the police were called.

Ten minutes later, two disgruntled police officers were getting rather frustrated at Luke's confusing answers and his persistence to explain every detail of the popcorn machine. Luke, himself, was getting even more confused that he was being asked over and over again whether he 'did it' without a detailed explanation of what 'it' was.

Fortunately, the whole experience amused Luke. He said he felt as if he were part of a detective film and it was all rather surreal.

Things could have been very different. Ordinarily, the whole experience of being questioned by police and misunderstood could have been enough to traumatise anyone, and the whole series of events could quite easily have spiralled out of control if it wasn't for the fact that Luke's sister, Anna, had realised that Luke had disappeared. Knowing Luke's difficulties, Anna had set off to find him. Discovering where Luke was being 'interrogated' (his words), she spoke to the police officers and told them that Luke had AS and often misunderstood the way people spoke unless they were very clear and that he rarely made eye contact so always looked shifty. She then told Luke clearly what the police thought he had done and asked him to prove that he hadn't. Luke, of course, had no problems taking the police to the hole in the wall and discussing at great length the shape of the hole and the size of the wheelchair and the way the plaster was falling and made it quite clear that it couldn't have been damaged in the way he was being accused of.

So, what should he have done in this situation? Tell them he had AS before he entered the disco? Tell them he had AS as soon as the guard came over to him? Tell the police he had AS? That would have entailed explaining AS and all that that means when he was in a situation that was already highly stressful.

It seems to me that it is important for people with AS to carry some kind of card around that briefly explains AS and maybe gives a contact number in case of difficulties. Although such cards are available from the National Autistic Society (NAS) and other places, I think that a personalised card, given out on diagnosis (although, of course, this raises a problem for those who cannot get a formal diagnosis) would be beneficial for many reasons. Dennis Debbaudt's chapter in this book has detailed advice about making personal and general cards.

A sense of self

Luke often tells me that he wishes he were exceptionally good at something, like some autistic or AS people are. I tell him several times a day how brilliant he is at photography and digital art, how helpful and insightful his books have been, and how articulate he is when he speaks. None of it makes any difference. To him, if there is more to learn about his specialist subject, then he is not good at it. Writing his books was merely a way of learning about himself and helping others and, in Luke's words, was 'just something I did at that time of my life; after all, it is not like it was a fiction book.'

However, despite this apparent lack of self-esteem, Luke and many other people I have met with AS have a quiet, often disconcerting innate knowledge of who they are. The issue of self-esteem is one that I think is of supreme importance to all humans, especially children. Something that I have noted from living for nearly 16 years with Luke and spending a lot of time with many other AS children and adults is that although their self-esteem is extremely fragile, and often their self-confidence has been knocked by the blows of life, there is often a quietly confident, almost arrogant undertone to an AS character, which can be quite disconcerting. Many times it is apparent that Luke is confused and agitated by the fact that he is misunderstood and misunderstands others, but it is also clear that he knows exactly who he is and that although he knows he is different, he has a quiet confidence in himself as a person. Indeed, the nightclub scenario described earlier could have been extremely traumatic for the best of us, but Luke explains the whole experience with an uncanny detachment, rather as if he was watching the situation from the outside. As he knew who he was and he didn't do what he was being accused of, it didn't affect him adversely.

Just for fun

For any of you AS folks who are wondering how well you deal with the whole issue of when, who and how to tell folks about your AS, here is a quick quiz. Remember that this is purely for fun, although it might make you think a bit about your actions and reactions.

1. Proud of yourself for getting around a supermarket despite the flicker of the fluorescent lights and unpleasant hum of the chillers, you make your way to the checkout, only to find that there is an enormously long queue. Do you:

    (a) Abandon your trolley, dash out of the shop and rush home, only to sit and wonder what you are going to eat tonight.

    (b) Push to the front of the queue, shouting that you are disabled and need to go first.

    (c) Go and find an assistant and quietly tell them you have a disability that means that you cannot cope with queues so will he please open another checkout.

    (d) Stand in the queue and begin to sweat, fidget and panic. Dropping your money when you come to pay, you shove what you can into your shopping bag and then spend the rest of the evening a quivering wreck who is unable to eat anyway.

2.   You can't believe your luck. The girl/guy that you have fancied for ages has just come over and asked whether you want to go out with them. You don't want to blow your chances, but you are worried that they might want to go somewhere that you find difficult. Do you:

    (a) Weigh up the options and decide that it will all go horribly wrong so tell them thanks, but no thanks, and then spend the evening wondering about what might have been.

    (b) Tell him/her that yes, you would like to go, but they have to realise that you are disabled and then give them a pile of books about AS and a list of dos and don'ts to take into consideration for the date.

    (c) Agree to go, suggest a place yourself that is familiar to you and decide that if the subject arises or he/she asks any questions about your behaviour, then maybe the subject will be discussed.

    (d) Agree to go, cringe when the brightest, noisiest place is suggested, and then get so stressed by the unfamiliarity and sensory input that you spend the evening unable to speak and trying to control the rising panic inside you.

3.   You are wandering happily to a familiar shop, when a police officer suddenly taps you on the shoulder and asks whether you have any knowledge of an incident that took place in the street earlier today. Taken unawares, you immediately start to shake, sweat and panic uncontrollably. The policeman hisses that you obviously have something to hide and maybe you should go along with him. Do you:

(a) Turn in a blind panic and run off.

(b) Lash out at him, screaming that you are disabled and how dare he take you unawares like that.

(c) Realise that this is the right time to use one of those cards that says that you have Asperger syndrome, so manage to get one out of your pocket and pass it to the policeman.

(d) Become paralysed with fear and unable to explain or speak, begin to cry uncontrollably and get ushered into a police car and taken to the police station for questioning.

4. You see a job advertised in a computer-shop window and decide that it might be just the job for you. It's only a small place and it says to enquire inside about the position. Do you:

(a) Decide that it is a waste of time, as there is no way that they will give you the job anyway so go home feeling useless.

(b) Walk into the place, tell them you are disabled and quote the Disability Discrimination Act to them.

(c) Take a deep breath and go in, decline an interview there and then, ask for an application form, saying you need time to prepare and then determine that you will declare your AS on the form.

(d) Go into the shop and agree to be interviewed there and then, only to struggle to articulate your answers and sit, staring at the floor, fiddling with your clothes.

5. You have managed to make an effort to get some physical exercise and so have joined a gym. However, in order to cope, you have to follow the same routine and use the same locker and shower each time. You enter the changing room only to find that 'your' locker is just about to be used. Do you:

(a) Grab your things and turn straight back home and vow never to come again.

(b) Push straight past and shout that you are disabled and *need* this locker.

(c) Pluck up the courage to quietly tell the other person that
you have difficulties with change and could you possibly
swap lockers.

(d) Put your things in a different locker, begin to shake and
panic, and become unable to do anything other than
break out into a cold sweat at the thought of repeating
the whole experience again.

Mostly As

Although you are playing it safe and are unlikely to get yourself into too
many difficult situations, it may be time for you to think about taking
more of a chance in life. You may miss out on some golden opportunities
by letting your AS disable you. Only *you* know what you can cope with,
but it might be worth taking a deep breath and venturing into the
unknown occasionally.

Mostly Bs

Although your confidence, acceptance and willingness to disclose your
AS are definitely admirable, there may be situations when overdosing
others with too much information can make them put up barriers or feel
uncomfortable. You may want to stop and assess each situation and decide
whether it is really necessary to disclose your AS. Sometimes, a more
subtle approach can be better.

Mostly Cs

Congratulations! You seem to have found a balance between knowing
your own limitations and the need to tell others without bombarding all
with too much information. Although there are bound to be times when
you are unsure and may get it wrong, you give yourself the optimum
chance of accepting and being proud of your AS but refusing to let it rule
your life.

Mostly Ds

Although you should certainly congratulate yourself for taking a chance
and stepping into difficult situations, sometimes it may be better for you

to take more of an active rather than a passive role. By taking more of a lead in your own life and, perhaps, disclosing your AS at times when things are getting too much to bear, you will almost certainly feel more in control and able to enjoy life to the full.

After getting Luke to take this little quiz, it seems that he is of the 'mostly D' category and, more often than not, enters into situations that he cannot cope with. Again, the answer is not clear-cut. No one can ever know when is the right time to disclose your, your child's or your partner's difference, and it is impossible to predict one's reactions. However, I do think that if local authorities were to produce cards that explained a little bit in those difficult situations and took the onus off the individual, then life might be easier for all. So, come on, any representatives from health, education and social services – get a move on and help the whole issue of disclosure to be at least marginally easier for all!

References

Jackson, J. (2003) *Multicoloured Mayhem: Parenting the Many Shades of Adolescents and Children with Autism, Asperger Syndrome and ADHD.* London: Jessica Kingsley Publishers.

Jackson, L. (2002) *Freaks, Geeks and Asperger Syndrome: A User Guide to Adolescence.* London: Jessica Kingsley Publishers.

14.

Coming out, various[1]

Wendy Lawson

Introduction

Diagnosis seems like an easy word to define. One looks at the symptoms and characteristics and concludes that they amount to this or that pattern, which matches this or that diagnostic criterion. This might seem like a simple procedure, but I know from personal experience that it is not. I was not diagnosed with an autism spectrum disorder (ASD), in particular Asperger disorder (AD), until I was 42 years old. This has meant that most of my life I didn't have the appropriate label that matched my experiences.

As a small child, I was initially diagnosed with intellectual disability. I didn't talk until I was four years old; I was obsessive, ritualistic and prone to tantrums. Had I been given an assessment then, I would have qualified for a diagnosis of classic autism. I'm writing this here because I know from personal and professional experience that the characteristics of ASD change over time. Some of us in the world of ASD have different understandings of an individual according to their diagnosis. One is either an 'autie' or an 'Aspie'. However, there is much solidarity among us, and we are more alike than we are different. I don't think that a diagnosis of high-functioning autism, Asperger autism or any other type of autism is separated according to our difficulties as much as it is in the minds of other people who don't know us. Just like everyone else, we have our own personalities, dispositions, skills and abilities. Just like everyone else,

---

1   This chapter appears in almost identical form in Lawson, W. (2004) *Sex, Sexuality and the Autism Spectrum*. London: Jessica Kingsley Publishers.

these change over time. Disclosure should not be a fearful thing, where one's label is positive in one vein and negative in another, but a true sharing of the value that exists between human beings. We are fighting the same battle, we are on the same side. In many respects, it's all for one and one for all.

I survived my childhood, adolescence and a big chunk of my adult life knowing I was 'different' but not knowing why. My scattiness, lack of understanding of others, inability to organise myself and difficulties with people were attributed to learning difficulties and schizophrenia. I didn't do well at school, and most of my academic learning occurred after leaving school. Not being convinced that my 'diagnosis' was accurate, in 1994 I sought reassessment. Not long before my diagnosis of AD, I was also coming to terms with my sexuality as a gay woman. The impact of both of these events has meant a dramatic change of vocation and lifestyle for me. This chapter will explore the above with particular emphasis on disclosure.

Disclosure, or the revealing of something previously hidden, has a number of benefits and pitfalls. For me, it was a relief to be given a label that made sense to me. After my diagnosis, I had the resources to explore what the label meant and, in particular, what it meant for me. The depressing realisation, though, was that AD was a lifelong disability and it was not going to go away. Here I was with all of this insight, but I couldn't make it change who I was.

Just a year earlier, I had gone through similar emotions and realisations while coming to terms with my sexuality. I didn't choose to be gay. It chose me! There was no way out of this. I remember saying to a person at church, 'How easy would it be for you to give up being heterosexual and become gay'? They laughed at me. At first, even though I disclosed to the pastor that I was gay, she said that I was mistaken and that I just needed lots of 'mothering'. Why was it so difficult to get other people to believe me? Why was it so difficult to be taken seriously and have someone acknowledge my experience? It is true that I had not been involved sexually with women and that I was married at the time. However, it was increasingly evident to me that I was not attracted to the male sex – never had been and didn't want to be. I was attracted to the female form, though – always had been – and this reality was beginning to filter though my emotions and into my physical responses.

I have always been a person with strong sexual desire, but for all of my adolescent years and some of my early adult life this was unconnected to any other person. I did not fantasise about sex with another person, and I didn't like to notice intimacy among others. Seeing other people physically close, hugging one another or kissing caused me discomfort, and I avoided such behaviour however it was being expressed – written, film or in person.

Coming to terms with my sexual identity and initially disclosing this to myself caused me huge discomfort and left me doubled up with pain. I was forced to admit that I couldn't stay married. I needed to be honest with my church, where I was an associate pastor, and tell my family and my friends. I had no idea of the impact it would have on them or on my future.

Initial disclosure

It took six months after my AD diagnosis to get the written report. I was so sure that having a report in writing would mean that the treating psychiatrist would say I could stop my neuroleptic medication, seeing as how I was not psychotic and didn't have schizophrenia. This was my first disappointment. The psychiatrist thought that the medication, which I had been taking on and off for more than 25 years, should continue. 'After all, it was probably helpful.' I sought the support of the autism association in my area. They said that such medications were helpful for lots of individuals but that I should talk this over with my doctor and aim at reducing it to see how I went. Eventually, the psychiatrist agreed to this idea. It took another five years before the doctor finally agreed that I could cease taking the medication all together. This was done abruptly and without any consultation with me about possible side effects. With the antipsychotic medication withdrawal came a lack of motivation, seemingly endless 'tummy upsets' and increased difficulty with concentration. At times I thought I was mad. My doctor prescribed an antidepressant called Zoloft™ (sertraline). No one explored the possibility that my experiences were probably connected to fast withdrawal from neuroleptic medication. I took Zoloft for 12 months, but with each day of taking it I felt nauseated and had a strange icy feeling around the inside of my head. I was relieved to stop this medication, even though it probably took the edge off my anxieties and helped me cope with my daily life.

Telling my family that I was autistic didn't seem difficult to me. I thought that they would welcome the diagnosis and realise, as I had done, that it made sense. I expected that everyone would feel the same way that I did. This was a mistake. For the most part my children (then 12, 14, 18 and 20) seemed really interested and happy for me. My youngest son was also being assessed; in lots of ways, although we were very different people, we were also quite similar. Tim received his diagnosis of AD within months of me receiving mine. The children's father (we were separated at this time) dismissed the diagnoses and said that we were just looking for a way out of our responsibilities. My mother, who had admitted to a close friend 'Wendy was never normal' reneged upon her statement and said that she only had 'normal' children and that she treated us all the same.

Continuing education and disclosure

I had returned to school to study for my year 11 and 12 qualifications. I wanted to go to university and this was one of the prerequisites. I did well as a nearing-40-year-old among 17–18-year-olds. I found the group of students I was part of to be accepting and supportive. I spoke freely to them of my difficulties with academic study. They helped me with putting my essays on to the computer and with developing and structuring my ideas. The teacher for Australian history was interested in me because of my choice of topic for my project. Instead of the usual range of historical study, I chose 'women in the 1930s and cross-dressing'. Although I was not fully 'out' to my friends at this time, I found that my studies enriched my understanding and helped me to appreciate the battles of other women who had struggled to exist in earlier years.

It was during my first year at university that I fully accepted I was gay. My divorce came through, and my partner and I seriously decided to set up home together. We had been soulmates for more than ten years and she was all I dreamed of. I knew we had to tell the children that their mum was now going to live as a lesbian, not just in name but in actuality, with another woman. This woman was like an aunt to them, and they loved her. For the first time, the children began to understand the reality of their situation. What would their friends say? How could they bring friends home and have them realise their mother was gay? What did it all mean? They were furious with me. 'How dare you do this to us Mum?' my daughter said. I tried to explain that I was not doing it to anyone. She didn't understand, and because I wouldn't change my mind she left home. My oldest son also left home. My daughter went to live with a lady from church. My son went to live with his father. The impact of this on me was devastating. I had thought that my children would see that this was good for us all. I failed to appreciate that they were embarrassed by me and, in their still childlike way, believed that I should put them first above any other. I had no income (only an education allowance), two of my children had left home and I felt completely isolated.

I turned to my friends at church. They were astounded. 'How can a reasonable and intelligent person like you be doing this?' they said. 'Men were designed to relate sexually with women; not women with women,' said a close friend. 'I mean, only a man has the right appendage for the job.' I failed to see what 'the right appendage' had to do with loving and being yourself. A meeting was called at church, and the committee asked me to resign. I complied. From that day to this, most of the 'friends' I thought I had removed themselves from our friendship. I still feel sad about this today.

At university, I found a very different culture. At uni, I experienced respect and support. In particular, my academic work was respected. I still had lots of difficulties with social events and avoided them, but my desire to learn was welcomed by the lecturers. I found other students who were gay and would involve myself in debates about religion and homosexuality. I obtained an assessment for my academic difficulties with reading, writing and mathematics. As well as being an AD person, I was diagnosed as being dyslexic and dysmathic (my word for difficulties with maths); much later in my career, I discovered I had attention-deficit/hyperactivity disorder (ADHD). The university made provision for my difficulties. They were never seen as a problem.

The university was happy to use my abundant energy and enthusiasm. Instead of constantly being told to 'Sit still, Wendy', it was 'What do you think you might like to do to contribute to uni life?' No one had ever asked me what I wanted; most of my life, I had been told what to do by others who knew what was best for me. Had I been asked, I might have said that I wanted to become an artist, a writer or a missionary in some distant place. My dreams might have seemed a bit out of reach at some points in my life, but this is not a good reason to stamp on them.

As a keen writer and researcher, I was offered the role of editor for the university newspaper. I was so excited! This was the first time in my life I had ever been offered a job of this nature. In the past, I had been considered with some contempt as not being able to do anything. As a child at school, for example, when it came to other students choosing the members they wanted for their team, I was never chosen and teacher had to intervene to put me in a team. I was not good at appreciating the social complexities of human relating, and it was easier to walk around the playground following the white line than join in with children's games that made no sense to me and failed to facilitate any of my interests. The only games I was welcome in were those that other children found fun in through teasing or bullying me.

I was glad that I had disclosed my sexuality to my fellow students, and I was fortunate to have a positive response. I know that not all of my friends found this true for their situation. I wonder if it was easier for some to accept my sexuality because I was a woman. How would it have been if I were a man?

When I received my diagnosis of AD, I went to the disability liaison officer at uni and gave them my written report. Again, I was very fortunate: I had a person who was willing to listen. 'Wendy, what difficulties do you experience?' she asked me. I said that it was very difficult to listen to a lecture and take notes at the same time. I explained that I wasn't good at doing two things at once. 'Oh, that's easy,' she said. 'We'll get you a note-taker.' I also told her how I got lost easily and didn't cope with finding my way around or with lots of noise, lights and people. She assigned me to a peer-support person, who showed me around campus and waited to assist me in locating places. I also was allowed to take exams in a separate room to other students, given extra reading time and allowed to check with the invigilator that I had the right understanding of the questions.

Disclosure and family

My children were finding it very difficult to accommodate their mum's new lifestyle. Not only was Mum home less often, she also had a really keen interest in understanding homosexuality and the world of disability, especially autism. In the past, they had been used to Mum's obsessive disposition towards insects, birds, animals and Christianity. In fact, being a Christian had been Mum's preoccupation ever since they could remember. Suddenly, Mum was not attending church more. No more Bible-study groups. No more prayer meetings. They were quite worried that their mum had lost her mind. I don't know whether they stayed away from our home because of their need to remain in a more familiar environment or whether they just couldn't fathom what else to do.

At first, I experienced waves of a very uncomfortable feeling. It would just whoosh up from inside my tummy and I couldn't eat or sleep. I felt like I had failed my children, failed my husband and failed my Heavenly father. 'What kind of a Christian does this to her family?' I asked myself. The truth, as I saw it, was that I had to be honest. Somehow, I believed that my Heavenly father loved and understood me. If anyone accepted me for who I was, He did. I took comfort in this belief and in my studies.

My mother made it very plain to me that she didn't accept my sexuality, my chosen partner or my lifestyle. Whenever I shared with her some of my academic success she seemed pleased to have me as a daughter. Whenever my autism presented me with a problem, however, she became cross and removed herself from me. I so often felt abandoned and despairing. Fortunately for me, my few remaining friends stayed loyal and supportive.

Disclosure and the world of academia

I continued to do well in my studies and began to envisage a career in the behavioural sciences. I started a support group for parents of children with autism. The parents said that my talking of my experiences helped them to understand their children better. They suggested that I write about my experiences and even consider a career as a teacher. 'Wow! What a concept,' I remember thinking. 'Who would have ever thought that Wendy, diagnosed as being intellectually disabled, as having autism and learning difficulties, would be thought of as an individual with skills useful to others?' I was ecstatic.

I had always found written expression a great medium for arranging my thoughts and reviewing an understanding. I spent a couple of years putting together a manuscript as an autobiography and then set about finding a publisher. At the same time, I travelled overseas to continue with my social work studies as an exchange student. During the five months at the University of Bradford in the UK, I concentrated on my studies from Monash University Australia, by distance education, managed the compulsory studies at Bradford and pursued my writing. I eventually found a publisher and gained a literary agent. Sheila, my agent, encouraged me to keep writing. After my second book was published (I self-published my first book – a book of poetry), Sheila told me that it would be the first of many. To have such faith in my work, my ability and me was totally foreign to me. I cried a lot at that time. Disclosing critical aspects of my life experience in my book *Life Behind Glass* was quite painful for me. Revisiting my growing up, schooling, teenage experiences, getting married and then becoming a divorcee all opened up wounds that I had wanted to forget. However, maybe my life today needed me to revisit my life then. Maybe I am wiser and stronger for having faced those times. It seems to me that writing and then reading what I write helps me to cement my understanding. My experiences take on meaning; they get connected to reality and I am even more able to make sense of things. I know that my learning is delayed and I seem to be slower than many others at adjusting to understanding, either of self or of other. The great thing about this understanding, though, is that once it gels, it really sticks.

It has been a gradual process of writing, getting my work published and completing the various studies that I have undertaken at different universities. I love to study, research my material and write about it. At times, I have been so excited about a topic that it has been hard to contain it. I talk incessantly to others and have got myself into trouble because they are not interested. When I tell other students 'I got an A!', I expect them to rejoice with me. I've been known to talk on and on and on about the things that interest me. This failure to pick up on or be sensitive to the fact that another person might not share my interest has taken me years to realise. Disclosure is one aspect of 'telling', but I am learning that there is a time to disclose and a time to refrain from disclosure.

Academically, I still wrestle with what aspects of my knowledge I should or should not share. Learning to be honest while being discreet and sensitive to others is not my forte.

Disclosure or non-disclosure?

I am aware that once I have spoken, I cannot take the words back. However, what I have difficulty recognising is which situations I should share with another, who that 'other' should be and when I should share. For me, when something is on my mind it completely takes over my thoughts and there is no space for anything else. Thus, it will be those thoughts that get expressed and, at times, it is not appropriate to tell the person those thoughts. I know this after the event because the person might say 'I don't need to know that Wendy.' Sometimes the person will become 'different'. I can tell that something has changed for that person, but I might not be able to define what that change is, or what caused it, or what the implications of that change might be.

When I chose to actively engage in the gay lifestyle, I found it much easier being 'out' when I was among others who were like me. This has been true also for my autism. I find that being with other individuals 'on the spectrum' gives me a freedom to be myself. I don't need to struggle to hide my emotions or to wear myself thin trying to perform so as not to upset someone.

It is only this year (I am now 51 years old) that I realised it is OK not to disclose all my thoughts and feelings to my partner. I believed that a partnership meant sharing every aspect of myself with the other. When I discovered that it was OK to have thoughts, ideas, dreams and interests that were one's own and didn't automatically need to be shared, I was intrigued. I still felt some discomfort with this realisation, but I also felt some relief. It was a relief to know that if I chose not to disclose my thoughts, then it was OK. I have come to understand that I am not lying if I choose to keep some information to myself. In fact, at times, other individuals are not interested in what's happening for me and they prefer it if I just take time to listen to them.

Telling

A story's not a story, unless it can be told.
In order to share with another,
I need to know when to be bold.

A story's not a story, unless it can be shared.
A story might be helpful,
When it's well prepared.

A story's not a story, unless identified with.
Life that's easy, life that's hard,
We each have a life to live.

I want to share my story.
I want to do it for free.
I need to know that others,
can accept the real me.

If I only give parts of the story,
The picture will be incomplete.
If I give too much of my story,
I might send the people to sleep.

Oh, to find the balance,
Of what to say, where, and when.
I might keep myself out of trouble.
I might have some friends once again.

But then there is a problem,
A real friend stays true just the same.
I want my story to make a difference,
I don't want it to be just a game.

Disclosure and emotional growth

'No pain, no gain' a friend states. How I wish this were not true, but I
think it probably is right. I know I have felt the joy of satisfaction from

eating after I have experienced hunger. I know the relief I have experienced once I realised my anxiety was unfounded. Then there is the ecstasy of discovering a good grade written on the results board in the hall at the university. If I hadn't first felt the hunger, the anxiety, the discomfort of waiting, I could not have known the relief. This is also my experience with disclosure. There have been moments of utter despair; times of sheer agony, heartache and helplessness. I have experienced huge disappointment, frustration and physical torment. Today, I can look back over those episodes not with gladness that they happened but with some comprehension and appreciation of the outcomes they have brought for my life. How will we ever educate others or assist them in their understanding if we don't 'disclose' to them? We need to start by acknowledging self to ourselves; then we can begin to acknowledge self to others. Accepting who I am, warts and all, is the best gift I can give to myself and to others. Self-confidence can only reign well in a culture of self-acceptance. This depends on me, not on the value I receive from others. Obviously, my self-confidence is endorsed and enhanced by the positive actions of others, but it cannot begin there. The responsibility of my accepting me is mine to begin with. This is the foundation for my current and future life. I know that some would argue that self-confidence begins with having others believe in us first, then we can believe in ourselves. Maybe it's that old question of what comes first: the chicken or the egg? I don't know the answer. I only know that I need to believe in me. If I wait for others to promote my abilities and take no action until they do, then I could be waiting a very long time and I might be missing the moment, and hence the opportunity might be lost.

It isn't very comfortable to realise one has certain difficulties. I know I have huge problems with working out my money. I manage to shop and buy the things I need, but I'm hopeless at working out how much things cost and what change I should have. I depend on the honesty of others. Quite often, I am 'left behind' in a conversation. I might get the gist of what the conversation was about, but usually I need longer for full meaning to sink in. This means, especially in social get-togethers, that I can't successfully join others in their conversations. I'm not fast enough to keep up and respond appropriately. If a conversation is based on information that is of interest to me, however, then I already have most of the building blocks to participate and can feel fully involved with the topic.

Knowing my limitations is one thing. Accepting those limitations is not so easy and it is something that I revisit constantly.

Disclosure and relationships

In my experience, sometimes other people are uncomfortable around me. It would seem that my very presence 'exposes' them in some way or another. Maybe my behaviour causes them to feel embarrassed, or they just don't feel that comfortable with themselves, and this is more evident when they are with me. This seems to have been the situation with some of my friends in the past. For me, coming to terms with this understanding has been very difficult. I know that the aspects about myself that are not pleasing to others seem to be the things that I cannot change. This means that by disclosing who I am (gay and autistic), I am exposing any potential relationship to the risk of not developing. It is, therefore, tempting to conform to expectation and not upset the delicate balance of human need and demand. I'm just not good at this! I have tried to be the wife; the good Christian woman; the mother. I actually think I did a good job while it lasted. The crunch came when I could no longer live a lie. It was OK for a while, because I didn't have the right name for who I was. I conformed to the label I'd been landed with, even though it was very uncomfortable. But, once reality set in and I knew the truth, I could no longer hide behind the make-believe set-up I'd grown up in and adopted as 'my life'.

'You shall know the truth and the truth shall set you free.' This quote from scripture holds true for me and I am glad. I'm not glad that others are embarrassed by the 'truth' that is Wendy. I'm not glad that some are disappointed and saddened by this truth. However, these are their difficulties, not mine. Their problems with who I am are for them to solve and sort out. I know that my real friends are bigger and stronger than the discomforts they feel with any of Wendy's 'Wendy-ness'. They are committed to my wellbeing and to our mutual friendship. At times, my own disclosures of difficulty and doubt set others free to share their difficulties too. If we only share our achievements and successes, then I think we set the standard too high and others may feel as if they cannot be themselves. It's as if being who they are means accepting and disclosing to themselves that they are imperfect beings. Surely we all need to know that this is true for each of us and it's OK?

Disclosure, self and the future

In this chapter, I have disclosed to you, the reader, much about my being autistic, gay and 'happy' with who I am. This has required courage and honesty from me. I hope it has been useful to you. I hope that you will have the courage of your convictions, whatever they may be, to stand up and be counted. If we stand together, it is easier to face the foe. None of us need be in this battle alone. There is some evidence to suggest that the incidence of homosexuality is higher among individuals on the autistic spectrum than it is in the typical population. There is evidence to show that the population of people with autism is growing. If we want to be involved with the building of a better future for our children, and for the human race in general, then we need to be involved with disclosure. No longer can we afford to sit on the fence and let others do the jumping. We need to be jumping with them. Self-confidence may develop as one takes the plunge, dives in and learns to swim. If you want to be left behind, that's up to you. But think about what you are missing. Why should everyone else have all the fun? I reckon the future looks rosy if we can build it together. Out there on our own, though, that's not so promising. Maybe you could think about disclosure and what it might mean for you? Could be the beginning of a whole new journey! Are you game?

Bold, bright and beautiful

> It isn't easy being green,
> Buried beneath the earth's crust.
> I've been down here long enough,
> Surface now I must.
>
> It's only when I spread my wings,
> That I may learn to fly.
> I mightn't be very good at it,
> But I know I want to try.

Yes, I'll surface quietly,
Knowing that you might not see.
But as I take flight to the trees
And catch that early morning breeze,
You'll notice me without a doubt.
With my legs I'll make a shout.

My disclosure heard by all,
Causes me to sing.
I know it's dangerous flying tall,
Ravens might upon me spring.

But this is how I tell my story.
Attracting others to my plight,
All cicadas bathe in glory
Singing out created life.

15.

Diagnosis, disclosure and self-confidence in sexuality and relationships

Lynne Moxon

There is a general consensus (Jones 2001; Shore 2003) about the type of questions that need to be considered when making decisions on disclosure, and this needs particular consideration in the area of building relationships:

- Who is it I am going to tell?
- Is the person ready for the discussion? Is my autism having a significant effect on the relationship?
- What underlies this judgement?
- What changes am I looking for following disclosure?
- Are significant others, e.g. colleagues and friends, aware of the diagnosis? How have they reacted?
- How will I initiate the discussion?
- What are the likely benefits to me and to others?
- What are the potential risks or negative consequences?
- How will I illustrate what Asperger syndrome (AS) means?

Sometimes, being scrupulously honest will not work. 'I want to get married so that I don't have to masturbate anymore and I'll have someone to cook for me.' This comment was made by a young man with AS and it would not endear him to most women, in spite of its frank disclosure. Uta Frith (1991) suggested that the lack of relationships, attachments and friendships that typifies people with AS does not mean that they do not want to interact but that they have not instinctively learned how to do it appropriately or how to appreciate social cues. I work with young people with AS on sociosexual development to teach those skills picked up automatically by ordinary young people but perhaps not recognised by people with AS. These skills can help friendship development; they can also prevent imprisonment if overtly unacceptable sexual behaviour is shown. If you have been given a diagnosis of AS, you or someone else has noticed a difference, perhaps in the area of friendships or sexual relationships. How, then, do you tell someone in a relationship that you have AS, and when is this necessary?

Asperger (1944, translated in Frith 1991, p.80) recognised that there were difficulties in sociosexual skills and wrote that:

> Thus, with the sexual aspects of an affective life there is often a disharmony, either a weakness or precocity and perversion, but no harmonious integration of sexuality into the developing personality.

This is a very negative perspective, but if a diagnosis can unlock resources and self-knowledge, rather than stigmatise, then it is worth it. Think of the bumper-sticker phrase, 'Aspies do it differently', not they can't do it.

Many young people with AS want relationships; a few do not. It is the lack of social understanding, which forms part of the diagnostic criteria for AS, that can make it difficult to form relationships. The inability to look at things from another person's perspective can make relationships difficult to sustain and the need to disclose your diagnosis difficult to understand. In some circumstances, a person's sensory sensitivity can lead to problems with the intimate side of sex. If your boyfriend with AS refuses to touch you in foreplay because he does not like the feel of stimulating a female sexually, then there will be less enjoyment all round. Social understanding is the vital issue. Most people with AS can learn basic social skills, but it is when and how to put these into practice that matters, i.e. social confidence. This will include when and how to tell – or not to tell – another person that you have AS. One glance at the popular website www.bbc.co.uk/relationships shows that it is not only people with AS who worry about understanding partners and finding compromises, improving dating techniques and self-confidence. There are areas of knowledge that will make anyone a better friend or partner.

The academic area of a diagnosis is unambiguous in comparison with the practical implications of living with an autism spectrum disorder

(ASD). I frequently discuss with my students whether they would prefer, as a partner or friend, someone with AS or a person without AS. The discussion focuses on confidence and understanding. They feel that a partner with AS would understand their problems better and they would feel more confident in the relationship. There would be a shared experience; sensory difficulties would be understood. On the other hand, they could not live, for example, with a person who collected beer cans or played computer games for hours! As with all young adults perceived similarity, good looks, sense of humour, kindness and unselfishness rate high for males and females as traits associated with friendship and popularity (Coleman and Hendry 1999).

Some potential areas of difficulty in disclosing ASD to a potential partner are discussed below. You need to consider how to manage these areas, in order to avoid damaging your self-confidence. Make sure you build in a possibility of success in what you do before you set out; recognise your attributes and make the most of them rather than dwelling on imperfections. Self-esteem has a powerful influence on adjustment across a wide range of areas. Achievement in education and work, social relationships, mental health and the ability to deal with stress are all influenced by self-esteem. All people with low self-esteem are character- ised by a sense of incompetence in social relationships, social isolation and the belief that people neither understand nor respect them.

The consensus from research is that it is satisfaction with one's physical appearance that contributes most to overall self-esteem, followed by social acceptance by peers and, to a lesser degree, academic success and sporting achievement. Peer group (workmates, fellow students) opinion seems to be more important than that of close friends, ahead of parents. Look at the way you present yourself, how you dress, the topics of con- versation you have, the new experiences you are prepared to try.

Emotions

People with AS are not emotion-free robots, but they may need to learn to recognise, use and control their emotions. Without some disclosure, it is difficult to help a friend. Emotions impact on work, relationships, creativity and achievements. Philosophers such as David Hume (Mossner 1986) and Adam Smith (2000) believed emotions to be vital to social and individual existence. More recent thinkers have examined the premise further. Evans (2003) writes: 'Intelligent action results from a harmonious blend of emotion and reason.' To have an understanding of when to go along with our feelings and when to ignore them is a valuable asset that is now called 'emotional intelligence'. To be able to recognise and control anger is vital in relationships, and many young adults with AS find this difficult. Evans goes on to suggest that as emotions are vital for intelligent action, a Vulcan such as Mr Spock – all logic and no emotion – would be, on the whole, less intelligent than a human. It can be emotionally difficult to disclose our imperfections, which may be needed with a prospective partner.

Sex and relationships

Sexuality comes with being human. It is not something we can easily cut out of out lives. Grandin (1996), an exceptionally able person with AS, decided not to complicate her life with sexual relationships, although she sometimes wonders what she has missed. However, Armstrong (2003), in his work on the philosophy of intimacy, states that the 'need to love and be loved is deeply placed in human nature'.

Cohen (1980, p.388), writing before AS had a separate diagnostic category (AS was added to the *Diagnostic and Statistical Manual IV* in 1994), quotes a young man with autism:

> I really didn't know there were people until I was seven years old. I then suddenly realised that there were people. But not like you do. I still have to remind myself that there are people… I never could have a friend. I really don't know what to do with other people really.

When this personal experience is considered alongside the diagnostic criteria for AS the likelihood of attaining and maintaining any relationship, let alone a sexual relationship, may seem remote. This is particularly so, as most parents report that their child with AS has never had a friend. Older outcome studies looking at the prognosis for adults with autism (Rutter 1970; Kanner 1971) showed no marriages and few dating. There is still little research about frequency of marriages and long-term relationships. More recent outcome studies of high-functioning adults (Szatmari *et al.*1989; Larsen and Mouridsen 1997) found some marriages and long-term relationships, but Hellemans and Deboutte (2002) found a high percentage of relationships in high-functioning autism, perhaps reflecting the wider diagnosis now made. Clinical experience, books by people with AS (e.g. Slater-Walker and Slater-Walker 2002) and their partners, and increasing research now show many examples of long-term successful relationships. Hénault and Attwood's (2002) research found that people with AS and high-functioning autism have levels of sexual desire and imagery comparable to those of the general population. However, the AS sexual profile differed in several respects from that of the general population. Body image, sense of belonging to one's sex and the erotic imagery of individuals with AS seem to be less influenced by social norms. Adults with AS would appear to act according to their internal desires, regardless of whether they are directed to a person of the same or the opposite sex.

Young people with AS need to learn the rules: that there is more than one way of saying 'no' and to understand that there are subtle, non-verbal signals of encouragement. Verbal interactions can be complicated; the phrase 'Would you like to come up for coffee?' needs knowledge of context to be interpreted correctly. Standard school sex education is not sophisticated enough to help an adolescent with AS. If diagnosis happens early, then the extra time gained should be used to teach useful social skills.

Sexuality and autism spectrum disorder (ASD)

Sexuality encompasses more than sexual behaviour. It includes self-image, emotions, gender, values and attitudes (Downs and Craft 1997; Hellemans and Deboutte 2002). This is sociosexual behaviour in all its complexity. Society's view of sexuality changes constantly in response to experiences, education and cultural values. Discriminatory attitudes to the sexuality of people with developmental disabilities have in the past interfered with sex education for this group of young people (Shakespeare 1996), and for many years sexuality was denied to people with autism (Dewey and Everard 1974). As a result, literature on the sexuality of people with autism or AS is sparse in comparison with that available for people with learning disabilities.

Although Hénault and Attwood (2002) found that the majority of people with ASD are interested in sex and show a wide range of sexual behaviours, they also found that individuals with AS and high-functioning autism have poor levels of knowledge regarding sexuality. Clinical experience shows that in some individuals and couples, the specific areas of difficulty in autism cause relational and sexual problems. Accurate information is needed, and deficits in perspective-taking mean that an understanding of reality is important; what is seen on TV does not always reflect the world around.

Adolescents with AS have less social experience than their peers and are less tuned to social rules. They see no problem in being attracted to people of the same gender (Hénault 2003) and may express a wish to change sex if they feel they would be more comfortable as such. However, gay groups have social rules too, and a male with AS who takes on an overly camp persona, imitated from TV, may find he is rejected by mainstream gay people. Some young people confuse the comfort and enjoyment of friendship with sexual attraction. If you have never had a close friend until your late teens, then the newly developed intimacy and caring for another may cause confusion. Again, if it is difficult to interpret your emotions, then fear and sexual arousal may be confused. Many young people have a wide vocabulary of sexual words but little knowledge of what they mean – e.g. 'petting', 'blow job' – and will need guidance if they are not to be teased or bullied in school or work. Young people with AS need to experience an environment that welcomes healthy sexual expression.

There is some evidence that a young person with AS can gradually acquire relationship skills by intellect rather than intuition, especially if they have motivation and guidance in the areas of friendship and relationships (Attwood 2000).

Masturbation

Masturbation is normal and healthy and gives pleasure (Hingsburger 1995). Many of the young adults I work with have had problems simply because no one has told them these facts. The data suggest that people with ASD, even when normally intelligent, do not always discover spontaneously how to masturbate. Difficulties in achieving orgasm and/or incorrect masturbation techniques include not using the hand to masturbate because they have been punished for 'touching oneself', and so the person rubs against hard surfaces and receives friction burns or tears the testicles. A person might be unable to ejaculate and become sore because they cannot relax enough to come, which may sometimes provoke stress and hypermasturbation. Masturbating excessively may also become a problem, perhaps because climax cannot be reached because of poor sensory sensitivity or because of antidepressant medication.

Lack of awareness of the use of the imagination for sexual fantasy can lead to the use of more physical forms of stimulation, such as the vibration of washing machines or public transport, or the use of vacuum-cleaner pipes, holes in chair backs, socks, bottles and more unusual items, such as TV remote controls and golf clubs. Females unaware of the use of sex toys have used deodorant cans, scissors, keys and candles.

Real difficulties arise by not maintaining secrecy in sex play as most of the population do. Young adolescent males with AS may tell of touching or masturbating together in school. If the police become involved, the young person may be put on the sex offenders register. Lack of understanding may also lead to bizarre behaviour, e.g. mixing sugar with milk to resemble semen and drinking it to keep up the supply of sperm following frequent masturbation. Occasionally, the feeling of an orgasm is so overwhelming that it frightens the person.

Fetish behaviour

Studies have indicated that there is a tendency towards repetitive behaviour, stereotyped interests, and sensory fascinations, which may influence the sexual development of people with ASD. Many people with and without AS use fetish objects to maintain or stimulate sexual response. In autism, there may be a ritual use of objects, fascinations with a sexual connotation and unusual fears associated with sex. Fetish items can range from the usual silk or leather to very individual items that have come to be associated with sexual response often at an early age, e.g. TV theme tunes or the smell of petrol. There can be difficulties if the sexual response is conditioned to public places; in this case, the person will need imagery training and work on the context of sexual behaviour.

In a relationship, your partner has to agree to be involved in unusual sexual behaviour and will need to understand why such stimulation is needed.

Sensory sensitivity

Sex is touching, holding, cuddling and stroking, much more than inserting A into B, but some forms of sexual stimulation may be uncomfortable or even painful for the person with AS. Sensory problems may lead to difficulties, e.g. not wanting to touch your partner in foreplay, disliking the feel of condoms, not wanting to be hugged, or regulating the force applied with the hands and fingers, which will need the support of your partner. Disclosure of specific sensory differences is important.

Inappropriate behaviour

Research suggests that inappropriate behaviour in individuals with ASD, e.g. touching the genitals and masturbation in public, talking inappropriately about sex, inappropriate person-oriented behaviour, and stalking, occurs quite often (Hellemans and Debaoutte 2002). Deviant behaviour 'may arise from living in a system in which appropriate sexual knowledge and relationships are not supported' (Schwier and Hingsburger 2000). I would endorse this statement. When people do not have an appropriate place in which to engage in sexual behaviour or appropriate knowledge of what is acceptable, they will not stop the behaviour but they may get into severe trouble. For most of us, feeling embarrassed helps to teach us social distinctions and to build barriers that enable the determination of the appropriate from the inappropriate. Many of my students get into difficulties because no one has told them the correct way of behaving – they often have no friends in adolescence when most information on sex is picked up informally. Occasionally, they have received counselling in which behaviour that can get them into trouble or disgust partners (hiding in bushes, naked and masturbating; collecting poo and storing it under the bed) has not been addressed as inappropriate. 'A healthy environment for adults is one in which people are given accurate information regarding sexuality and sexual expression' (Hingsburger 1995). A number of the young adults I have worked with find children sexually arousing. This may have arisen as part of sexual attraction to young adolescent peers when growing up and has not moved on, or it may be to very young children (Hellemans and Deboutte 2002). This is inappropriate and needs to be addressed professionally.

People with Asperger syndrome do fall in love

Love is not just a feeling. The evolutionary theory of the development of this emotion is that it aids survival of the species, because this strong emotion lasts about 18 months to ensure the birth of children in a male/female relationship. Love 'matures' over time (Armstrong 2002) and turns into a feeling that will sustain a partnership through a long, mutually supportive relationship. Many neurotypical people place too much importance on finding 'the one' – the right person for their affections. The perfect partner does not exist. Incompatibility makes relationships break down, but it is illogical to conclude that you can avoid pain by waiting forever in search of a totally compatible partner. If you love someone, then you need to put them first, to make their needs a priority. This might mean that you have to change some of your routines to accommodate a long-term partner and, possibly, children. If a partner in a relationship receives a late diagnosis of AS, then the non-AS partner might blame all the difficulties of the relationship on AS. Stanford (2003) discusses this in her book on AS and long-term relationships. Stanford suggests ways for finding solutions to such problems. All relationships hit troughs at one time or another; the key to overcoming them is communication. Within your relationship, there needs to be a genuine capacity for disclosure, sharing and expressing your thoughts and feelings in a way that feels right for both of you. There also needs to be a way in which to resolve conflict and to discuss unmet needs. If a partner with or without AS does not agree that there is a problem, then they will not change.

However, a late diagnosis might lead to a flowering of social development and relationships as the person finds the courage to move forward in work and life, no longer blaming themselves, afraid of making mistakes and learning how to interpret other's behaviour.

Computer dating

Online communication is wonderful for many people with AS (Harpur *et al.* 2004). It can provide easy access to friendship and support for people who struggle with shyness or low self-esteem, and it gives the opportunity to build confidence and social skills in a non-threatening environment. Online relationships can and do last. But this same accessibility can lead to problems, e.g. it is hard to know whether the person is lying. It is easy to misrepresent yourself online, to pretend to someone you are successful and good-looking, or a female rather than a male. You do not have to disclose your AS. If someone is desperate for love or friendship, then they are more likely to imagine that the person they are talking to is their perfect partner. The Internet can become a tempting distraction from the difficulty and hassle of making real rather than virtual relationships.

Will diagnosis help?

If people with ASD are to form friendships and be a part of society as adults, knowledge of relationships and the skills to make them must develop during childhood. We find our adult friends later in life, usually through work or social activities. However, only 12 per cent of higher-functioning adults are in full-time paid employment, over a third go out only 'rarely' to any social event, and half will go out only once or twice a month (Barnard *et al.* 2001). These figures for lack of engagement in social activities were even higher for people in their teens and twenties.

However, although integrated classrooms and recreational activities are important, what is needed is teaching of skills. Relationships between people with ASD and others are not formed simply by grouping people together. Some individuals need assistance with fitting into certain settings and activities, and although children are integrated in school, they may have few friends. Others may need someone to facilitate their involvement or to interpret social interactions for them. Without supports – and this includes diagnosis – some people with ASD may never have the opportunity to know other people.

When it all goes wrong

Is the problem in a relationship something you can let go, or is it funda-mental to your happiness? If it is the former, you have to ask yourself whether you can change, e.g. can you give up your hobby of plane-spotting every weekend and holiday? If it is the latter, can your partner do the changing, e.g. will your partner come with you? Do you insist on turning the TV channel over to something you want to watch? Do you insist on having your meal on the table at 6 o'clock? Do you make sure you have sorted out all of *your* jobs and routines before you feed the crying baby?

If you enjoy being with your partner, agree with how they think and behave, and share the same opinions about life, then you are doing well, whether you have AS or not. If your partner is also someone whom you respect, trust and feel affection for, then you have the basis for a long-term relationship.

> Difficulties in interpersonal functioning can arise when someone is not aware of his or her feelings, has trouble expressing emotions, expresses them inappropriately, or misinterprets the feelings of his partner. (www.bbc.co.uk/relationships)

The website mentioned above is to help the general public improve their relationship skills, but the description could be specific to AS social functioning and the difficulty in recognising emotions in oneself and others. This will happen at times in any relationship, but more often in AS. Diagnosis might help you realise early on that a partner is reacting negatively to what you are doing. This can help to guide your behaviour and perhaps help you to avoid more serious confrontations in the future.

Even when you have learned skills such as eye contact and joining colleagues for a drink after work, things can still go wrong. Many people with AS have difficulty in listening to one person speaking in a noisy social setting and need to lean in closely and watch the person's mouth,

> The more intense the flirting, the more intensely we'll look from eye to eye – and the more time we'll spend looking at their mouth. If someone is watching your mouth while you're talking to them, it can be very, very seductive. It could be that they're imagining what it would be like to kiss you. (Cox, n.d.)

In the scenario above, a woman colleague made a pass at a man with AS who had learned good eye contact but found himself in a noisy pub where he had to watch her mouth; she kissed him on the lips.

Aston (2003) discusses many problems associated with a diagnosis of AS and how this challenge to a family or a relationship can be positively overcome.

To tell or not to tell?

It is natural to want to know the cause of your difficulties. Without a clear diagnosis you can feel in limbo, trying to come to terms with what is happening and unsure what the future holds for you and perhaps the rest of your family. After a diagnosis, you may learn skills you have missed, but that does not signal the end of your problems. Should you tell everyone you meet, 'hoping that they will automatically make a needed adjustment' (Shore 2003).

If you do choose to tell a friend or partner of your diagnosis, then it is best not to leave it until a crisis makes it necessary, as this makes it more likely that an uninformed person will assume that it is just an excuse. You do not need to make a list of all the things you find difficult; just disclose what is relevant at the time.

Some people choose not to pursue a formal diagnosis. This is a personal decision, especially if they are concerned about privacy or think others may be unsympathetic or even rejecting or if they are certain that their condition will not lead to any problems. Perhaps the more important question that an individual with AS should consider is not whether to tell or not to tell, but rather what are the consequences of *not* getting a formal diagnosis or not telling? Aston (2003, p.46) says from her wide experience of couples, 'The only time I have seen AS men change their perception of themselves [as always being right] is when they have had a diagnosis and realised that what their partners were saying was true.'

A person may have struggled with AS without ever knowing exactly what their problems were, learning over time a number of techniques that make life easier for them. Over the years, they have developed ways to get and keep track of the information they need and developed systems for helping them get and stay organised. A diagnosis may enable them to find even more avenues to success at work, in relationships and in the community.

Even if people with AS are knowledgeable about their disabilities and their rights, there are issues of to tell or not to tell. And if you do tell, when is the right time? Jones (2001) suggests that giving a diagnosis to individuals functioning at the higher end of the autistic spectrum is important, because they are likely to live and work independently and need an awareness of their own style in order to develop problem-solving strategies and to be able to describe the nature of AS to other people. In general, therefore, better outcomes are likely to result from giving the diagnosis as early as practicable.

Remember that you do not have to choose between telling everyone and telling noone. You can choose to tell a few people you trust or who really need to know and ask them to keep it strictly confidential. What matters is:

- How severe is the AS?

- How much does the nature or difference of AS conflict with the wish to further the relationship?

- How open is the other person to recognising and accommodating individuals with disabilities?

A colleague with AS has written of situations where he feels it necessary to reveal his AS, 'such as when applying for jobs and more informally, when someone notices something "unusual" about me. In my case, it is usually obsessiveness.' Here is an example of when he felt it necessary to put others in the picture:

> ...when having dinner on a cruise ship. When eating meals, I often like to stick to a preference, in my case steaks and ice cream for desert. One of my table-mates noticed that I took the steak option each time for my main course and ice cream for desert and 'had become used to it'. When she noticed this, I thought that it was necessary to tell others that I had Asperger syndrome.

Jones (2001) describes how very little has been written about giving the diagnosis of AS or high-functioning autism to the young person concerned. There is even less advice on informing others of your diagnosis, although Shore (2003) has developed a series of worksheets to enable adolescents with AS to give information about themselves to others. Professionals need to recognise the logical consequence of increased feelings of helplessness, hopelessness, lower self-esteem and lack of assertive skills that arise as the result of living day in and day out with AS, particularly as this difficulty, for many adults, is either identified inadequately or not identified and is even less likely to have been given appropriate educational input. Jones (2001) and Shore (2003) both write about sharing the diagnosis with others but suggest caution about the people with whom you discuss the diagnosis and the nature of AS in order to avoid a situation where other people constantly want to talk about it or to seek signs of ASD behaviour. More people think they know what AS is due to the increased exposure in the press and books such as *The Curious Incident of the Dog in the Night-time* (Haddon 2003). If you are going to make a disclosure, you need to understand yourself first and then consider why you are doing this.

> Other cases where I feel it necessary to tell people that I have Asperger syndrome are when others notice that I can memorise events day by day, whether news events or family events, as well as being able to memorise everything everybody says word-for-word. One of my uncles is intrigued by this. When people notice how well I can memorise dates, general knowledge, etc., I often say that I have Asperger syndrome. (see Mitchell 2005)

The major responsibility for the discussion and sharing of a diagnosis rests with the person with AS. It would be unethical to 'out' a partner without their consent. In this regard, there needs to be some discussion as to whether there are likely to be benefits from a more general sharing of the diagnosis with fellow students at college, colleagues in the workplace, as well as friends. It is also important not to use AS as an excuse, as in 'You can't expect me to do that: I have AS!'

While most individuals enjoy meeting new people, some people with ASD find this stressful. They are sustained by those they have known over time and who accept their difference. The continuity of relationships over the years is an important source of security, comfort and self-worth. In order to nurture continuous relationships, to do all the things that maintain and promote friendships some understanding of the topics discussed above is important.

References

Armstrong, J. (2002) *Conditions of Love: The Philosophy of Intimacy.* London: Penguin.

Aston, M. (2003) *Aspergers in Love.* London: Jessica Kingsley Publishers.

Attwood, T. (2000) 'Strategies for Improving the Social Integration of Children with Asperger Syndrome.' *Autism 4,* 85–100.

Barnard, J., Harvey, V., Potter, D. and Prior, A. (2001) *Ignored or Ineligible? The Reality for Adults with Autism Spectrum Disorders.* London: National Autistic Society.

Cohen, D. (1980) 'The pathology of the self in primary childhood autism and Gilles de la Tourette syndrome.' *Psychiatric Clinics of North America 3,* 83–402.

Coleman, J. and Hendry, L. (1999) *The Nature of Adolescence*, 3rd ed. London: Routledge.

Cox, T. (n.d.) 'Singles and dating – Techniques: Flirting and body language.' *Relationships*. www.bbc.co.uk/relationships/singles_and_dating/techniques_flirting.shtml

Dewey, M. and Everard, M. (1974) 'The Near Normal Autistic Adolescent.' *Journal of Autism and Childhood Schizophrenia 4*, 348–56.

Downs, C. and Craft, A. (1997) *Sex in Context*. Brighton: Pavillion Press.

Evans, D. (2003) *Emotion: A Short Introduction (Very Short Introductions)*. Oxford: Oxford University Press.

Frith, U. (1991) *Autism and Asperger Syndrome*. Cambridge: Cambridge University Press.

Grandin, T. (1996) *Thinking in Pictures and Other Reports from My Life with Autism*. New York: Vintage.

Haddon, M. (2003) *The Curious Incident of the Dog in the Night-time*. London: Random House.

Harpur, J., Lawlor, M. and Fitzgerald, M. (2004) *Succeeding in College with Asperger Syndrome: A Student Guide*. London: Jessica Kingsley Publishers.

Hellemans, H. and Deboutte, D. (2002) 'Autism Spectrum Disorders and Sexuality.' Paper presented at the Inaugural World Autism Congress, Melbourne, Australia, 10–14 November 2002.

Hénault, I. (2003) 'The Sexuality of Adolescents with Asperger Syndrome.' In L.H. Willey (ed) *Asperger Syndrome in Adolescence*. London: Jessica Kingsley Publishers.

Hénault, I. and Attwood, T. (2002) 'The Sexual Profile of Adults with Asperger Syndrome: The Need for Understanding, Support and Sex Education.' Paper presented at the Inaugural World Autism Congress, Melbourne, Australia, 10–14 November 2002.

Hingsburger, D. (1995) *Hand Made Love: A Guide for Teaching about Male Masturbation through Understanding and Video*. Toronto: Diverse City Press.

Jones, G. (2001) 'Giving the Diagnosis to the Young Person with Asperger Syndrome or High Functioning Autism.' *Good Autism Practice 2*, 65–73.

Kanner, L. (1971) 'Follow up study of eleven children originally reported in 1943.' *Journal of Autism and Child Schizophrenia 1*, 112–145.

Larsen, F. and Mouridsen, S. (1997) 'The Outcome in Children with Childhood Autism and Asperger Syndrome Originally Diagnosed as Psychotic: A 30-year Follow-up Study of Subjects Hospitalized as Children.' *European Child and Adolescent Psychiatry 6*, 181–90.

Mitchell, C. (2005) *Glass half-Empty, Glass Half-Full: How Asperger's Syndrome Changed My Life*. London: Sage.

Mossner, E.C. (1986) *A Treatise of Human Nature: David Hume*. London: Penguin.

Rutter, M. (1970) 'Autistic Children: infancy to adulthood.' *Seminars in Psychiatry 2*, 435–450.

Rutter, M. and Lockyer, L. (1969) 'A Five to Fifteen Year Follow Up Study of Infantile Psychosis.' *British Journal of Psychiatry 115*, 865–82.

Schwier, K. and Hingsburger, D. (2000) *Sexuality: Your Sons and Daughters with Intellectual Disabilities*. London: Jessica Kingsley Publishers.

Shakespeare, T. (1996) 'Power and Prejudice: Issues of Gender Sexuality and Disability.' In L. Barton (ed) *Disability and Society: Emerging Issues and Insights*. Harlow: Longman.

Shore, S. (2003) 'Disclosure for People on the Autism Spectrum: Working Towards Better Mutual Understanding with Others.' In L. Willey (ed) *Asperger Syndrome in Adolescence*. London: Jessica Kingsley Publishers.

Slater-Walker, G. and Slater-Walker, C. (2002) *An Asperger Marriage*. London: Jessica Kingsley Publishers.

Smith, A. (2000) *The Theory of Moral Sentiments (Great Books in Philosophy)*. New York: Prometheus Books.

Szatmari, P., Bartolucci, G., Bond, S. and Rich, S. (1989) 'A Follow-up Study of High Functioning Autistic Children.' *Journal of Autism and Developmental Disorders 19*, 213–25.

Further Reading

Haracopos D. and Pederson L. (1992) *Sexuality and Autism*. Danish Social Ministry Preliminary Report.

Home Office (2003) Sexual Offences Act. London: HMSO. www.legislation.go.uk/acts/acts2003/20030042.htm

Kanner, L. (1943) 'Autistic Disturbances of Affective Contact.' *Nervous Child 2*, 217–50.

Koller, R. (2000) 'Sexuality and Adolescents with Autism.' *Sexuality and Disability 18*, 125–35.

Konstantareas, M. and Lunsky, Y. (1997) 'Socio-sexual Knowledge, Experience, Attitudes and Interests of Individuals with Autistic Disorder and Developmental Delay.' *Journal of Autism and Developmental Disorders 27*, 397–413.

Rubble, M. and Dalrymple, N. (1993) 'Socio/Sexual Awareness of Persons with Autism: A Parental Perspective.' *Archives of Sexual Behaviour 22*, 229–40.

Stanford, A. (2003) *Asperger Syndrome and Long-Term Relationships*. London: Jessica Kingsley Publishers.

16.

Diagnosis in adulthood
and community disclosure

Dora Georgiou

Introduction

The focus of this chapter is disclosure in the community, and how disclosure affects the individual and their family when a diagnosis of Asperger syndrome (AS)/high-functioning autism (HFA) is made in adulthood.

Disclosure affects people on many levels, including emotional, cognitive and practical, both at the point of the initial disclosure of a diagnosis and again when the person with AS or their family discloses information to others in the community, such as to family, friends, neighbours, colleagues or professionals. Some of these aspects will be explored.

Receiving a diagnosis in adulthood

The term 'Asperger syndrome' was introduced to describe more cognitively able individuals who did not readily fit classic autism (Wing 1981) and was based on the descriptions of Hans Asperger, who in 1944 worked with children he described as having autistic psychopathy. The identification of the syndrome is, therefore, still a relatively recent phenomenon; as a consequence, diagnosis and support for people affected by AS/HFA is relatively new. This means that the adult with AS/HFA has commonly gone through childhood without a diagnosis, or more importantly, without the necessary support and guidance to navigate an incomprehensible social world, often misunderstanding others and in turn being misunderstood by them. In parallel, the family struggles with the impact that AS/HFA has on the whole family, coupled with the lack of appropriate support and advice.

Adults with AS/HFA and their families frequently express the distressing journey that they have taken until a correct diagnosis is made. For some, it is experiences of incorrect diagnosis and subsequent inappropriate support and treatment. For others, it is the constant 'stonewalling' that they experience as their concerns are rejected time and again by the various professionals involved, their concerns being explained away as the overreactions of a highly strung or overprotective parent. In school, the child with AS/HFA is recognised as being different, but the nature of this difference is not appreciated and the child is often labelled inappropriately as lazy, odd, gifted or wilful. Experiences of bullying from peers and teachers are common, especially in secondary school, and adults with AS/HFA have written poignantly about devastating school experiences (Gerland 1997; Sainsbury 2000; Williams 1992).

The earlier a diagnosis is obtained, the greater the chances are for the child to be supported appropriately. However, obtaining a diagnosis and an appropriate assessment for an autism spectrum disorder (ASD) is difficult (Howlin and Moore 1997). Adults and their families searching for answers are being made aware of AS from the increasing information that is now available from the Internet, mass media, first-person accounts and academic literature; as a consequence, more adults are seeking a diagnosis. In addition, some parents are reporting that having received a diagnosis for their child they are able to appreciate that difficulties they have experienced, either with themselves or with their spouse, may stem from the reality that they too have been living with AS (Holliday Willey 1999).

There are many variables that influence how a person with AS/HFA will react to a diagnosis. The clinician's manner when offering a diagnosis can do a lot with regard to how the disclosure will affect the individual and their family and how they deal with this information (Cunningham *et al.* 1984; Lingam and Newton 1996; Quine and Rutter 1994; Sloper and Turner 1993). Clarifying concerns and being provided with information about helpful organisations and local services is useful. The person's age, personal characteristics, support systems and previous experience with health, education and welfare professionals will also play a part. The impact on the family is also complex. ASD is little understood, not least by professionals (such as health visitors, general practitioners (GPs), educators and others), and this is especially so when the child is likely to be high-functioning or have AS. Brogan and Knussen (2003) found that parents were more likely to be satisfied with the disclosure if they gave positive ratings to the manner of the professional and the quality of the information provided; if they had been given written information and the opportunity to ask questions; and if their earlier suspicions had been accepted by professionals. Their results, they suggest, underline the importance of the interaction between parents and professionals during the disclosure interview.

A family seeking support from the paediatrician in their health authority was informed that their child just needed a 'bit of discipline'. Given their concerns, the doctor referred the child for a psychological assessment. However, after the first meeting, when the child had pulled the psychologist's hair, the family was informed that they should be ashamed of the lack of discipline regarding their child and under such circumstances it would not be appropriate for the psychologist to carry on. After years of grappling with a number of inaccurate labels, the family eventually received an AS assessment for their son when he was in his early thirties. They expressed their relief that they were finally talking to specialists who understood clearly what they had gone through and who could answer their many questions. They continue to struggle, however, as they fight in order to receive appropriate support. Their son's ability to manage has reduced significantly over the years, and the chronic stress of living with the condition and constantly fighting for an accurate assessment and support has had a debilitating effect on all the family.

When a parent is informed that their young child has a disability they experience a complex range of emotions, a sense of sadness and loss for the 'normal' or 'fantasy' child, a sense of relief that their concerns have been taken seriously, and a sense of fear coupled with courage and a determination to find the right support (Sicile-Kira 2003). Receiving a diagnosis in adulthood however, is a more bitter-sweet process. In contrast to the parents of a younger child being told, in adulthood there is less a feeling of loss and more a feeling of relief to finally receive a diagnosis that makes sense. It is a validation that there is something specific and that it has a name. Having someone explain why things may have occurred as they did can be very helpful for both the person with

AS/HFA and their family; and it allows one to look at the future in a new way (Midence and O'Neill 1999). Entangled with feelings of relief is the realisation that AS/HFA is a disability that is lifelong, that there is no 'magic pill' to be taken, no therapy or treatment that will make the AS/HFA go away. The relief of having a diagnosis is coupled with feelings of sorrow and trepidation as everyone tries to come to terms with a new reality. Often, on talking to parents, it is a sense of sadness that they share, because in retrospect they can see all the behaviours in their child with a new perspective and in this process they begin to see their own interactions with a more critical eye.

For some, diagnosis spearheads a new sense of purpose, which is driven by the desire to find out everything that there is about the condition. The person and their family can begin to search for information and to try to put the pieces together, allowing the family to start on a new journey with at least a semblance of a road map. For others, there is a complex process of helplessness, anger and denial. Helplessness is evident in those who do not have specific guidance and information about options available after a diagnosis, where networks in their community are sparse, and where the person with AS/HFA or another family member has additional difficulties that have been precipitated by the condition thus complicating the picture further and making it harder to know where to turn for the right help. Anger is also a common response that takes hold after the initial feelings of relief and is linked with feelings of sadness. With the benefit of hindsight and armed with new knowledge, parents often feel the loss of the years when they could have achieved so much more. Parents commonly direct this anger at the many professionals who previously had failed the family and current representatives of these professions within their local area. The adult receiving a diagnosis may also direct their anger towards his or her parents for not managing to find out sooner. Unlike parents whose children are diagnosed early, parents of people diagnosed as adults are less in denial of the condition. However, denial is more likely to be evident where the adult son or daughter appears to be managing relatively well; at this point, parents prefer less onerous descriptions: one parent preferred an alternative diagnosis of dyspraxia with the addition that his son was a little eccentric. The family was very wealthy and academic, so the son's behaviour was accepted more easily under this construct.

For the person with AS/HFA, denial is mostly evident in those receiving a diagnosis in adolescence, when the young adult is more aware of their differences and more compelled to fit in and become like others. The adolescent may be angry and reject their parents for accepting such a pervasive diagnosis.

The level of acceptance will be determined in part by how the condition has been described. It is harder for people to accept the condition when it is described in terms of autism, as this conjures up images of children who do not speak or relate. This image rarely bears any similarity with the experiences of the person with AS/HFA.

After diagnosis

A diagnosis enables the person with AS/HFA and their family to focus on the specific support and resources that may be needed and that will specifically take account of the AS or HFA. Unfortunately, many parents report an uphill struggle after a diagnosis is obtained. Trying to access specialist support is difficult enough for parents with young children with ASD, but for those who fight for their adult son or daughter, and for the adult with AS/HFA who makes their own request, the picture is usually worse still. There are a number of reasons for this; some relate to the nature of the disability and others to policy and the nature of funding.

The nature of Asperger syndrome/high-functioning autism

Even 15–20 years ago, many education, health and social services professionals had not heard of AS. Social and health services disputed that the condition existed; where it was acknowledged, there were debates about whether it came under the umbrella of 'learning disabilities' and was the responsibility of social services or whether it was a mental illness and hence came under the auspices of the health authority (there are remnants of this debate even now).

Children were difficult to place because they did not show signs of a learning disability but did show skewed patterns of achievement, both developmentally and academically. Because of this, many children found themselves in special schools because they were considered to suffer from emotional or behavioural difficulties, or else they struggled through mainstream school. Very few children were placed in specialist ASD environments. Frith (1989) talks of the enigma that is autism; and this is especially true when we look at the person with AS/HFA. While the child struggles to make sense of and manage their sensory, physical and social environments, the very nature of the social and communication differences means that the child finds it difficult to express this conflict other than behaviourally. Unlike many physical disabilities, AS/HFA is not immediately obvious to the observer, and the behavioural characteristics are often misinterpreted. Over the years, the child either finds more sophisticated ways to manage or mask their differences or becomes more entrenched and anxious, reducing their ability to successfully engage in day-to-day life. Not understanding the depths of the disability and not having clear and tangible signs of its acuteness has meant that few professionals appreciate just how potentially devastating the disability can be.

In most cases, families have been able to provide an 'invisible safety net' to allow the person to navigate through life. However, as children reach adulthood, they are faced with greater challenges, such as accessing higher education, employment, finding relationships outside of the family, and grappling with issues of autonomy and independence. In order to make the best use of the options available to the person, a level of support will be required that reflects what was offered by the family. The UK Disability Discrimination Act makes it clear that people with disabilities have a right to support to enable them to live independently and to access community resources. Support may be in the form of specialist aids, facilitators or environments to accommodate special needs. Professionals, however, find it difficult to look beyond the box of physical, learning or sensory disabilities.

Policy and funding
The availability of specialist support for adults with AS/HFA varies greatly from one area to another. This is, in part, a reflection of the limited knowledge and awareness of the condition by professionals in the statutory sectors, coupled with a finite amount of money to commission services. Today's culture is dictated by resource management; this commonly translates into care managers apportioning limited resources

to only those assessed as having high priority needs. Adults with AS/HFA and their families commonly experience great difficulty when trying to access funding and support because statutory professionals have difficulty appreciating the potentially disabling aspects of AS/HFA, especially when confronted with a physically able and articulate individual. Often, resources are available for adults with AS/HFA only at the point of crisis, which sadly presents in the form of mental health difficulties such as depression (Ghaziuddin and Greden 1998), addiction or inappropriate or unacceptable behaviour in the community, at work, at college or within the family unit. The person's behaviour is little understood, and the person may be incarcerated, lose their job, or lose their home.

A young man living with his parents spent much of his life staring at the outside world, yearning for an ordinary life, of having a girlfriend and of one day having a family. Unfortunately, his inappropriate attempts at meeting women resulted in him being incarcerated for sexual assault and later being sectioned in a secure psychiatric unit. Luckily for this young man, a recommendation that he be assessed for an ASD was made, which resulted in a diagnosis. After a year in a secure environment, where his social interactions were analysed within the construct of a sex offender, his difficulties were finally placed within a new construct of AS, and his behaviours suddenly made more sense to the professionals managing his care. Both his behaviour programmes and the attitude of the staff were reconstructed to meet his actual needs. This young man was able to move on from this secure environment back to his community; he is now living in a home run by a charity offering specialist support for adults with ASD and using community resources such as mainstream classes in the local further education college. What is clear for him and those who support him is that he must come to terms with his diagnosis, accept that strict guidelines are in force because of his history, and work within clear boundaries that will enable him to move forward. For him and the staff who support him, disclosing his disability is one issue, but it is compounded further by his specific difficulties around relationships. The question of how much to disclose and to whom becomes a matter of anxiety and concern; there is a need both to balance his needs and to protect his privacy.

In this instance, diagnosis and disclosure may facilitate a more positive future for the individual; it has also raised the awareness of the psychiatrist, psychologist and care staff in the secure unit. In future, they may be more willing to look beyond the initial presentation of an offender and check what may underlie certain behavioural characteristics.

As diagnosis increases, so will the demand for appropriate services and support from knowledgeable and trained professionals in the statutory sector. In the UK, the All Party Parliamentary Group on Autism (APPGA) has now presented their manifesto. It states five general principles and 11 objectives to be achieved by 2013. Included in this is to have a named senior manager in each local authority responsible for the commissioning and delivering of services to children and adults and a named member of each community mental health team with expertise in ASD to be assigned the responsibility of meeting the mental health needs of children and adults with an ASD. In addition, they propose that effective training in understanding ASD is the prerequisite for the implementation of the manifesto. The APPGA wants all professionals working in health, social care, education and the criminal justice sector to receive autism-awareness and job-specific training as part of their continuing professional development.

Specialist support needs to be available to enable the person with AS/HFA to access higher education, vocational or prevocational training and counselling and the opportunity and guidance to meet and interact with others in a social context and to live independently from one's family. Given that such support is commonly both difficult to find (Howlin 2000) and even more difficult to fund, improved training and awareness may have a more positive impact on how resources are allocated. Inevitably, in seeking to secure the right support, a level of disclosure will be necessary.

Improving understanding through disclosure

Disclosure plays an important part in enabling the community to open its eyes to difference, in increasing understanding, and in improving provision in order to translate the rhetoric of equality into reality.

Rhetoric aside, such disclosure may involve sharing information, which can make the person feel vulnerable and add to them feeling different. The success of disclosure will depend on how comfortable the person feels with such disclosure and how able those who have informa-

tion disclosed to them are to deal with the information: one is intrinsically related to the other. Disclosing your disability articulates your
difference to others, and our society does not always deal sympathetically
with difference.

Who needs to know?

There are individual differences that will determine the way in which the
person comes to terms with their diagnosis and that will affect their
feelings about disclosing to others. There are also cultural, practical and
circumstantial events that will influence this. Some adults with AS/HFA
have both the intellectual and the emotional capacity to live fairly successfully with AS/HFA. Many have talked about the importance of
having a few people who have stood by them and supported them. In
such instances, the need to disclose is often limited to a small number of
people, such as parents, spouse and friends. Alternatively, the access to
greater knowledge and information that becomes available after a
diagnosis empowers others; rather than limiting who they disclose to,
they are instead driven by the desire to educate others about their
disability (Willey 1999).

However, necessity may dictate a need rather than a choice to
disclose. Not all adults are able to cope with the difficulties of growing up
with AS/HFA; some may not have the cognitive or emotional resources
to manage effectively; and practical and financial resources may also have
an impact. The isolation and the stress that some people place on
themselves just to get through the day means that they can become more
susceptible to additional mental health difficulties such as depression,
severe anxiety, fears, phobias and suicidal tendencies. Managing anger
will also be more difficult (Gillott et al. 2001; Kim et al. 2000; Tantam
2000). These difficulties reduce the whole family's ability to relate to
others. Social and leisure pursuits are avoided and, as a consequence,
alienation, desperation and hopelessness dictate family life, adding to the
stress (Gray 1994). People with greater needs will, inevitably, have
greater dependence on their family. Once a diagnosis is made, specific
specialist support can be requested; this inevitably means having to
disclose to a number of professionals in order to secure such services.
Lack of specialist services poses further difficulties for some people, who

may have to travel long distances to receive appropriate support, and using public transport can be very problematic.

A specialist counselling service for people with AS/HFA had a number of clients using the service who had to travel 20–30 miles. Many of these clients had severe difficulties with public transport. Some clients preferred to use local taxi services and felt disclosure helped them because they could request one or two drivers with whom they felt comfortable. For them, disclosure helped to reduce some of the anxiety of the journey because they could trust the drivers not to distress them further, either in what they did or what they talked about.

Thus, the fullness of disclosure will vary from individual to individual, and with the complexity of their specific difficulties and needs. The more complex these difficulties are, the more the person and their family may have to disclose in order to receive support from statutory and voluntary organisations.

The value of disclosure

Negative experiences over the years can make the person suspicious and sensitive to criticism (Aston 2001). Consequently, there are risks to disclosing, such as further exposing oneself, which can be difficult for those who are hypersensitive; a fear of being further ostracised; or, worse still, being made to feel that the AS/HFA is an excuse for poor behaviour. Cultural differences in how disability is perceived will also influence how much a person and their family feels is appropriate to disclose and to whom, and what level of support will be sought outside of the family. The level of disclosure may be influenced by an extended family and religious or cultural parameters. The benefits of disclosure, however, are likely to outweigh the costs: disclosure encourages professionals and organisations to increase their knowledge base and to identify resources or meet a deficit in resources where this is highlighted. Irrespective of the level of perceived need, various laws and rulings are in place to ensure that people's specific disabilities are being recognised and that opportunities are available to support access and inclusion (e.g. Disability Discrimination Act 1995; DfEE 1997; FEFC 1996; Tomlinson 1996).

Disclosure can enable the individual to find potential sources of support at school or college and in the workplace and interested others who are willing to learn more about AS/HFA and to be of assistance. Individuals in higher education or employment may not be comfortable with disclosing, preferring instead to mask their difficulties and to continue to work at blending in or avoiding potentially difficult situations. The psychological cost of such effort can never be underestimated, however. Thus, although it may not be necessary to disclose to everyone, it may be helpful to know that disclosing to one or two key people may provide greater support in specific areas of need. College and workplace environments may make appropriate adjustments to meet the needs of the individual, for example in trying to accommodate for perceptual and sensory difficulties and adapting the way social demands and changes of schedule are made in order to be more AS/HFA-friendly (Ozonoff *et al.* 2002). In turn, this can lead to better communication and interactions, further increasing self-confidence and opening people's minds. Sharing information and knowledge enriches everyone's quality of life and makes us all a little more tolerant of difference.

Self-confidence

Increased confidence comes with positive life experiences, supportive relationships and the influence that these have on our sense of self and our self-esteem. Many people with AS/HFA talk about the fog that shrouds them; others have written about feeling as though they are behind glass, not quite able to make the connection with the neurotypical world (Lawson 1998), or of never quite feeling like a real person (Gerland 1997). Such feelings become most apparent during adolescence; during this stage of life, young people begin to explore issues of individuality and identity in relationship to others; this is no different for the person with AS/HFA (Bashe and Kirby 2001). For many, this is a time when being part of a peer group, experiencing different relationships and grappling with issues such as dependence versus independence becomes a focus; the success of such resolutions will be integral to the positive development of self. For many people with AS/HFA, it is during adolescence that their differences to others become more challenging to their identity and sense of self; it is one of the more difficult times to receive a diagnosis.

A young man who was diagnosed in adolescence had difficulty coming to terms with the diagnosis, both because of the association with autism and because he rejected the pervasive and labelling aspect of the diagnosis. His family, on the other hand, was relieved to have a description that explained the difficulties. Their desire to disclose to professionals, the school and members of the family in order to receive appropriate support was in conflict with his wish not to disclose. This was a critical time for him, as he struggled for independence and the desire to be like his friends. Given his age, the issue of disclosure was a sensitive area. Fortunately for him, his family was able to discuss how best to deal with this conflict with a specialist counsellor; in so doing, they found a balance between respecting his right for privacy and finding ways of helping him in areas of need. The compromise reached was that his parents would maintain their involvement with a local group fighting for services for people with AS/HFA in the borough while agreeing to accept his view as valid. The son then agreed to attend some of these meetings with his parents when certain topics were discussed. Once the turmoil of adolescence is over, he may be in a better position to acknowledge his specific difficulties. The fact that he is involved in the AS network, if only on the outskirts, means that he will be assimilating information that is salient for him.

Once adults begin to put their experiences in the context of AS, they have tangible evidence for why they have been unable to fit in and further, that they are not alone, that they are not to blame for their difference. Restructuring one's experiences in order to make some sense of them increases self-awareness and improves self-confidence. In addition, finding friends or professionals who are sensitive to the condition can do a lot to enable the person to explore the specific issues and difficulties that they may have, either with themselves or with others.

A young woman was constantly upset by the fact that a young man she knew from her local pub was friendly with other women. This caused a number of difficulties in the pub when she became upset. After seeing a counsellor specialising in AS/HFA, she was able to talk through and understand the nature of this relationship and to find ways to manage her feelings when the young man talked to other women. Counselling was instrumental in helping her both to understand this specific social situation and to look at other issues that had reduced her ability to live successfully in the community. Clear and structured support for her and information regarding AS/HFA to her support workers enabled her to deal with a number of areas of conflict in her life. This had a significant impact on her self-esteem.

The more people become aware of AS/HFA, the more comfortable the person with AS/HFA will be with disclosure in the community. Unfortunately, the very nature of the disability often means that people with AS/HFA limit their opportunity to be involved in the community. Part of this is related to the social communication difficulties and people's different processing and learning styles; as a consequence, environments in which the social demands cannot be controlled can lead to anxiety and panic, whether at college or work, in the supermarket or a leisure environment. Given that individuals are likely to meet and make friends in such environments, avoiding such places will consequently reduce their opportunity to make friends and further reduces their ability to learn the social rules and ways of interacting that are likely to help in building relationships and improving self-confidence and self-esteem. Friends who are informed of AS/HFA can offer more targeted support in situations in which the person with AS/HFA may feel uncomfortable or out of their depth; in this way, individuals do not have to avoid situations where there are opportunities to meet others and to share interests. Many people with AS are now making contact with others via the Internet or joining social groups, thus reducing the potential isolation and loneliness that can significantly harm self-esteem and self-confidence.

For the family, a diagnosis also improves confidence, because it allows them to describe more effectively that their son or daughter has specific difficulties that are recognised clinically and that can be supported. There is a vindication that their worries and concerns over the years were real and that many of the complexities of family life could be attributed to AS/HFA and not to poor parenting, which they may have feared or which may have been overtly or covertly ascribed to them. In parallel to the individual with AS/HFA, being made aware that there are many other families like them reduces the sense that they are alone and opens the door to meeting and sharing experiences, to fighting to improve services, and to finding opportunities for mutual support and problem-sharing, both for the practical and the emotional aspects that families are confronted with. Rather than travelling alone in an unknown territory both the individual with AS/HFA and their family can begin to call on a larger network of support and feel more confident that they have more control of the future with a diagnosis than they did of the past without one.

References

Aston, M.C. (2001) *The Other Half of Asperger Syndrome*. London: National Autistic Society.

Bashe, P.R. and Kirby, B.L. (2001) *The Oasis Guide to Asperger Syndrome*. New York: Crown Publishers.

Brogan, C.A. and Knussen, C. (2003) 'The Disclosure of a Diagnosis of an Autism Spectrum Disorder.' *Autism: International Journal of Research and Practice 7*, 31–46.

Cunningham, C.C., Morgan, P. and McGucken, R.B. (1984) 'Down's Syndrome: Is Dissatisfaction with Disclosure Inevitable?' *Developmental Medicine and Child Neurology 26*, 33–9.

Disability Discrimination Act (1995). London: TSO.

DfEE (1997) *Excellence for all Children: Meeting Special Education Needs*. London: HMSO.

Frith, U. (1989) *Autism: Explaining the Enigma*. Oxford: Blackwell.

Further Education Funding Council (FEFC) (1996) *Inclusive Learning: Report of the Learning Difficulties and/or Disabilities Committee (Principles and Recommendations)*. Coventry: FEFC.

Gerland, G. (1997) *A Real Person: Life on the Outside*. London: Souvenir Press.

Ghaziuddin, M. and Greden, J. (1998) 'Depression in Children with Autism/Pervasive Development Disorder: A Case–Control Family History Study.' *Journal of Autism and Developmental Disorder 28* 111–15.

Gillott, A., Furniss, F. and Walter, A. (2001) 'Anxiety in High Functioning Children with Autism.' *Autism: International Journal of Research and Practice 5*, 277–86.

Gray, D.E. (1994) 'Coping with Autism: Stresses and Strategies.' *Sociology of Health and Illness 16*, 275–300.

Howlin, P. (2000) 'Outcome in Adult Life for More Able Individuals with Autism or Asperger Syndrome.' *Autism: The International Journal of Research and Practice 4*, 63–83.

Howlin, P. and Moore, A. (1997) 'Diagnosis in Autism: A Survey of 1200 Patients in the UK.' *Autism The International Journal of Research and Practice 1*, 135–62.

Kim, J.A., Szatmari, P., Bryson, S.E., Streiner, D.L. and Wilson, F.J. (2000) 'The Prevalence of Anxiety and Mood Problems among Children with Autism and Asperger Syndrome.' *Autism: International Journal of Research and Practice 4*, 117–32.

Lawson, W. (1998) *Life Behind Glass*. Lismore, NSW: Southern Cross University Press.

Lingam, S. and Newton, R. (1996) *Right from the Start: The Way Parents are Told that their Child has a Disability. Paediatric Practice Guidelines*. London: British Paediatric Association.

Midence, K. and O'Neill, M. (1999) 'The Experience of Parents in the Diagnosis of Autism a Pilot Study.' *Autism: International Journal of Research and Practice 3*, 273–85.

Ozonoff, S., Dawson, G. and McPartland, J. (2002) *A Parent's Guide to Asperger Syndrome and High Functioning Autism*. New York: The Guilford Press.

Quine, L. and Rutter, M. (1994) 'First Diagnosis of Severe Mental and Physical Disability: A Study of Doctor–Parent Communication.' *Journal of Child Psychology and Psychiatry 35*, 1273–87.

Sainsbury, C. (2000) *Martian in the Playground*. London: The Book Factory.

Sicile-Kira, C. (2003) *Autism Spectrum Disorders: The Complete Guide*. London: Vermilion.

Sloper, P. and Turner, S. (1993) 'Determinants of Parental Satisfaction with Disclosure of Disability.' *Developmental Medicine and Child Neurology 35*, 816–25.

Tantam, D. (2000) 'Psychological Disorder in Adolescents and Adults with Asperger Syndrome.' *Autism: International Journal of Research and Practice 4*, 47–62.

Tomlinson, J. (1996) 'Inclusive Learning. Responding to Tomlinson: The report of the Further Education Funding Council Committee on Learning Difficulties/Disabilities.' Conference held at the University of Cambridge Institution of Education, Cambridge, November.

Willey, L.H. (1999) *Pretending to be Normal: Living with Asperger Syndrome.* London: Jessica Kingsley Publishers.

Williams, D. (1992) *Nobody Nowhere.* New York: Time Books.

Wing, L. (1981) 'Asperger Syndrome: A Clinical Account.' *Psychological Medicine 11*, 115–30.

17.

Coming out autistic at work

Jane Meyerding

Should I? Should you? Should all of us? How much choice do we actually have about it? Depending on how our autism manifests, or, to put it another way, how "normal" we are capable of acting and for how long, just getting a job may be a humbling experience.

An article in the *Guardian* (13 May 2001) quoted autie Ian Wombell as saying: "If I put on a job application that I am suffering from Asperger syndrome (AS), I don't get an interview. If I don't tell people about my disability when I go for the interview, they cannot understand what is wrong with me."

Here is a small selection of autie experiences with job interviews, drawn from an online survey I did:[1]

> It seems NTs [neurotypicals] are only interested in people's personalities. They don't care about what you can actually do. Since to them I look like a nut or a zombie, they won't hire me; they judge me because of my slightly off body language. (Jeanette H.)

> I am absolutely horrible at an interview. I can't explain myself or answer questions on the spot.

> Interviewees are supposed to "sell themselves," which I've never known how to do. I think I am bad at interviewing. (Terry Walker)

> I have often found it difficult to understand the nuance of the questions when the questions have several meanings, so the answer I have given has not captured the nuance.

---

[1]   I am grateful to all who participated in this survey. Throughout this chapter, unattributed quotations are from respondents who prefer to remain anonymous.

I don't interview well, as I sometimes need time to answer questions. I also sometimes don't immediately understand what it is I am being asked. This is worse when I'm stressed.

Symptoms [of autism] make me appear odd at interviews.

I think my autism affects my ability to make good first impressions at job interviews. I have had bosses who have said things like, "I didn't think much of you when you first started, but you've turned out really well." (Dirk Brugman)

I may not conform to expectations of search committees in terms of non-verbal communication and literal interpretation of language. (Stephen)

I typically have little trouble getting an interview based on my qualifications and résumé. However, in person I send the wrong non-verbal signals to the people interviewing me. Most of the work I've managed to find has been the result of knowing someone who already works there. Of course, I know less people than most people know, so this doesn't make things much easier.

To get an academic [professor] job, you have to do an interview that is unlike most interviews in the non-academic world. In some cases, it involves spending a full 12 hours…with the department faculty … I'm sure some faculties are expecting me to be more social/extroverted than I naturally am; while I can have good conversations with people on relevant topics, I'm lousy at "shooting the breeze", especially with people I barely know. So the other candidate comes in and is more social and talkative, and s/he gets the job instead of me.

The biggest problem by far is the interview. The pendulum has swung way too far in the "must be a team player" direction. Individuality is rarely valued anymore. (Fred)

My own experience agrees. Until I was in my thirties, I never succeeded in getting a job through an interview – and even then, the job I got was one for which I had established a record of experience as a temp. My first two jobs were obtained for me by my mother, starting when I was 16. Later, when I tried to get a job on my own by showing up at businesses in response to newspaper ads, no one would even give me an application to fill out. Maybe it was because I looked too young, or because I didn't have the appearance of a person seriously looking for work. I did (and do) tend to become vague in unfamiliar places, because I am overloaded. Too much newness all at once leads to a back-up in processing and, as a consequence, I have less capacity left over for interactions. Whatever it was, something made me appear to potential employers as not worth even minimal consideration.

Once we get a job, as Ian Wombell noted, we still need to deal with being perceived as non-standard units. We may be "high-functioning" (in some ways, at some times), but our problems at work tend to fall into the same categories as those identified among people labeled "low-functioning autistics": communication, social skills, sensory sensitivities, focus-shifting, meltdowns. Some of us are able to maintain an NT interface at work that enables us to pass as normal, or near enough, and those are the auties who can take the advice of autistic employment advocate Roger Meyer. According to Meyer (2001, p.45): "Autism is not something that most people understand. High functioning autism, or AS, is something that fewer people understand. Telling everyone about your Asperger syndrome will leave a lot of folks confused, often wondering why you bothered to tell them in the first place." Most times, he advises, you will be better off keeping quiet about autism and seeking instead to solve your workplace problems on a need-by-need basis. Not "I'm autistic so I need a quiet place to work" but "I work better in a quiet place. OK if I close the door?"

On that basis, sensory challenges may be the easiest to address. Not all workplaces will accommodate all sensitivities, but at least we can talk about those problems without mentioning autism. (Of course, if you are being driven mad by the invisible-to-others flickering of your workplace lighting, or by the inaudible-to-others keening of your equipment, then coming up with a persuasive explanation that does not include autism may be a stiff test of your conversational abilities.) Many of us, however, have a history of problems at work that cannot be hidden effectively enough or consistently enough to make a pretence of normality a reliable long-term strategy. From what I have seen, heard, and experienced myself, I suspect that the early years of employment and the later years of life may present especially difficult challenges for autistics like us. Our non-standard communication makes it harder for us to "acclimatize" to workplace standards and practices when we start out. And when we are getting on in years (as I am), our store of energy may wane to the point that we lose the ability to perform our NT emulation with 100 percent coverage of the workday.

Staying in the closet will be easiest for those with good communication skills who also get along well with the supervisor or co-workers with whom one must negotiate changes in the workplace. Unfortunately, those characteristics are far from universal among autistics. My online survey (30 autistic respondents) asked about AS/autism-related reasons for being fired. "Lack of ability to network or socialize with co-workers" was the most frequently ticked option, followed closely by "Not liked by co-workers or supervisor" and "Seen as weird or odd."

The difference in communication styles can be a major problem at work. For NTs, every contact with a co-worker has a social element. (NTs are the reason humans are described as "social animals.") Autistics, on the other hand, are more likely to converse only (or primarily) about substance, not recognizing that the manner of conversing is perceived by the non-autistic person as forming part of a personal, social relation. What I say is much less likely to be determined by my relationship with the other person, and more likely to be determined by the subject matter and my relationship with the subject matter. Part of what that means is that I am less likely to (think to) tailor what I say to suit/match the person to whom I am talking. As a result, I may be seen as pedantic, condescending (if I am going into too much detail, given the other person's background), or overly esoteric, when, in fact, what I am doing is processing/organizing the subject in my own mind, talking to myself as much as to anyone else.

When social aspects intrude into the workplace, our deficits (by NT standards) are likely to spring into relief. We may find ourselves standing around feeling stupid due to the lack of overt analysis and discussion. In an online group, Gail described how lost she felt during a party:

> A lot of times when I don't do something, it is not necessarily because I am unwilling. Often, I don't know what to do or how to do it. With many things, I have to be given very specific instructions or I am lost... I do not do well with vagueness. For someone to say to me "Do something" without telling me in detail what it is that they expect me to do can leave me completely lost. Out to sea. In a boat with no oars.

The same "lost-at-sea" experience can happen to an autie whenever work colleagues socialize. Either we stand around looking helpless/lazy/witless, or we ask someone to instruct us. One solution might be to confide in a co-worker beforehand so that someone would be primed to tell us what to do. Unfortunately, telling someone what to do has implications for most NTs that may make asking for this kind of help counterproductive for autie workers. The autie becomes less able in the eyes of the NT, which would not be a problem if the NT were autistic, because the autie brain's basic operating system is piecemeal rather than global. We can accept the idea of someone who is an idiot with "simple" things and a whiz at complex tasks that stump the majority. For the NT operating system, which uses a far more global basis, an idiot is an idiot. Anyone who can't figure out how to join in a simple activity is someone globally defective. The information "Jane can't do x" (e.g. figure out what to do at a potluck in the conference room) is integrated into the co-worker's overall perception of Jane, to produce a helper-versus-helpless dynamic that lives on in the mind of the NT long after the specific instance is history. No matter how helpful the assistance may be at the time, becoming known as in-need-of-help may not be to the advantage of one who hopes for good evaluations and/or promotion.

Executive dysfunction and weak central coherence lead to a variety of problems at work, including inability to multi-task, to see the forest instead of the trees, to prioritize and organize tasks with many steps, and so on. When we do learn new skills, we may fail to recognize other situations to which those skills might be transferred effectively. Knowing how to behave in a meeting does not ensure that one will come away from it knowing how to apply the substance of the meeting to one's work. A successful meeting for an autie may be one in which nobody noticed he or she was there, or in which he or she managed to answer a question appropriately. Or in which he or she managed not to monologue when a topic of interest came up. Culling the substantive wheat from the social chaff, applying the relevant bits to one's own assignment, inferring the importance and priority of the various parts of the work from conversation framed in polite suggestions rather than declarative statements...it's enough to wear an autie out even before they get back to their workstation.

Focus can be a great advantage for an autie. When I asked in my online survey for people to choose the characteristics they had that helped them "perform well as an employee," only "I am reliable and honest" was chosen more often than "I can hyper-focus and work undistracted." (The other choices, in descending order, were "I am logical," "I have specialized knowledge," "I have special abilities," and, written in by one or more respondents, "perfectionist," "perseveration," and "punctual.") The trouble with having hyper-focus, of course, is that one is harder to rouse – which can be annoying for bosses and co-workers – and one has a harder time re-focusing on something else, such as one's impatient boss. Auties who function best with the support of routines and who hyper-focus also may be the hardest to dislodge and face the worst consequences when derailed successfully. Coming out of a hyper-focus can leave one stranded momentarily in an incoherent world. One man, responding to the lead-in, "The main advantage of being open about AS/autism at work would be…" wrote: "So people at work would understand why it sometimes takes me a while to answer their questions, especially if they are shouting at me. This also happens when I have to switch tasks quickly. I usually come across as being stupid, despite having an IQ of around 140."

Being left alone to hyper-focus can be a joy for those autistics whose job coincides with a perseveration. Many of us aren't so lucky, though. Given how much interaction is required by most jobs, it can feel as if we are working two jobs simultaneously. We need to do our work, but we also must expend huge amounts of energy on generating and maintaining a social interface. That's why I have been working part-time most of my life: if I try to work a full-time job, I need to spend the rest of my waking hours recuperating. Literally. It wasn't so bad when my mother was alive; she provided a lot of support with what the therapists call "activities of daily living." Food, cleaning, planning, organization (of time as well as effort and effects), everything from opening mail to keeping track of what food was in the house. No doubt more autistics would be willing and able employees if it were possible for more of us to get along on what a part-time job pays, or if it were possible to combine a job with receiving "daily living" assistance. Unfortunately, being employed part-time usually eliminates all access to supplemental income (e.g. "disability") as well as to "chore services" and other kinds of publicly funded support. The theory seems to be that either you are disabled and need both financial and practical support or you can work and therefore need/deserve nothing. For many employed autistics, the result of that dichotomy is steadily accumulating stress, which, sooner or later, spills over into the job.

The workplace itself can be a hugely frustrating environment for autistics. Frustration may lead to overload, which may cause us to attempt decompression through stimming. Or, as Smith *et al.* (1995, p.9) put it, "Workers with autism sometimes display behaviors that make co-workers uneasy."

Whether we are able to stim at work or not, some of us must live with the problem of frustration leading to meltdowns. An autie forced on to permanent disability status described the way he lost the last job of his working life:

> I had no problem doing the work; in fact I was doing over twice the amount of work as anyone else (for half the pay). The problem was my frequent meltdowns. One of the [company's] owners understood that I had a disability (it was still unnamed then), but the other owner had no tolerance. That second owner would often tell me that I was "lucky to even have a job." One day I had a meltdown, and he called it "the last straw." I was fired on the spot. I have not worked since.

Obviously, there is a wide range of experience in this area. Some auties never melt down in public. Others learn when they are young to suppress the full eruption and therefore don't need to deal with the problem in their adult working lives. Many of us, though, are stuck somewhere between no meltdowns at all and the kind of frequency that makes sustained employment impossible. I once wrote out my own thoughts on the subject when another autie woman asked for suggestions on what to tell a new support worker in a group house. For me, I told her, it would be helpful to talk about anger:

> What's important for the NT to understand is that my anger (which actually I don't usually feel/see as anger at the time) is *not personal*. It is the *situation* that is making me so frustrated that my inner "switch" is flipped and I am put into a mode of behavior that I can't escape from for the moment. Usually I need to retire to a quiet place where I can be alone for a while so I can decompress and wait for the inner switch to flip back to calm mode.

Being in meltdown is being stuck. My meltdowns have been explosive only a few times (and never at work), and the only violence I've ever done has been to my own property. At work, my meltdowns take the form of inarticulate sputtering and gesturing. A dry-land version of somebody going down for the third time. My voice may sound angry (rather than frustrated), but that seems to be true at times even when I am not in meltdown (and not angry, either). For auties whose meltdowns take a more physical form, even if all the frustration is directed against property rather than people, and perhaps especially for male auties and those whose size is seen as potentially intimidating, meltdowns can be an instant ticket to unemployment – unless, perhaps, the individual is lucky enough to be "out" as an autie and to have a workplace ready to recognize the reasons behind all the noise.

Increasingly, there is another reason to "come out" autistic at work: as a principled contribution towards the eventual liberation of us all (autie and normie alike) from the coercive oversimplification of societal standards, particularly as those standards affect "non-standard" individuals' ability to participate fully – and with due respect – in the lives of their communities. Advocating for the value and importance of a "neurodiversity movement," autist Terry Walker (2003) said:

> Our own lives can easily be the example that we present as we make the argument that some people are inherently incapable (not just recalcitrant but actually incapable) of functioning by the dominant social rules and expectations… Teach us how to "fit in" when necessary, yes, for those moments when social conformance is truly important. But don't try to suppress or eliminate our native behaviors entirely… We are better served by learning to keep ourselves intact amidst a world designed for different standards; we are better served by changing those standards so that we have a proper home in society.

Before I can get very far along this road, however, I need to figure out exactly what I am talking about, what I am asking for. Is autism a disability? Many of us would answer "Yes" if the autistic in question looks like the low-functioning profile presented in the books and articles of professional autism experts. Some of us would answer "Yes" if the question was asked with respect to someone seen as high-functioning but not Asperger. A few would include even Aspies in that "Yes", although I imagine a majority of that few would prefer the euphemism of "different" rather than "disabled."

The relationship (if any) between autism and disability must be clarified before we can ride off on our high horses into the new world of the neurodiversity revolution. Because it will come up. Those of us who can pass as NT or as AS or as high-functioning will find ourselves in the population of those with "invisible disabilities." We don't look disabled; most of us don't use a white cane or a wheelchair (and those of us who do probably have a hard time getting anyone to see past those tools to their autism). As Cal Montgomery (2001), has written, because we do not match the majority's expectations about what disability looks like, "people ask us why we need accommodation rather than what accommodation we need." We may find ourselves in the position of trying to "prove" we are disabled in order to be taken seriously as autistics. On the other hand, we do not want to erase in our public language about autism the real differences that exist among us. We can't have our goal be to substitute one false stereotype for another. Disability is not a single attribute; it is one form in which we give each other information about ourselves in the universe of human diversity. Autistics are not all alike, but neither can we each be assigned a specific static point on a linear continuum from high to low. Pick an analogy: visual (differences in vision and in need for adaptive equipment such as eye-glasses and audio-books do not correlate with much of anything else about anyone as a person), audio (ditto), mobility (from Olympic sprinter to electric-chair user: can't assume anything useful on that basis), and so on, as far as the imagination can reach.

About a third of the autistics I surveyed online reported that they were "out" at work. Another handful have disclosed their autism to one or a few co-workers; most have not. When those who answered "No" about being open at work were asked why, their answers varied like this:

> I will become unemployable, as my boss would fire me and make sure I don't get another job by telling potential employers of my problem. (Jeanette H.)

> I choose not to because of the inevitability of being treated as a Case. Instead, I'm slowly opening up about my individual AS traits, without giving them a label, so that people can treat me as a "person who is

overfocused and can't develop routines and has a really quirky way of looking at some things," etc., rather than as "autistic."

I told my boss and someone in personnel about my autism, but I regret it now. I feel my boss is going to use it against me. They have made absolutely no allowances for me at all, so it wasn't worth it for me to "come out" about it. I will not come out about it with future bosses/employers.

I don't want to be treated badly. (Being treated differently might be good if it included coping concessions.) I have seen other people treated cruelly if it became known that they were simply taking antidepressant drugs. I suspect that more significant neurological differences would also be handled poorly. (Terry Walker)

Those respondents to my survey who had "come out" on the job were much more likely to do so by talking one-on-one with a co-worker than by any more formal means. Given how hard it can be for one autie to make any headway on his or her own, how do we get beyond the delicate, one-by-one, post-hiring method of unfurling our autistic blossoms in our isolated workplaces? We can hope that, eventually, the cumulative effect of all the separate disclosures will add up to enough societal awareness of autism that "coming out" will not be so risky for anyone. Until we get to that eventuality, however, what about all of us who cannot get or keep a job because of our autism, whether we are open about it or not? It seems to me that the very least those of us who are employed, and who do have sufficient job security, can do on behalf of ourselves and other autistics is to keep learning and teaching. Most of us have been isolated from other autistics for much of our lives. As we think about making room in the workplace for ourselves, we can try to imagine opening the workplace to other autistics also. Part of the challenge lies in figuring out how to discuss autism itself, how to present autism to the world. If we fall back on stereotypes such as "Well, I am mildly autistic" (in response, perhaps, to a co-worker's surprise that we talk and don't look like Dustin Hoffman in *Rainman*), we may make the workplace more accepting of us while simultaneously reinforcing an image of "real autistics" or "low-functioning autistics" as outside the circle of social value.

Undoubtedly, the most common reaction we get from NTs when we make the attempt to start talking about what autism means in our lives is

"Oh, I do that too" or "I feel that way too," or "I have that problem too," or "That happens to me all the time." Well-meaning NTs automatically take that route because doing so is the best way to maintain and build the kind of NT relationship they are used to, and because they probably mishear what we say, re-interpreting what we say about our own experience in the light of their own lives. Prosopagnostic people (who have a deficit in the neurology with which normal people recognize human faces) quickly learn that at least 50 percent of the population hears "I can't recognize faces" as being identical to "I have trouble remembering people's names." If you want someone to understand what it is like to be face-blind, you must perfect a particular kind of story. Don't say it took you three years to figure out your five co-workers. That's not dramatic enough to get through. Instead, use the time your mother (father, sister, brother, spouse …) spoke to you in the grocery store and you didn't know who it was. The only way to escape the generous NT assumption that "we're all alike" – and that the only acceptable way for a decent person to react to difference is to refuse to acknowledge it – is to "hit them over the head" with an example too outrageous to be reinterpreted as "normal."

And that's a shame. As Larry Arnold has written, "Nobody turns around and says to someone that they can't have arthritis because they are not in a wheelchair." And, yet, we autistics who have been able to reach a certain level of independence are denied the reality of our experience. It's not supposed to count. We're supposed to be able to "overcome" by sheer force of will any autism-related problems we have – as if our mere presence in the NT world was not already a continuous act of will and adaptation. An autie who used to work in the tech world but finds himself unable to get a job these days has written:

> Now on job applications, they all put *must have interpersonal skills, must be able to work as part of a team.* In other words, you have to be not on the spectrum. It discriminates against auties, but what can we do? If the job description said *must not be blind* or *must be able to walk*, there would be an outcry as that would be against people with those disabilities. But when it comes to AS, I do not think any companies understand.

When I was in my 20s, a change was underway in large segments of US and British groups working for social change. Women began to insist that they be included fully at all levels and in all functions of the groups to which they devoted their time and energy. What's more, they declared their intention to participate on their own terms. Women shouldn't have to "act like men" (e.g. adopt stereotypically "male" communication styles) in order to gain access to full participation. The changeover from old- to new-style ways of organizing and running social change groups was by no means universal; nor, where it did occur, was it without problems. Indeed, some groups were unable to cope with the challenge and dissolved – or exploded. Even the most rigidly old-fashioned sectarians were affected to some extent, however. It was a change in culture, a change in what attitudes and behaviors could expect to pass unchallenged as "normal," as 'matter of course."

What we spectrumites need, I think, is an analogous cultural change. We need there to be a space (and time) where those who are "different" are able to teach the "normal" how their unexamined assumptions, attitudes, and ways of doing things have been holding us at a disadvantage. We need a chance to demonstrate how relaxing the boundaries of what is considered "normal" will benefit everyone. It's not only autistics who are "weird," after all. And even the most normal of normies will benefit when society becomes able to integrate more of the marginalized into greater participation in society, whether that participation be in the form of paid employment, volunteer advocacy for self and others, or the more private success of a quiet, self-occupied life.

AS adult (and father of an HFA son) Phil Schwarz (personal communication) says:

> I think the question boils down to striking a balance between expectations upon the individual to change, and expectations upon the society to change… I think on the whole that that balance should be – and can be – pushed further in the direction of societal change. It is not an easy task and it is a slow process, and we need allies far beyond our own numbers as a nearly invisible minority in order to accomplish such change on more than an immediate, local scale… We have a long way to go before our sensory, aesthetic, and social preferences cease to be dismissed by the medical and professional establishment as disordered and therefore meaningless. But nevertheless, by winning over hearts and minds among potential allies, one open mind at a time, eventually our ranks will be amplified by enough on-message allies to change the "conventional wisdom."

Coming out autistic at work can be part of that long process. Not all of us will be able to take this step in the here-and-now of our lives today. Some of us will find ways to come out elsewhere first, if we judge the risk too great at work. A few may be lucky enough to have a co-worker do it first, not knowing beforehand that he or she's not the only autie on the premises. When we do come out autistic at work, we can try to do it not only for our own advantage (or survival), but also as part of a broader current of social change, a "neurodiversity movement" that will pave the way for other autistics to have a smoother ride as they enter the workplaces we have pried a little bit wider open.

References

Meyer, R.N. (2001) *Asperger Syndrome Employment Workbook*. London: Jessica Kingsley Publishers.

Montgomery, C. (2001) "A Hard Look at Invisible Disability." www.raggededgemagazine.com/0301/0301ft1.htm

Schwarz, P. (2004) "Building Alliances: Community Identity and the Role of Allies in Autistic Self-Advocacy" In R.E. Joyner Hane, K. Sibley, S.M. Shore, R. Meyer and P. Schwarz (eds) *Ask and Tell: Self-Advocacy and Disclosure for People on the Autism Spectrum*. Shawnee Mission, KS: Autism Asperger Publishing.

Smith, M.D., Belcher, R.G. and Juhrs, P.D. (1995) *Guide to Successful Employment for Individuals with Autism*. Baltimore: Paul H. Brookes Publishing Company.

Walker, T. (2003) "Square Pegs: Autism in the Workplace." http://home.earthlink.net/~mellowtigger/conf/SquarePegs-20031002.html

18.

Disclosing to the authorities

Dennis Debbaudt

Everybody gets a little knot in their stomach when they see in their rear-view mirror the flashing lights of the police car. Is that for me, we think? When the patrol car speeds by, we exhale a sigh of relief. When it stays behind us, and the officer is now motioning with turn signals or their arm out the window for us to pull over, that knot in the stomach quickly joins a racing pulse and thoughts of "What did I do wrong?"

We pull over, grip the steering wheel, and wait for the officer. When instructed, we reach into our pocket, purse or glove box and produce our driver's license, car registration, and proof of insurance. We sit and wait again while our documents and driving record are checked out. Then the officer returns to our car. If we don't know by now, we ask the officer why we were pulled over. We find out our fate – ticket, warning, broken tail light, or expired plate – move on and deal with it. It is a routine and yet harrowing experience for most of us.

Beyond the traffic stop, people on the autism spectrum can expect more contact with uniformed or plain-clothes police and customs and immigration, airport, building, and event security staff (Curry *et al.* 1993). But coping with the stress of these sudden contacts will be compounded for those living on the spectrum. Questions will be more difficult for the spectrum person to decipher and answer. Problems with sensory overloads, poor social awareness, semantic misunderstandings, inability to deal with changes in routine or structure, and little to no understanding of non-verbal communications are the very kinds of things that make more appropriate responses to society very difficult for someone with autism spectrum disorder (ASD) (Debbaudt 2004).

What can and should the independent person living on the autism spectrum expect during sudden or even expected interactions with a law enforcement, customs and immigration, or security professional? With few exceptions, these professionals will have no training about how to recognize, communicate, and respond when they meet or interact with a person on the spectrum. There will be little understanding of the significance of the words "Asperger syndrome" or "autism" when they hear them. You can expect a higher-level scrutiny from law-enforcement and security personnel when traveling in the twenty-first century community.

Expect public- or private-sector scrutiny at:

- airports
- security checkpoints, such as government buildings, schools, and secured facilities
- guard shacks
- building entrances
- campuses
- shopping malls and districts.

In fact, in these days of heightened security, anywhere!

So, what are the best options for the independent spectrum person during a sudden interaction with a law enforcer during an emergency or non-emergency situation? Should you disclose your Asperger syndrome (AS)? When? To whom? When should you not disclose? First, consider a few key points about risk during these contacts: increased anxiety, restraint or physical harm, arrest, incarceration – jail or secured mental health facility, being delayed unnecessarily.

Increased anxiety

Expect your anxiety level to increase. Everyone who has a sudden contact with a police officer, security guard, customs and immigration official, or other public-service or private-sector professional will have increased anxiety and diminished ability to communicate. For those on the spectrum, be prepared to disclose your condition.

Restraint or physical harm

Those that choose to flee from an approaching law enforcer should expect to be pursued and restrained. Closing into a police officer's personal space may also be met with physical restraint. *Don't run!* Concentrate on the officer's questions and try to answer them directly. Learn to expect and tolerate casual touch, such as a hand on the arm, shoulder, or back, without overreacting to it (Debbaudt 2003).

Arrest

If you are arrested, even unjustly, be prepared for this. *Do not resist or attempt to flee!* Ask to be represented by an attorney before answering any questions. Exercise your right to remain silent. If you have decided to disclose your AS, then a good law enforcer – even one who is untrained about AS and autism issues – should take your condition seriously.

Incarceration: jail or secured mental health facility

If for any reason you find yourself in custody and choose to disclose, then ask the officer to alert jail authorities about your AS. At least for short-term confinement, it may be better for you to not be held in confinement with others. Ask the officer to immediately seek professional AS advice.

Being delayed unnecessarily

Do not let this affect how you deal with a sudden contact with police. A successful resolution of this contact is now your only goal. Successful resolution of the contact is your new mission. Focus on this only. Resist bringing up personal delays with the officer.

The sudden contact is now your only priority. Any delay, such as being late for work or an appointment, can be dealt with later. Delays are not important factors when interacting with the police.

So, what's the best tool to use when you make the decision to disclose the condition of AS to a police officer? Consider developing a handout card that can be easily copied and laminated. Carry something replaceable that you can give to the officer on the scene. Carry several at all times. The handout card can be generic or person-specific. Work with an AS support organization to develop a generic handout. Work with people whose opinions you trust and value to develop a person-specific handout.

Here's an example of what a handout could look like:

Asperger Syndrome Alert

I have Asperger syndrome.

I will be anxious in new situations or with new people.

Please read this card for information about how to communicate with me and how I communicate with you.

Below are some common characteristics of Asperger syndrome and some tips for you:

- Use concrete, direct language: I may take your expressions literally.

- Be patient. Allow me sufficient time (10–15 seconds) to answer your questions.

- Don't be offended when I repeat what you say. This is common for people with Asperger syndrome.

- I may try to change the subject of conversation to a topic of my choice.

- I may not understand your questions or commands. My good vocabulary may give you a false impression of my comprehension.

- Try to display calm body language. I am likely to model your body language.

- I may avoid eye contact. This is common and may not mean I have guilty knowledge.

- Try to ignore my self-stimulatory behavior, such as pacing or talking to myself.

- Avoid slang, jokes and sarcasm. I do not understand them.

- I may make unintentional socially inappropriate comments or gestures.

- I may display extreme distress for no apparent reason, such as, shouting, yelling, crying or physical agitation.

- I may be extremely sensitive to touch, sounds, lights or other sensory input.

Remember: each individual with Asperger syndrome is unique and may act or react differently.

Contact the following doctor to confirm diagnosis: _____

Contact this Asperger support group for information:

_____

Restraint

Try to de-escalate behavior through geographic containment. Consider removing person from an area with multiple sensory inputs, such as flashing lights, sirens, crowds, dogs, perfume, and smoke, to an area free of sensory input.

If restraint or physical contact becomes necessary, be aware of associated medical conditions, including seizure disorder and hypotonia or weak trunk muscles.

Avoid positional asphyxia. After takedown, turn person on their side often to allow normal breathing to occur.

Alert jail authorities about the person's Asperger syndrome. Strongly consider initial segregation from general prison population.

This person would be at extreme risk of injury or abuse within general prison population.

Document Asperger syndrome in the initial report.

Alert supervisor, detective bureau, and prosecutor about the condition of Asperger syndrome.

Interview

May not understand constitutional rights or legal warnings.

May have difficulty recalling relevant facts or details of a specific incident.

May be confused by standard interview or interrogation techniques and produce a misleading statement or false confession.

May not fully understand the consequences of their actions.

Consider contacting a professional who is familiar with Asperger syndrome.

Call the following professional: _____

What's the best way to tell the officer that you have a handout? Do not make sudden movements to reach for the handout card! Obtain permission or signal your intentions before reaching into your coat or pants pockets, briefcase, or bag, or vehicle glove compartment. Verbally, let the officer know you have AS and have an information card for them to read. If you are non-verbal, or if sudden interactions render you non-verbal or mute, consider using a medical alert bracelet for an officer to read about your condition of AS and the fact that you have an information card (Debbaudt 2001).

You've made the decision to disclose. Should you disclose to:

- a police officer?
- at customs and immigration?
- your lawyer or attorney?

Disclosure to a police officer

The decision to disclose will always be yours to make. If you know through experience that disclosure would be helpful, then choosing to disclose to a police officer is a good idea. Law enforcers report that they make their best decisions when they have their best information. A good, strong AS disclosure that includes the use of an information card, contact information for an objective AS professional, and proof of diagnosis should be considered.

At customs and immigration

You give up many legal rights when you seek entry into a foreign country. People with AS have reported extreme difficulties at customs and immigration checkpoints, including being mistaken as psychotic by customs or immigration officials, which ended in incarceration in a secured mental health facility.

Before embarking on international travel, research customs and immigration rules and regulations through a travel agency, airline, or government agency. Carrying an AS informational handout, but not disclosing your AS, may increase your chances of explaining if something goes wrong. Again, you are the final judge of when and when not to disclose. Discuss international travel and disclosure with a person that you trust.

Your lawyer or attorney

If you've been arrested and taken into custody, then the best advice is to disclose the condition to him or her. Even if you are self-diagnosed and have no official diagnosis, disclose this to your attorney. Work with your attorney, a trusted family member, an advocate, or an AS professional to develop a defense strategy that's based on good AS knowledge and information.

Self-diagnosis

Be aware that a strong disclosure to a law-enforcement officer, prosecutor, or judge carries with it the responsibility that the disclosure is accurate and truthful. Every and any responsible police officer – certainly their supervisor or a prosecuting attorney – will want to verify that the information you provide is accurate and truthful. While we in the spectrum know that self-diagnosis is common, and often very accurate, we cannot expect those that work in the criminal justice system to have the same belief.

Diagnosis as the result of a criminal justice contact is not uncommon. But do not expect a law enforcer to take your word that you have AS. It will be checked, perhaps while you wait in custody. It will have to be diagnosed by a qualified professional. Understand that if you disclose a self-diagnosis, then this could lead to a formal diagnosis, finding of no AS, or finding of another condition.

When not to disclose

The soft disclosure

There will be times when a full, strong disclosure may be too much, for instance during a discrepancy or misunderstanding with a ticket agent, shop clerk, bus or cab driver, restaurant waiter, or other travelers.

These may be good opportunities to offer what can be called a soft disclosure. That is, sharing information with a stranger that will help you navigate through your journey safely and swiftly, but without using the stronger – hard – disclosure techniques. A soft disclosure could be done without using any spectrum-specific terminology or explanation. For example, saying "I have a disability that makes certain sounds hurt my ears," or "My disability makes it hard for me to read this print or hear your words clearly" (or whatever point it is you are trying to make). This soft disclosure could get you what you need on the spot: understanding and accommodation.

Traffic stops

In the opening paragraph of this chapter, we discussed the perils of a routine traffic stop. Although disclosure to a law enforcer, in most cases, should be considered, is disclosure during a routine or other traffic stop a good idea? Should AS be offered as an explanation for driving violations, improper vehicle registration, or not maintaining your vehicle?

Driving is a privilege. As uncomfortable as it may be to consider, does any part of your AS make driving dangerous for you and other drivers out on the road? Other conditions in life, for instance seizure disorder, vision and hearing problems, sleep apnea, and medications, have caused others to take into account their ability to drive and address their responsibilities on our roads. Of course, drivers with AS as well as neurotypical people are good and responsible citizens. But a disclosure of AS on a traffic stop might not not be advisable and would be difficult to defend as an explanation.

One exception would be during a police roadblock or sobriety checkpoint. The symptoms of AS could be confused by a police officer as drunkenness, illegal drug use, or evasive responses. If you are asked to take a field sobriety test – and you know that you aren't drunk or high – compliance is recommended. Disclosure should also be an option if necessary.

Plan and practice disclosure techniques

Plan your response and practice with others for a sudden encounter. They will happen to all of us. Your preparation is your best chance to have a successful interaction with law enforcement. Will these interactions be free of anxiety? Are misunderstandings going to occur? Will you be quizzed and questioned more often than others? Should you expect higher scrutiny from police and other law-enforcement professionals? Yes to all of those questions! Can you prepare yourself to minimize these risks during a sudden and predictable interaction with police? Yes, again!

We've identified risk factors for you to be aware of. We've examined some of the tools and techniques you can use during a law-enforcement interaction. So, what are the best ways you can manage these everyday risks? Plan and practice!

- Discuss these risks with people that you trust.

- Develop a hard, person-specific disclosure handout.

- Develop a personal plan of how you will use the handout.

- Practice through role-playing with people you know and trust.

- Develop some soft-disclosure handouts and role-play when you would use them. Field test whenever you can to see how effective the handout and soft disclosure can be.

- Adapt and amend both soft- and hard-disclosure handouts. It's only paper. They're not written in stone.

Ask your AS support group or advocacy to develop a generic AS handout for law enforcement, distribute the handout to law-enforcement agencies, and develop an approved training program for law enforcers. Examples and spectrum training issues are detailed in *Autism, Advocates and Law Enforcement Professionals* (Debbaudt 2001).

Encourage your advocacy organizations and people of trust to create opportunities where you and other people with AS can interact with law enforcers in a safe, structured, non-threatening, low-anxiety environment. People with AS and law enforcers can learn from each other how best to interact. These educational opportunities will need to be discussed, planned, and carried out. Advocacy groups should be encouraged to embrace these issues and form partnerships with law enforcers and educators to ensure that these best practices are acted on and carried out. Mutual education and information-sharing will always be the keys to successful resolutions of contacts between law-enforcement professionals and people with AS.

You cannot expect a law enforcer to take your word on the spot that you have AS. Your disclosure of AS may not prevent you from being arrested or detained. But, in the long run, it can save you from a criminal justice nightmare.

References

Curry, K., Posluszny, M. and Kraska, S. (1993) *Training Criminal Justice Personnel to Recognize Offenders with Disabilities.* Washington, DC: Office of Special Education and Rehabilitative Services News In Print.

Debbaudt, D. (2001) *Autism Advocates and Law Enforcement Professionals: Recognizing and Reducing Risk Situations for People with Autism Spectrum Disorders.* London: Jessica Kingsley Publishers.

Debbaudt, D. (2003) "Safety." In L.H. Willey (ed) *Asperger Syndrome in Adolescence: Living with the Ups, the Downs, and Things in Between.* London: Jessica Kingsley Publishers.

Debbaudt, D. (2004) *Beyond Guilt or Innocence.* Waltham, Mass: Devlopmental Disabilities Leadership Forum of the Eunice Kennedy Shriver Center at the University of Massachusetts School of Medicine. Online (April 2004) at: http://www.mnip-net.org/ddlead.nsf/TrimTOC/BeyondGuiltorInnocen.

Contributor biographies

David N. Andrews BA, PgCertSpEd (pending) is a postgraduate applied educational psychologist living and working in Finland, where he specialises in autistic spectrum difficulties in adulthood. Among his main interests are mental health issues in Asperger syndrome, psychoeducational assessment (developmental diagnosis and potential academic/working ability), and the application of environmental psychology in educational and occupational settings.

He has a diagnosis as an Asperger autistic person, as does his daughter. His main reason for becoming an applied educational psychologist lies in the fact that he was let down very badly by professionals as a child and still carries some serious psychological scars resulting from this.

He has lectured on the applied psychology of adult autism at a few universities, including Birmingham and Oulu, and has designed and presented short courses on his specialism.

Tony Attwood is a clinical psychologist whose original qualifications were achieved in England and who now lives in Queensland, Australia. He has specialised in autistic spectrum disorders since 1975, and he achieved a PhD from the University of London in 1984. He currently works in private practice and is Adjunct Professor at Griffith University, Queensland. His book *Asperger Syndrome: A Guide for Parents and Professionals* has become one of the primary texts on Asperger syndrome. The book has been translated into 20 languages and sold over 300,000 copies worldwide. His current clinical interest is in developing diagnostic procedures and cognitive behaviour therapy (CBT) for children and adults with Asperger syndrome. His current research studies are the design and evaluation of a diagnostic scale for Asperger syndrome and the evaluation of a new CBT programme to manage anxiety and anger. He has also been invited to be keynote speaker at several international conferences on autism.

Penny Barratt has been working with young people with autistic spectrum disorders (ASD) and Asperger syndrome for 20 years in a range of different roles and provisions. She has worked in autism specialist provision, a special school nursery and a mainstream secondary school, as a local education authority (LEA) officer and as a coordinator of outreach provision for pupils with autism. She presently works as a deputy head teacher in an area special school, which provides autism-specific and generic special education.

Penny has also tutored students on the University of Birmingham distance learning courses in autism for the past ten years, many of these at master's level. She has co-written a number of practical books aiming to support parents and teachers in addressing the needs of young people with ASD and Asperger syndrome.

Tom Berney is an NHS consultant psychiatrist in learning disability and child psychiatry who has specialised increasingly in autism spectrum disorder over the last 25 years across the whole range of age and ability. Besides providing a regional specialist service for adults and children, he is the honorary psychiatrist to two charities that provide specialist schools, colleges and residential care in the community.

Michelle Dawson, like many autistics, can do difficult things easily but finds simple things impossible. She can't tie her shoes or safely own a toaster (much less cook), but she does law and science without formal training. Her severe self-injuring and poor self-care means that her freedom and autonomy remain at all times precarious, but she has gone to the Supreme Court of Canada as an intervener in an autism case and she is affiliated with an internationally respected autism research group. With help from other autistic Canadians and a wide variety of contributing researchers and critics belonging to various countries, professions and diagnoses, she posts some of her work and its consequences on the website No Autistics Allowed, at www.sentex.net/~nexus23/naa_02.html.

Dennis Debbaudt in the 1980s, wrote for the *Detroit News*, researched for *Monthly Detroit Magazine*, worked with network television in the US, UK and Canada, and operated a busy private investigative firm. Dennis turned his attention to autism spectrum disorders (ASD) in 1987 after his son was diagnosed with this condition.

Debbaudt's book *Avoiding Unfortunate Situations* became the first to address the interactions between children and adults with autism and law-enforcement professionals. In 1999, he helped develop the state of Maryland's Police and Correctional Training Commission's curriculum, 'Why Law Enforcement Needs to Recognize Autism' and consulted to ABC News 20/20 for a segment about false confession and autism. Over the past decade, he has authored numerous articles and books, including *Autism, Advocates, and Law Enforcement Professionals: Recognizing and Reducing Risk Situations for People with Autism Spectrum Disorders*, published by Jessica Kingsley Publishers, and articles for the FBI Law Enforcement Bulletin. A member of the American Society for Law Enforcement Training (ASLET), he presents his acclaimed ASD workshops for law enforcement throughout the world, and has provided training to the US Department of Homeland Security. He is a lively, well-informed and creative conference presenter.

Dora Georgiou has a background in behavioural psychology and counseling. She has spent most of her professional life working with people with an autism spectrum disorder (ASD). During her ten years as director and chief executive of the Hoffmann de Visme Foundation, one of the first London charities for people with ASD, Dora took a lead in developing the community outreach and counselling service to people with

Asperger syndrome and in providing training and assessment, both to the foundation and to other agencies.

Dora currently works with various health, social services and voluntary agencies as a freelance consultant and trainer on ASD. She also offers advice and counselling to people with ASD and their families. She is involved with various organisations that are trying to promote awareness of the needs of people with Asperger syndrome, her primary interest being to establish working practices that are appropriate for people with Asperger syndrome.

Jacqui Jackson is a single parent raising seven lively children and has a first class degree from the Open University. She is also nearing the end of a PhD on sensory environments and autism. She is a frequent speaker on autism issues and author of *Multicoloured Mayhem: Parenting the Many Shades of Adolescents and Children with Autism, Asperger Syndrome and ADHD.* published by Jessica Kingsley Publishers.

Wendy Lawson, a well-known author, poet and public speaker in both northern and southern hemispheres, is an adult with an autism spectrum disorder. Wendy has been married, separated and divorced. Currently, she lives with her partner and long-time companion Beatrice. Wendy brought up four children and has experienced the death of one of her teenage sons. Wendy's younger son, now aged 23, also has Asperger syndrome. Wendy returned to school and then to university as a mature student. Becoming a psychologist and sharing her knowledge, understanding and experience of autistic spectrum disorders has been Wendy's occupation over the past 11 years.

Mike Lesser is a mathematician, author and computer graphics expert. He has worked on the model of mind as a dynamic system of interests for over two decades. He worked on the model's equations at NASA's Goddard Jet Propulsion Laboratory, Washington DC, USA, at the Institute for Ecotechnological Research at Cranfield University, UK and at the Rutherford Appleton Laboratories, UK. The model has illuminated significant aspects of, yielded insights into and suggested helpful approaches to autism. He co-founded Autism & Computing, a non-profit organisation, with Dinah Murray. He is also the co-author of several scientific papers on dynamical systems theory with Professor P. Allen. In 1992, he was the co-author of *The Global Dynamics Of Cellular Automata*, published in the Santa Fe Institute's Reference Volumes. He spent his seventeenth birthday in Wormwood Scrubs Prison in connection with Unilateral British Nuclear Disarmament. He has also served three spells as editor of London's anarchist journal *International Times*.

Jane Meyerding contributed to the anthology *Women From Another Planet? Our Lives in the Universe of Autism* (Jean Kearns Miller (ed); see www.womenfromanotherplanet.com). She lives in Seattle, USA, and works part-time in an office of a state university. Since discovering her autism in 1996 at the age of 46, she has participated in online groups of autistics and allies. She has been writing for decades, mostly on various aspects of social change and non-violence.

Lynne Moxon obtained a first degree in psychology and then trained as a teacher and educational psychologist in Newcastle upon Tyne. She worked as an educational psychologist from 1976 but built up an interest in autism from 1980 when she was asked to provide consultancy work to a new residential school specialising in autism. Lynne currently works in independent practice, providing specialist consultancy to European Services for People with Autism (ESPA), training for schools, voluntary organisations and health trusts. ESPA, a Sunderland-based charity, runs a specialist further education college for young adults with Asperger syndrome and autism, where Lynne directs courses in sociosexual skills and affective education. Lynne is a senior lecturer and course leader for the master's degree in education studies and autism at Northumbria University. She is presently taking a doctorate at Newcastle University.

Dinah Murray is a worker, researcher, writer, campaigner and teacher re. autism and its variants. She is a person-centred planning consultant based in north London. She has years of hands-on experience with both children and (mainly) adults who have attracted autism spectrum diagnoses, and she has published extensively, both as sole author and with Mike Lesser and with Wendy Lawson. Dinah has written material and been a tutor for two courses about autism run by Birmingham University: distance education re. adults with ASD and Internet-based WebAutism. A critique by Murray, Lesser and Lawson of the diagnostic criteria, 'Attention, Monotropism, and the Diagnostic Criteria for Autism', appears in *Autism*, May 2005. To find out more, visit www.autismandcomputing.org.uk.

Jennifer Overton is a graduate of York University, Toronto, with a master's degree in theatre performance. Her career as a professional actor and director has spanned 20 years, including productions at leading regional theatres in Canada as well as major film, television and radio roles. She is currently Assistant Professor in the Theatre Department at Dalhousie University in Halifax. In 1997, her son was diagnosed with autism and for the past eight years she has been writing about how the condition has affected her family. *Snapshots of Autism: A Family Album* is her first book. Jennifer lives with her husband David, son Nicholas, dog Vanna and cat Christine in Halifax, Nova Scotia.

Heta Pukki was formally diagnosed with Asperger syndrome (AS) in 2000. This was several years after she had figured it out herself and after she had already crashlanded a brief career in plant molecular biology. Over the past seven years, she has participated in various forms of activities for AS adults, including co-writing a guide to the effective use of social services and initiating a yearly AS seminar funded by the Finnish Autism and Asperger Association. In 2002, Heta started a two-year course in autism-related special education at the University of Birmingham, obtaining a postgraduate diploma. She now does translating, consulting, lecturing and course planning related to the subject. Heta's five-year-old daughter also has the AS diagnosis, as does her ex-husband and her daughter's father, David Andrews, with whom she collaborates closely, both professionally and in childrearing.

Stephen Shore, diagnosed with 'atypical development with strong autistic tendencies', was viewed as 'too sick' to be treated on an outpatient basis and recommended for institutionalisation. Non-verbal until the age of four, and with much help from his parents, teachers, and others, Stephen Shore is now completing his doctoral degree in special education at Boston University, with a focus on helping people on the autism spectrum develop their capacities to the fullest extent possible.

In addition to working with children and talking about life on the autism spectrum, Stephen presents and consults internationally on adult issues pertinent to education, relationships, employment, advocacy and disclosure, as discussed in *Beyond the Wall: Personal Experiences with Autism and Asperger Syndrome*, *Ask and Tell: Self-advocacy and Disclosure for People on the Autism Spectrum*, and numerous other writings.

A current board member of the Autism Society of America, Stephen also serves as board president of the Asperger Association of New England as well as for the Board of Directors for Unlocking Autism, the Autism Services Association of Massachusetts, More advanced individuals with Autism, Asperger's syndrome, and Pervasive developmental disorder (MAAP), and the college internship program.

Philip Whitaker has been employed since 1979 as an educational psychologist in Northamptonshire, Leicestershire and Toronto. His interest in autism was originally sparked during his initial training, through involvement in Elizabeth Newson's assessment and diagnostic clinics at the University of Nottingham.

Building on experience with youngsters with complex learning and communication difficulties, he took on a specialist role for youngsters with autistic spectrum disorders in 1996 within Leicestershire's Educational Psychology Service. He was involved closely in developing the role of the county's autism outreach team and in supporting the team's casework and training activities. He was also responsible for the initial development and management of the local education authority's provision for pre-schoolers with autism and their families. Since April 2004, he has worked for Northamptonshire in a similar specialist role.

Philip is the author and co-author of a number of books and articles on the management and education of youngsters with autistic spectrum disorders.

Liane Holliday Willey EdD is an internationally respected speaker and writer on Asperger syndrome and a researcher who specialises in the fields of psycholinguistics and learning style differences. She has worked as an elementary education teacher, a waitress, a retail sales clerk and a university professor. Following years of improper diagnoses, she was diagnosed properly with Asperger syndrome in 1999. She is the author of *Pretending to be Normal: Living with Asperger Syndrome* and *Asperger Syndrome in the Family: Redefining Normal* and is the editor of *Asperger Syndrome in the Adolescent Years: Living with the Ups, the Downs and Things in Between* (all published by Jessica Kingsley Publishers). When Liane is not presenting information on Asperger syndrome, she is likely to be found at her children's functions, working on her first novel, tutoring children with reading problems, or consulting with businesses that are interested in building more effective communication paradigms.

Subject index

Author Index